The Longman Companion to
America, Russia and the
Cold War 1941–1998

Longman Companions to History

General Editors: Chris Cook and John Stevenson

Now available

The Longman Companion to

America, Russia and the Cold War, 1941–1998

Second Edition

John W. Young

LONGMAN
London and New York

Addison Wesley Longman Limited
Edinburgh Gate,
Harlow, Essex CM20 2JE, United Kingdom
and Associated Companies throughout the world.

*Published in the United States of America by Addison
Wesley Longman, New York.*

First published 1993
Second Edition 1999

ISBN 0-582-36901-0 PPR

Visit Addison Wesley Longman on the world wide web at
http://www.awl-he.com

British Library Cataloguing in Publication Data

A catalogue entry for this title is available from the British Library

Library of Congress Cataloging-in-Publication Data

Young, John W., 1957–
    The Longman companion to America, Russia, and the Cold War,
1941–1998 / John W. Young. — 2nd ed.
      p. cm. — (Longman companions to history)
    Rev. ed. of: The Longman companion to Cold War and detente,
1941–91. 1993.
    Includes bibliographical references and index.
    ISBN 0–582–36901–0 (pbk.)
    1. World politics—1945– 2. Cold War. I. Young, John W., 1957–
Longman companion to Cold War and detente, 1941–91. II. Title.
III. Series.
D840.Y68 1999
909.82′5—dc21
                                             98–39550
                                                  CIP

Set by 35 in 9½/12pt New Baskerville
Produced by .
Printed in Malaysia, PP

Contents

List of maps

Acknowledgements to the first edition

I am grateful to John Stevenson of Worcester College, Oxford for first suggesting that I contribute a volume to the *Longman Companion* series. I would also like to thank Chris Cook and the staff at Addison Wesley Longman, for helping to bring the project to fruition.

The book is not of course a work of original research, but draws heavily on the work of others, especially *Keesing's Contemporary Archives* and other reference books. My debt to staff and students at my previous universities is immense, but I would particularly like to thank Robert Frazier, who first awoke my interest in the early Cold War, Christopher Andrew, Geoff Berridge, David Dilks, Mike and Saki Dockrill, John Kent, Scott Lucas, David Stevenson, Phil Taylor, Donald Cameron Watt and Geoffrey Warner. The manuscript was typed up by Janet Smith and Mary McCormick with their usual speed and care. Last, but not least, thanks to Brigette for all her support.

John W. Young
6 October 1991

Acknowledgements to the second edition

The second edition has principally allowed me to add sections to many chapters on the post-Cold War period, including entries on the Bosnian war, the START II treaty and such figures as Bill Clinton, Boris Yeltsin and Saddam Hussein. I have also corrected some errors from the first edition, expanded some points and revised the bibliography. To those thanked in the first edition I would like to add Michael Cox, Pauline Elkes, Keith Hamilton, Karen Henderson, Mike Hopkins, Jan Melissen and Wyn Rees. I would also like to renew my thanks to Janet Smith, who typed up the new sections, and to my family for their support.

John W. Young
27 March 1998

List of abbreviations

ABM	Anti-Ballistic Missile
ANZUS	Australia–New Zealand–American Alliance
ARVN	Army of the Republic of (South) Vietnam
CENTO	Central Treaty Organisation (Baghdad Pact)
CFE	Conventional Forces in Europe Treaty
CIA	American Central Intelligence Agency
Comecon	Council for Mutual Economic Aid
Cominform	Communist Information Bureau
CSCE	Conference on Security and Co-operation in Europe
EDC	European Defence Community
EC	European Community
EEC	European Economic Community
Ex Comm	Executive Committee of the NSC
FNLA	National Front for the Liberation of Angola
GATT	General Agreement on Tariffs and Trade
ICBM	Inter-Continental Ballistic Missile
INF	Intermediate-range Nuclear Forces
KGB	Soviet secret police
MBFR	Mutual Balanced Force Reductions
MIRV	Multiple Independent Re-entry Vehicle
MPLA	Popular Front for the Liberation of Angola
MX	Missile Experimental
NATO	North Atlantic Treaty Organisation
NSC	National Security Council
NVA	North Vietnamese Army
PFP	Partnership for Peace
SALT	Strategic Arms Limitation Treaty
SDI	Strategic Defence Initiative
SEATO	South-East Asian Treaty Organisation
SLBM	Submarine-Launched Ballistic Missile
START	Strategic Arms Reduction Treaty
SWAPO	South-West African People's Organisation
UN	United Nations
UNITA	National Union for the Total Independence of Angola
UNRRA	UN Relief and Rehabilitation Administration

With thanks to
Robert Frazier and
Christopher Andrew

SECTION ONE

Chronology

1. Origins of the Cold War, 1917–41

7 November 1917. (25 October under old calendar.) The Bolsheviks, led by Lenin, seize power in Russia.

c. April 1918–November 1920. Period of Allied intervention in Russian civil war in opposition to Bolsheviks: British, French, US and Japanese forces side with the 'Whites' against Lenin.

15 March 1919. Formation of Communist International, by Lenin, to encourage Communist revolution worldwide.

21 January 1924. Death of Lenin.

January 1928. Stalin becomes the dominant leader in USSR.

17 November 1933. US opens diplomatic relations with USSR for first time.

23 August 1939. Ribbentrop–Molotov Pact made, dividing Poland between Germany and USSR and establishing 'spheres of influence' in Eastern Europe.

1 September 1939. Hitler invades Poland.

3 September 1939. Britain and France declare war on Germany.

17 September 1939. USSR joins in invasion of Poland, and seizes half the country.

30 November 1939–12 March 1940. 'Winter War' fought between USSR and Finland. The war is hard-fought, but results in Soviet territorial gains.

15–16 June 1940. Soviet forces occupy Baltic states of Latvia, Estonia and Lithuania (independent since 1918), claiming there is a military threat to the Soviet Union; formally annexed on 1–8 August.

22 June 1940. France agrees to armistice with Germany, after German advances since May; Britain faces Germany alone; Italy allied to Germany.

11 March 1941. US begins 'lend-lease' economic and military aid to Britain (to USSR in November).

22 June 1941. Germany launches invasion of USSR.

11 August 1941. After meeting at sea off Newfoundland, Roosevelt and Churchill issue Atlantic Charter, promising restoration of independence to conquered states.

August–September 1941. British and Soviet forces occupy Iran, needed as a supply route from the West to Russia.

2. The 'Big Three', 1941–45

7 December 1941. Japanese attack US forces at Pearl Harbor, forcing America into the war.

15–18 December 1941.   Visit by British Foreign Secretary, Eden, to Moscow; he finds that Stalin hopes to retain gains made under Ribbentrop–Molotov Pact.

22 December 1941–7 January 1942.   'Arcadia' conference of Roosevelt and Churchill in Washington plans war strategy and agrees to set up Anglo-American Combined Chiefs of Staff.

1 January 1942.   Twenty-six Allied countries sign 'United Nations' declaration and agree not to make a separate peace with Germany, Italy and Japan.

26 May 1942.   Twenty-year Soviet–British alliance against Germany signed.

12–15 August 1942.   Churchill and Stalin meet in Moscow to discuss war strategy.

8 November 1942.   US and British forces land in North-West Africa; first US military involvement on land against German forces.

12 December 1942.   Soviet–Czech alliance signed, showing Czech desire to work with Soviets after the war.

1943

14–24 January.   Casablanca Conference of Roosevelt and Churchill sees announcement that Germany and her allies must surrender 'unconditionally'.

1 February.   Siege of Stalingrad ends, marking turning point in war on Russian front, after large German forces surrender to the Soviets.

27 April.   Stalin suspends relations with Polish government-in-exile after arguments over whether Germany or USSR carried out 'Katyn massacre' of Polish officers, after their occupation of Poland in 1939.

12–25 May.   'Trident' conference of Roosevelt and Churchill, in Washington, discusses possible invasion of France.

15 May.   Stalin dissolves Comintern to please the Western allies.

18 May–1 June.   Hot Springs conference near Washington discusses establishment of United Nations Relief and Rehabilitation Administration (UNRRA). Formally set up in November.

10 July.   Anglo-American invasion of Sicily begins liberation of Western Europe.

25 July.   Mussolini replaced in Italy by Marshal Badoglio, ending Fascist rule there.

17–24 August.   At Quebec Conference Roosevelt and Churchill decide to invade France in mid-1944.

8 September.   Italian armistice announced; Italy soon (13 October) changes sides in the war, joining the Allies.

18–30 October.   In Moscow 'Big Three' foreign ministers lay the ground for a leaders' meeting, discuss establishment of UN organisation and set up a European Advisory Commission to discuss policy in post-war Germany.

22–26 November. In Cairo Roosevelt, Churchill and China's Chiang Kai-shek discuss strategy in Far East.

28 November–1 December. First 'Big Three' Summit between Roosevelt, Churchill and Stalin in Tehran, discusses war strategy and future co-operation.

4–6 December. At second Cairo Conference, Roosevelt and Churchill decide Eisenhower should be Supreme Allied Commander in West.

1944

6 June. 'D-Day': Anglo-American invasion of France, code-named Operation Overlord, begins full-scale 'second front' in the West.

1–22 July. Bretton Woods Conference, of forty-four nations, on financial-economic issues, agrees to establish International Monetary Fund (to stabilise currencies) and World Bank (for reconstruction and development). Soviets refuse to join.

21 July. Red Army sets up a Communist 'Committee of National Liberation' in Lublin, Poland, after 'liberating' eastern areas of the country.

1 August–2 October. Warsaw rising of Polish resistance's 'Home Army' against Germans. Soviets fail to provide support for it and the rising is eventually crushed.

23 August. Germany's ally Romania signs armistice following Soviet invasion.

8 September. Germany's ally Bulgaria changes sides in war following Soviet invasion three days earlier.

11–16 September. At second Quebec Conference Roosevelt and Churchill discuss post-war occupation of Germany.

19 September. Germany's ally Finland signs armistice with USSR.

3 October. British forces begin to arrive in Greece; its liberation is completed by 11 November.

7 October. Dumbarton Oaks Conference in America of US, USSR, Britain and China (begun 21 August) results in draft UN charter.

9–18 October. Moscow Conference of Stalin and Churchill includes 'percentage deal' creating British and Soviet spheres of influence in the Balkans.

7 November. Roosevelt re-elected president for fourth term, beating Thomas E. Dewey.

3 December. Fighting breaks out between British forces and the Communist resistance movement in Greece, who oppose the restoration of the Greek monarchy.

10 December. In Moscow France's General de Gaulle signs twenty-year Anti-German Treaty with Stalin.

25 December. After the fighting in Greece Churchill himself arrives in Athens to settle the differences.

1945

1 January. Soviets recognise their puppet Communist administration in Poland as the 'provisional government'; America and Britain refuse to recognise it.

13 January. Truce between British and Communist forces in Athens is followed (February) by the Varkiza Agreement promising a referendum on the return of the monarchy and other reforms.

20 January. Germany's ally Hungary signs armistice with USSR.

4–12 February. Yalta Summit in Crimea of Roosevelt, Stalin and Churchill discusses post-war Europe, UN and Far East.

6 March. Petru Groza becomes head of Communist-led government in Romania.

15 March. Stalin criticises Anglo-American talks in Berne with local German commander about surrender of German forces in Italy: Stalin fears these forces will be sent to the Eastern Front.

4 April. Roosevelt condemns Stalin's criticisms of Berne talks as 'vile misrepresentations'.

11 April. Soviet–Yugoslav Treaty of Mutual Assistance signed. (Similar treaties were signed between all Communist Eastern European states including Soviet–Polish treaty on 21 April.)

12 April. Death of Roosevelt; succeeded by Harry S. Truman.

23 April. Truman strongly warns Molotov, in Washington, that Soviets must adhere to Yalta Agreements.

25 April. US and Soviet forces meet at Torgau on the River Elbe.

28 April. Mussolini captured and hanged by partisans.

30 April. Hitler commits suicide in Berlin.

1 May. Anglo-American and Yugoslav Communist forces arrive in Trieste (previously Italian) and contest its control; danger of an armed clash.

8 May. V-E Day: formal German capitulation in Berlin; placed under US, Soviet, British and French occupation.

11 May. With Germany defeated, Truman limits 'lend-lease' to goods needed for the war against Japan.

14 May. Austria, though under joint Allied occupation by US, Soviet, British and French is given an independent republican government under Karl Renner.

21 May. Tito, the Yugoslav leader, agrees to Anglo-American military government in Trieste.

6 June. Stalin agrees, in talks with US envoy Harry Hopkins, to expand the Polish government to include pro-Western elements.

21 June. Truman orders US forces in Czechoslovakia and Eastern Germany to withdraw to their own occupation areas, allowing Red Army to advance into preagreed areas of occupation.

21 June. Leaders of Polish resistance's 'home government' are jailed in Warsaw for 'anti-Soviet activities'.

26 June. At end of San Francisco conference (begun 26 April) fifty countries launch UN charter, establishing a new world peace-keeping organisation.

28 June. New Polish government includes some former members of London-based government-in-exile.

29 June. Czechoslovakia hands border area of Ruthenia to USSR.

5 July. US and Britain recognise new Polish government, despite continued Communist predominance.

16 July. First atomic bomb successfully tested at Alamogordo, New Mexico.

17 July–2 August. Potsdam Summit of Big Three leaders establishes joint policies for the occupation of Germany.

26 July. British general election results in defeat for Churchill.

6 August. Atomic bomb dropped on Hiroshima.

8 August. Soviet Union enters Far Eastern War against Japan, and begins to occupy areas of Manchuria.

9 August. Atomic bomb dropped on Nagasaki.

14 August. Soviet treaty with Chiang Kai-shek confirms Soviet territorial gains in China under Yalta Agreement.

15 August. Capitulation of Japan on understanding that Hirohito can remain Emperor.

23 August. End of America's 'lend-lease' programme.

2 September. Formal Japanese surrender to the Allies, on USS *Missouri* (V-J day).

3. The breakdown of the Grand Alliance, 1945–48

2 September 1945. Communist resistance leader Ho Chi Minh proclaims independence of Vietnam (then part of French Indo-China).

13 September. After an Allied agreement on areas of occupation, British forces arrive in Saigon, southern Vietnam. (Chinese occupy northern Vietnam.)

11 September–2 October. London Conference: first meeting of Council of Foreign Ministers (US, USSR, Britain, China, France) set up at Potsdam to draft peace treaties with defeated enemy states, breaks down in disagreement, after various arguments between Soviets and Western states.

5 October. French forces arrive in Saigon, and begin to take over from the British.

23 October. Communists emerge as leading party in first post-war French election, but Christian Democrats and Socialists are close behind.

24 October. UN formally comes into existence.

27 October. Truman's Navy Day address restates US commitment to Atlantic Charter principles and strong armed forces.

4 November. Smallholders' Party emerges well ahead of Communists in first post-war Hungarian elections.
11 November. Rigged elections in Yugoslavia give 90 per cent vote to Tito's 'People's Front' of Communists.
15 November. Truman, Attlee and Canadian premier Mackenzie King agree on basic plan to control atomic energy through UN.
17 November. Nationalist leader Ahmed Sukarno declares independence of Indonesia from Dutch.
18 November. Communist 'Fatherland Front' wins rigged elections in Bulgaria.
20 November. Soviets refuse to allow Iranian troops into Iranian Azerbaijan, then under Red Army occupation – leads to Anglo-American protest.
27 November. US General Marshall sent to China to negotiate a settlement between Nationalists and Communists, in the hope of avoiding a civil war.
6 December. US reconstruction loan to Britain finalised, after talks involving Lord Keynes.
16–26 December. US, Soviet and British foreign ministers meet in Moscow and agree to new talks on peace treaties.

1946
2 January. King Zog of Albania formally deposed by Communists.
5 January. Communists and Nationalists in China agree to end fighting.
10 January. First regular session of UN General Assembly opens in London.
30 January. UN calls for talks between USSR and Iran over their differences.
9 February. Stalin speech during Soviet elections launches new Five-Year Plan and describes Second World War as vindication of Communism.
11 February. Secret Yalta Agreement on Far East published, showing that Roosevelt ceded territories to USSR.
15–18 February. Arrests of a major Soviet spy ring in Canada.
22 February. From Moscow, US chargé George Kennan sends 'the long telegram' analysing Soviet expansionist tendencies, and urging American resistance.
28 February. Chinese agree to withdraw from northern Indo-China and restore French authority.
28 February. Speech by Secretary of State James Byrnes marks a toughening of US public stand against USSR.
2 March. Deadline passes, under wartime agreements, for Soviet troops to leave Iran; US and Britain begin diplomatic pressure to remove them.

5 March. Churchill's speech at Fulton, Missouri, condemns 'iron curtain' in Eastern Europe and calls for Anglo-American alliance. Criticised by Stalin on 13 March.

6 March. US note to Moscow complains about continued presence of Soviet troops in Iran.

24 March. Soviets agree to withdraw troops from Iran. (Last troops leave 6 May.)

31 March. Royalists triumph in Greek elections.

6 April. Fighting again breaks out, in Manchuria, between Chinese Communists and Nationalists.

20 April. East German Social Democrats forced to join Communists in 'Socialist Unity Party'.

25 April–16 May. Council of Foreign Ministers, meeting in Paris, resumes talks on peace treaties (US, USSR, Britain, France).

1 May. In Britain, Alan Nunn May jailed for giving atomic secrets to USSR.

3 May. US deputy governor General Clay suspends reparations from US zone in Germany and blames Soviet and French policy for lack of Allied agreement on Germany.

15 May. Albanians shell British ships off Corfu.

26 May. Communists are leading party (35 per cent) in Czech elections, and head a coalition government with democratic parties.

28 May. Large US reconstruction loan to France agreed.

1 June. French governor Thierry d'Argenlieu proclaims separation of Cochin China in Southern Vietnam, undermining French government's talks with nationalist leader, Ho Chi Minh.

2 June. Italian referendum puts an end to the monarchy.

14 June. US Baruch Plan for control of atomic energy published; criticised by USSR.

15 June–12 July. Council of Foreign Ministers meets again in Paris and finalises draft treaties with Romania, Bulgaria, Hungary, Finland and Italy.

4 July. US gives independence to its Far Eastern colony, the Philippines.

10 July. In the Paris talks, Molotov appears to make a bid for German popular support by making a speech favouring German revival.

17 July. Tito executes Yugoslav royalist leader Draja Mihailovic.

25 July. First underground atomic test explosion by US at Bikini atoll.

27 July–15 October. Allied nations meet in Paris to discuss the peace treaties drafted by the Council of Foreign Ministers.

1 August. McMahon Act by Congress prevents US sharing atomic secrets.

7 August. Soviet note to Turkey proposes Soviet role in defence of Dardanelles; offends US and Britain, because of danger of Soviet access to the Mediterranean.

1 September.   Greek referendum agrees to retain monarchy.

6 September.   Speech by US Secretary of State Byrnes at Stuttgart declares more sympathetic policy towards Germany and promises to retain US troops in Germany until peace is assured.

8 September.   Monarchy ended in Bulgaria by Communists.

10 September.   Greek Communists launch civil war against the royal government.

12 September.   Speech by US Secretary of Commerce Wallace calls for co-operation with USSR; as a result Wallace is forced to resign (20 September).

19 September.   Speech by Churchill in Zurich advocates European unity.

1 October.   End of major Nuremburg war trials: several leading Nazis executed.

20 October.   Berlin municipal elections won by Social Democrats; Communists get one-fifth of vote.

3 November.   New Japanese constitution promulgated.

4 November–12 December.   Council of Foreign Ministers meets in New York and accepts most of Paris Peace Conference amendments to peace treaties.

5 November.   Republican gains in US Congressional elections highlight need for 'bipartisan' foreign policy.

10 November.   French elections again leave Communists as largest party.

23 November.   French warships bombard northern Vietnamese port of Haiphong after unrest there.

2 December.   'Bizone' agreement fuses US and British occupation zones in Germany.

3 December.   Greece claims in UN that Albania, Yugoslavia and Bulgaria are aiding Greek Communists in civil war; UN sends a commission to investigate on 18 December.

19–20 September.   Viet-Minh nationalists attack French nationals in Hanoi; first Indo-China war begins.

1947

19 January.   Rigged elections (originally promised at Yalta) held in Poland, despite Western complaints.

25 January.   Beginning of blizzards in Western Europe, threatening popular morale and economic recovery.

10 February.   Allies sign peace treaties with Italy, Hungary, Bulgaria, Romania and Finland in Paris.

20 February.   British announce independence for India.

21 February.   British inform Washington that they can no longer provide financial aid to the Greek government.

4 March.   Treaty of Dunkirk, directed against revival of German aggression, signed by Britain and France.

10 March–24 April.   US, Soviet, British and French meet to discuss German and Austrian treaties, in Council of Foreign Ministers in Moscow; fail to reach agreement.

12 March.   Truman Doctrine speech, to joint session of Congress, requests aid to Greek and Turkish governments to help resist Communism; approved by Congress on 15 May.

7 April.   General de Gaulle forms right-wing 'Rally of the French People' (RPF), highlighting political divisions in France.

4 May.   Communist ministers are expelled from the French Cabinet by premier Paul Ramadier.

5 May.   Communist ministers are expelled from the Italian government by premier de Gasperi.

23 May.   US and Britain decide to allow German political representation in an 'Economic Council' in the Bizone.

30 May.   Hungarian premier Ferenc Nagy resigns under Soviet pressure; criticised by Truman on 21 June.

5 June.   Launch of the Marshall Plan: Harvard speech by Marshall offers US economic aid for a European recovery plan, which Europeans should draw up.

27 June–2 July.   Soviet, British and French foreign ministers meet in Paris to discuss the Marshall Plan; Molotov eventually walks out of the talks.

July.   George Kennan's 'X' article is published in *Foreign Affairs*, providing intellectual justification for US policy of 'containment'.

4 July.   British and French invite other European countries to discuss the Marshall Plan.

10 July.   Under Soviet pressure, Poland and Czechoslovakia turn down the invitation to discuss the Marshall Plan.

12 July–22 September.   Sixteen Western European nations meet in Paris to draw up an economic recovery plan for submission to the US.

15 August.   India and Pakistan become independent.

29 August.   US and Britain increase industrial output of the Bizone, despite Soviet and French criticism.

31 August.   Rigged elections ensure Communist victory in Hungary.

2 September.   Rio Pact, on inter-American defence, signed by US and Latin American states.

22–23 September.   Soviet, East European, French and Italian Communists establish an Information Bureau (Cominform) at a conference in Poland; Soviet representatives declare that the world is now divided into two camps.

23 September.   Bulgarian Agrarian party leader Nikolai Petkov is executed, despite Western protests.

19 October.   De Gaulle's RPF scores major successes in French local elections.

20 October. US House of Representatives' 'Un-American Activities Committee' begins to investigate Communist influence on Hollywood.

26 October. Polish democratic leader Mikolajcyk flees the country.

30 October. GATT agreement signed by Western states in Geneva.

November. Wave of strikes breaks out in France and Italy; ends early December.

1 November. 'Benelux' customs union between Belgium, Holland and Luxembourg formed.

25 November–16 December. Council of Foreign Ministers meets in London and again fails to agree on German or Austrian treaties; no date is set for a further meeting; US, Britain and France begin to plan a joint policy in Western Germany.

23 December. Truman signs Bill to provide interim economic aid, especially to France and Italy, in advance of full Marshall Plan.

24 December. Communist Party sets up rebel government in Greece; party is banned on 27 December.

30 December. King Michael of Romania is forced to abdicate.

1948

6 January. Greek Communists defeated at Konitza.

21 January. Italian Socialists decide to fight a joint campaign with the Communists in the forthcoming election.

22 January. In London, Foreign Secretary Bevin calls for the creation of a 'Western Union' including a West European alliance system.

16 February. 'People's Republic' declared in North Korea (occupied by USSR at end of war).

19–25 February. Communist coup in Czechoslovakia; condemned by the West.

23 February. US, Britain and France begin talks in London on the future of Western Germany.

10 March. Czechoslovakia's democratic foreign minister, Jan Masaryk, dies after falling from a window.

17 March. Britain, France, Belgium, Holland and Luxembourg sign the Brussels Pact, including pledges of mutual defence.

18 March. Soviet military advisers are withdrawn from Yugoslavia because of resentment at Tito's independence.

20 March. French foreign minister Bidault, in Turin, announces that US, Britain and France favour the return of Trieste to Italy; leads to Yugoslav protests.

20 March. Soviet representative walks out of the Allied Control Council in Germany, accusing the Western powers of destroying it.

1 April. Soviet officials begin regularly to interfere with Western surface traffic into Berlin.

2 April. US Congress approves Marshall Aid; the Economic Co-operation Administration is established to manage it.

6 April. Finland signs a non-aggression pact with the USSR; Western states fear Soviet pressure on Norway and Denmark to sign similar treaties.

16 April. European countries establish Organisation of European Economic Co-operation to run Marshall Aid.

18 April. Christian Democrats win the Italian election with 48 per cent of the vote, after considerable US, British and French support.

30 April. Organisation of American States founded at Bogota, Colombia.

1 May. North Korean government claims jurisdiction over all Korea.

10 May. USSR publicises recent exchange of correspondence between Molotov and US Ambassador Bedell Smith on possible end to Cold War.

14 May. Israel proclaimed a state (after British leave Palestine and UN agrees to partition it between Jews and Arabs); first Arab–Israeli war follows.

19 May. Yugoslav leaders refuse to attend a Cominform meeting called by USSR.

1 June. US, Britain and France announce London Conference decisions including establishment of a West German state.

11 June. US Senate passes Vandenberg Resolution authorising government to enter regional security pacts.

16 June. Emergency declared in Malaya against Communist insurgents.

18 June. Western powers begin to introduce new currency in Western Germany.

4. The 'First Cold War', 1948–52

24 June 1948. Soviets launch full blockade of surface routes to West Berlin; Eastern bloc foreign ministers in Warsaw condemn Western policy in Germany.

26 June. Berlin airlift begins.

28 June. To Western surprise Yugoslavia is expelled from the Cominform; Eastern bloc denounces Tito as 'deviationist'.

6 July. US, Canada and Brussels Pact states begin talks on Atlantic security in Washington.

15 July. 'Atomic-capable' B29 bombers are sent by US to bases in Britain.

2 August. Western ambassadors discuss Berlin situation with Stalin.

15 August. South Korea declared a Republic and recognised by US.

15 August. UN Commission says Greek Communists *were* aided by Albania, Yugoslavia and Bulgaria.

26 August. Western powers decide to take Berlin issue to UN.

1 September. Western German representatives (in Bonn) begin to discuss 'basic law' of a new state.

3 September. Independent-minded Communist Gomulka is expelled from Polish government.

14 September. Death of Zhdanov, anti-Western hard-liner, who had been seen as Stalin's likely successor.

October–November. New strike wave in France and Italy.

31 October. Chinese Communists take control of all Manchuria after taking Mukden.

2 November. Truman narrowly re-elected president, defeating Thomas Dewey.

5 December. Social Democrats win West Berlin elections; Communists humiliated.

31 December. USSR and Eastern bloc launch full trade embargo against Yugoslavia.

1949

22 January. Chinese Communists capture Beijing.

25 January. Establishment of Comecon by the USSR and its satellites.

6 February. Soviet note to Norway, calling for a non-aggression pact between them, increases pressure on Western powers to include Norway in Atlantic security talks.

8 February. Cardinal Mindsentzy of Hungary condemned to life-imprisonment.

18 February. Berlin airlift carries its millionth ton of supplies.

8 March. France makes former Emperor Bao Dai the head of a new Vietnamese government.

4 April. North Atlantic Treaty signed in Washington.

8 April. In Washington, US, Britain and France reach agreement on terms for creating West German state.

20 April. Chinese Communist forces cross the Yangtze, shelling British naval vessels.

4 May. USSR agrees to lift the Berlin blockade in return for four-power talks on Germany.

5 May. West European countries, in London, sign Statute of Council of Europe, including a Consultative Assembly in Strasbourg; first annual session begins on 8 August.

8 May. West German representatives finalise 'Basic Law' of new state which comes into existence on 23 May.

12 May. The Berlin blockade is lifted.

23 May–20 June. US, Soviet, British and French foreign ministers meet in Paris to discuss future of Germany but cannot find common ground.

30 May. Soviets constitute an East German government.

29 June. US troops withdrawn from South Korea.

13 July. Pope Pius XII's Apostolic *Acta* condemns all who support Communism.

20 July.   Israeli–Syrian armistice ends all fighting in Arab–Israeli War.
25 July.   Truman asks Congress for military aid to NATO states.
5 August.   US ends aid to Chiang Kai-shek.
29 August.   Soviets explode their first atomic bomb; announced by Truman on 22 September.
8 September.   US agrees its first loan to Tito's Yugoslavia.
15 September.   Konrad Adenauer becomes first Chancellor of West Germany.
21 September.   Mao Zedong declares the Chinese People's Republic.
28 September.   Congress approves a 'Mutual Defense Aid Programme' to NATO.
28 September.   USSR abrogates its mutual defence pact with Yugoslavia; other Eastern bloc states follow suit.
7 October.   East German constitution proclaimed.
16 October.   Greek civil war ends in government victory.
2 November.   Holland gives independence to Indonesia.
22 November.   Petersberg Agreement between Western powers and West Germany eases economic restrictions on West Germany.
8 December.   Chiang Kai-shek sets up a government in Formosa (Taiwan).

1950
6 January.   British recognise Communist China.
10 January.   USSR's Yakov Malik walks out of UN Security Council in protest over continued presence of Nationalist China.
12 January.   US Secretary of State Acheson defines a 'defense perimeter' in the Far East, running from Alaska through Japan to the Philippines; later criticised by Republicans for omitting Korea.
14 January.   Ho Chi Minh establishes a 'Democratic Republic of Vietnam'; recognised by China on 19th and USSR on 31 January.
25 January.   Alger Hiss, former State Department official, is condemned for perjury, following allegations by Whitaker Chambers he was a Communist; the case makes Congressman Richard Nixon a household name.
31 January.   Truman announces that America is to build a hydrogen bomb.
7 February.   US and Britain recognise pro-French government of Bao Dai in Indo-China.
9 February.   Beginning of 'McCarthyism': Senator Joe McCarthy, at Wheeling in West Virginia, claims there are over 200 Communist sympathisers in the State Department.
14 February.   Sino-Soviet alliance signed by Mao Zedong in Moscow.
30 March.   Truman condemns McCarthy but cannot prevent beginning of an anti-Communist 'witch-hunt'.
7 April.   US policy document NSC-68 proposes large-scale arms programme.

9 May.   French foreign minister launches Schuman Plan for a European coal–steel authority.

23 May.   US, Britain and France complain that East Germany's 'police-force' breaches Potsdam agreement on German disarmament.

6 June.   East German–Polish treaty recognises the Oder–Neisse border.

25 June.   Start of Korean War: North Korean forces invade South Korea.

26 June.   US forces are sent to Korea (arriving 1 July); US Seventh Fleet is sent to defend Taiwan from Chinese Communists.

27 June.   UN, in Soviet absence, approves 'Uniting for Peace' resolution, to send forces to Korea.

26 July.   US makes major increase in military aid to French in Indo-China.

14 September.   In Korea, UN forces under General MacArthur begin landings at Inchon which force a North Korean retreat.

15–18 September.   The US proposes West German rearmament in meeting with Britain, France and NATO states in New York; the idea is opposed by the French.

28 September.   Zhou Enlai warns UN forces not to invade North Korea.

29 September.   UN forces begin to cross the 38th parallel into North Korea.

17 October.   US makes military aid agreement with Thailand.

20 October.   Eastern bloc foreign ministers in Prague condemn West German rearmament proposals.

21 October.   Chinese forces invade Tibet.

26 October.   Chinese 'volunteers' enter the Korean War.

26 October.   The French premier launches the Pleven Plan for German rearmament within a federal European Army.

3 November.   USSR proposes talks with US, Britain and France on Germany; they reject Soviet arguments in note of 22 December.

26 November.   Chinese intervene in force in Korea, driving UN forces back.

30 November.   USSR vetoes anti-Chinese resolution at UN; Truman announces there has been 'active consideration' of the use of atomic bombs in Korea.

8 December.   US ends all trade with China; Truman assures British premier Attlee in Washington that the atom bomb will not be used.

19 December.   NATO Council in Brussels agrees in principle to West German rearmament, but allows France to pursue this through a European federal army.

30 December.   USSR sends new note to Western powers proposing talks on Germany; receives another cautious reply on 23 January.

1951

1 January.   In Korea, Chinese forces cross the 38th parallel; capture Seoul on 4 January.

10 January.   Chinese advance in Korea reaches its furthest extent.

15 January.   Truman's budget request to Congress includes greater military spending.

1 February.   By large majority General Assembly of UN approves condemnation of China for aggression.

5 February.   Soviet note to the US, Britain and France calls for talks on Germany; on 19 February they suggest preliminary talks in Paris.

15 February.   France, West Germany, Italy, Belgium and Luxembourg begin talks on a European Army in Paris – later joined by Holland.

21 February.   First Communist 'Peace Council' begins in East Berlin.

5 March.   At the Palais Rose, Paris, deputies of the Soviet, American, British and French foreign ministers begin talks to draft an agenda for a foreign ministers' conference.

27 March.   In Korea, UN forces again reach the 38th parallel.

2 April.   Supreme Headquarters Allied Powers Europe (SHAPE) opened in Paris, under Eisenhower.

5 April.   In US Julius and Ethel Rosenberg are sentenced to death for passing atomic secrets to USSR during the Second World War (executed 19 June 1953).

11 April.   General MacArthur is sacked by Truman as UN commander in Korea after making unauthorised statements, including calls for attacks against China.

18 April.   France, West Germany, Italy and the Benelux nations sign the treaty to establish a European Coal–Steel Community (ECSC).

19 April.   Before Congress, General MacArthur criticises Truman's handling of Korean War.

30 April.   Iranian parliament votes to nationalise the mainly British-owned oil industry; Britain complains to International Court of Justice on 26 May.

23 May.   China takes control of Tibetan government, although the Dalai Lama remains there.

25 May.   British spies Guy Burgess and Donald Maclean flee to the USSR.

21 June.   End of the Palais Rose talks, begun on 5 March; no agreement on East–West foreign ministers meeting.

23 June.   USSR calls for a cease-fire in Korea; UN (29 June) and China (1 July) agree to talks, which begin at Kaesong on 4 July.

30 August.   US–Philippines mutual defence treaty signed.

1 September.   ANZUS Pact for mutual defence signed between US, Australia and New Zealand.

4–8 September.   San Francisco Conference, without USSR or Communist China, leads to peace treaty with Japan.

8 September.   US–Japanese defence treaty signed.

14 October.   Britain proposes a Middle East Command (to include Western and Middle East states) largely as a means to maintain Britain's presence in the Suez Canal; Egypt rejects this on 15 October and also abrogates its 1936 treaty with Britain.

16–17 October. British troops occupy Suez Canal base installations.

23 November. Armistice talks in Korea reach agreement on cease-fire line.

3 December. US Economic Co-operation Administration (set up to handle Marshall Aid) is replaced by a Mutual Security Agency (with the emphasis on military assistance).

1952

2 January. UN command says repatriation of prisoners of war in Korea should be on a voluntary basis; opens way for Communist prisoners to refuse to return home.

18 February. Greece and Turkey join NATO.

27 February. UN begins to meet in its permanent New York headquarters.

10 March. USSR puts forward the 'Stalin note' proposing a peace treaty that would reunify Germany; Western powers reply cautiously on 25 March.

9 April. A new Soviet note on a German peace treaty; Western powers delay reply until 13 May.

26 May. Treaty of Bonn signed by US, Britain, France and West Germany, to end the occupation and restore sovereignty to West Germany. (Entry into force depends on the Treaty of Paris below.)

27 May. Treaty of Paris between France, West Germany, Italy, Belgium, Holland and Luxembourg to establish a European Defence Community, placing German forces under federal control.

23 June. UN forces bomb hydroelectricity stations in North Korea.

23–26 July. Officers under General Neguib overthrow King Farouk of Egypt.

23 August. New Soviet note on German peace treaty; Western Allies reply on 23 September.

16 September. Soviets agree to restore Port Arthur and railway rights in Manchuria (obtained at Yalta in 1945) to China.

3 October. Britain explodes its first atomic bomb in the Montebello islands.

5–14 October. Nineteenth Soviet Communist Party Congress sees height of Stalin's 'personality cult'.

1 November. US explodes the first hydrogen bomb in the Marshall Islands.

4 November. Republican Dwight Eisenhower wins the US election over Adlai Stevenson.

27 November. Rodolf Slansky and other dissident Communists are condemned to death after a show trial in Czechoslovakia.

3 December. After intense debate, the UN Assembly adopts an Indian proposal on prisoners of war and a Korean armistice: rejected by Communist China on 15 December.

5 December. Eisenhower visits the front line in Korea, highlighting his determination to end the war.

5. 'The Thaw', 1953–58

1953

13 January. Moscow announces arrest of Kremlin doctors, who are accused of murdering the former Politbureau member Zhdanov in the 'Doctors' Plot'.

5 March. Death of Stalin; succeeded on 6 March by a 'collective leadership' led by Georgi Malenkov as prime minister and party leader.

14 March. Malenkov surrenders leadership of the Communist Party to Nikita Khruschev.

19 March. West German parliament ratifies the European Defence Community.

3 April. New Soviet government releases those accused in the Doctors' Plot.

16 April. Eisenhower speech on possibility of peace with new Soviet leadership, calls for Korean settlement and Austrian treaty.

20 April. First exchange of sick prisoners of war in Korea.

11 May. Winston Churchill speech calls for a summit meeting between Soviet and Western leaders; upsets US, France and West Germany.

25 May. First test of an atomic artillery shell by US.

17 June. The 'Berlin Rising': workers' demonstrations in East Berlin and other cities quickly put down by Red Army.

18 June. South Korean leader Syngman Rhee releases North Korean prisoners of war and thus threatens peace efforts (see page 91).

5 July. Imre Nagy, formerly criticised by the leadership, becomes Hungarian prime minister; introduces liberalisation measures.

10 July. Soviet security chief Beria is arrested and later (22 December) executed as a 'spy'.

10–15 July. Meeting of US, British and French foreign ministers in Washington invites USSR to a conference on Germany. In replies (5 and 16 August) USSR insists on Chinese representation in Great Power talks.

27 July. Armistice agreement signed at Panmunjom ends the Korean War.

7 August. UN nations involved in Korean War warn that if war is renewed it probably could not be confined to Korea.

8 August. US–South Korean mutual defence treaty signed.

8 August.   Explosion of first Soviet hydrogen bomb.

19–20 August.   CIA supports successful coup by supporters of the Shah of Iran, leading to the arrest of the radical prime minister Mossadeq.

2 September.   Further Western note to USSR proposing a conference on Germany; Soviets reply on 28 September.

12 September.   Khruschev is given the title 'First Secretary' of the Soviet Communist Party.

26 September.   Agreement on military bases between US and Franco's Spain.

27 September.   Japan decides to recreate military forces.

28 September.   Cardinal Wyszynski, head of the Roman Catholic Church in Poland, is arrested; leads to street protests.

2 October.   Iranian government begins crackdown against Communist *Tudeh* party.

8 October.   US and Britain announce that they will return Trieste (established as a free port in 1947) to Italy; followed by protests from Yugoslavia.

18 October.   US, British and French foreign ministers, following talks in London, send another note to USSR proposing talks on Germany; Soviets reply positively on 3 November; further exchanges on 16 and 26 November.

20 November.   French establish a military base at Dienbienphu in northern Vietnam as part of offensive operation by General Navarre.

4–8 December.   Eisenhower, Churchill and French premier Laniel meet in Bermuda; agree to accept proposal for a four-power conference on Germany in Berlin.

8 December.   Eisenhower's 'Atoms for Peace' speech given before the UN Assembly.

14–16 December.   At NATO Council in Paris Secretary of State Dulles warns of an 'agonising reappraisal' of US security policy if France does not ratify the European Defence Community.

1954

15 January.   Dulles speech says US will meet any threat through 'a capacity to retaliate instantly by means . . . of our own choosing': inaugurates policy of 'massive retaliation'.

21 January.   US launches first atomic submarine, *Nautilus.*

25 January–18 February.   US, Soviet, British and French foreign ministers meet in Berlin to discuss Germany; fail to agree.

5 February.   Viet-Minh forces surround the French garrison at Dienbienphu.

1 March.   Organisation of American States meets in Caracas and condemns the threat of Communism; major step in US isolation of radical Guatemala.

1 March. US tests first deliverable hydrogen bomb in Marshall Islands; fall-out affects the Japanese fishing boat, *Lucky Dragon*.

8 March. US–Japanese defence deal signed.

29 March. Dulles calls for 'united action' by the West to save Dienbienphu.

31 March. USSR proposes it should be allowed to join NATO: Western powers reject this on 7 May.

2 April. Turkish–Pakistani treaty signed; first step towards later Baghdad Pact.

7 April. Eisenhower in a news conference, talks about the danger of 'falling dominoes' in South-East Asia.

13 April. British agreement on 'association' with European Defence Community published; designed to encourage French ratification.

17 April. Nasser becomes head of Egyptian government.

26 April. US, Soviet, British and French foreign ministers, with Asian representatives, begin talks on Korea and Indo-China in Geneva.

28 April. Chinese–Indian trade agreement includes acceptance of the 'five principles' of non-alignment.

7 May. Dienbienphu falls to Viet-Minh, one day before Geneva talks turn to Indo-China.

8 May. French call for a cease-fire in Vietnam.

17 May. Communist leader, Luis Taruc, surrenders to the Philippines government after eight years of guerrilla insurgency.

19 May. US and Pakistan sign defence pact.

2 June. In US, Senator McCarthy makes new accusations about 'Communists' in government.

16 June. Emperor Bao Dai asks pro-American Ngo Dinh Diem to become Vietnamese prime minister; forms government on 5 July.

18 June. Pierre Mendès-France becomes French prime minister; promises an Indo-Chinese settlement within a month.

19 June. Guatemalan government appeals to UN over 'aggression' from Nicaragua and Honduras: actually a CIA-backed coup against the Guatemala government.

27 June. Radical President Arbenz of Guatemala agrees to resign; gives way to the pro-America Castillo Armas.

2 July. Churchill, without British Cabinet approval, sends telegram to Soviet foreign minister, Molotov, with idea of an Anglo-Soviet leaders' meeting.

21 July. Geneva conference ends with signature of agreements on independence of Indo-China.

24 July. USSR proposes a European security agreement, without US, in new note to Western powers; rejected by West.

30 July. US Senate debates possible censure of Senator McCarthy.

9 August. Balkan Pact signed by Yugoslavia, Greece and Turkey.

11 August. Communist China demands the 'liberation' of Taiwan from Nationalist rule.

19–22 August. Brussels Conference of signatories to the European Defence Community treaty fails to agree on French demands for amendments to it.

24 August. The American Communist Party is outlawed.

30 August. French Assembly refuses to ratify the European Defence Community: the whole scheme collapses, and German rearmament is thrown into limbo.

3 September. Chinese artillery begin to bombard the Nationalist-held island of Quemoy.

6–8 September. Manila Conference leads to Pacific Charter and creation of South-East Asian Treaty Organisation (SEATO).

28 September–3 October. London Conference of US, Britain, France, Germany, Canada, Italy and Benelux agrees on German rearmament in NATO, restoration of German sovereignty, and creation of Western European Union.

5 October. US, Britain, Italy and Yugoslavia settle the future of Trieste: the port to Italy, the hinterland to Yugoslavia.

19 October. Britain and Egypt sign agreement on the Suez military base: to be evacuated by Britain in 1956, but can be 'reactivated' by Britain within seven years if Middle East states are attacked.

20–23 October. Paris Conference of NATO countries finalises the London agreements on German rearmament.

23 October. Soviet note to US, Britain and France proposes a conference on European security again, rejected by West in notes of 29 November.

1 November. Algerian nationalist struggle against France begins in earnest.

13 November. In Egypt, Nasser arrests President Neguib; Nasser becomes President on 17 November.

1 December. US–Taiwanese mutual defence treaty signed.

2 December. US Senate condemns McCarthy's behaviour in hearings earlier in the year; clear sign of McCarthy's declining power.

20 December. USSR threatens to annul its treaties with Britain (1942) and France (1944) if Germany is rearmed.

30 December. French Assembly approves the Paris Accords on German rearmament.

1955

31 January. UN Security Council invites Communist China to discuss continuing tensions over the Quemoy and Matsu islands; China refuses.

7 February. Taschen Islands abandoned by Nationalist Chinese, who hold on to Quemoy and the Matsus.

8 February. Replacement of Georgi Malenkov as Soviet premier by Nikolai Bulganin.

24 February. Original Baghdad Pact signed by Iraq and Turkey.

16 March. America publishes its documents on the 1945 Yalta Conference, after accusations that Western interests had been betrayed there.

23 March. Eisenhower raises the possibility of a summit with the USSR.

4 April. Anglo-Iraqi treaty links Britain to the Baghdad Pact.

18 April. Reformist Imre Nagy sacked as Hungarian premier.

18–24 April. First conference of developing nations at Bandung, Java, condemns racism and colonialism.

25 April. In Bandung Zhou Enlai expresses readiness to discuss the Quemoy–Matsu crisis with the US; Dulles gives a positive reply on 26 April.

5 May. End of the Western Allies' occupation of West Germany.

7 May. USSR annuls its wartime treaties with Britain and France.

8 May. West Germany admitted to NATO.

10 May. US, Britain and France propose a conference to USSR; USSR replies on 26 May.

11–14 May. Eastern bloc countries meet in Warsaw and sign Warsaw Pact.

15 May. Soviet and Western foreign ministers sign the Austrian State Treaty.

26 May–2 June. Khruschev and Bulganin visit Yugoslavia and re-establish relations with Tito.

1–3 June. The 'relaunch' of Europe: the Messina Conference of European Coal–Steel Community members agrees to discuss a common market and an atomic energy agency.

6 June. US, Britain and France propose that a Summit meeting should be held with the USSR in July; USSR accepts on 13 June.

7 June. USSR invites Adenauer to Moscow.

11–25 June. Nehru of India visits USSR; USSR accepts the 'five principles' on non-alignment as the basis of future relations.

16 July. Premier Diem of South Vietnam cancels all-Vietnamese elections which had been due in 1956.

18 July. Pakistan joins the Baghdad Pact.

18–24 July. Geneva Summit meeting between Eisenhower, Khruschev, Eden and Faure.

1 August. US and Chinese begin talks at ambassadorial level in Geneva but cannot agree on permanent settlement of Quemoy–Matsu issue.

29 August–3 September. Serious Israeli–Egyptian clashes at Gaza highlight continuing Arab–Israeli tension.

8–13 September. Adenauer visits USSR; diplomatic relations established.

19 September. USSR and Finland renew their non-aggression treaty for twenty years.

20 September.   Soviet–East German treaty signed, recognising East German sovereignty.

23 October.   South Vietnamese referendum deposes Emperor Bao Dai and leads (on 26 October) to a republic under Diem.

27 October–16 November.   US, Soviet, British and French foreign ministers meet in Geneva; fail to agree on Germany and European security.

3 November.   Iran joins the Baghdad Pact.

12 November.   First West German troops are commissioned.

18 November–1 December.   Khruschev and Bulganin visit India, demonstrating greater Soviet links to developing states.

23 November.   USSR tests a deliverable hydrogen bomb.

1956

26 January.   USSR returns naval base at Pokkala to Finland.

14 February.   Twentieth Congress of the Soviet Communist Party begins.

25 February.   Khruschev's 'secret session' speech attacks Stalinism and leads to pressure for liberalisation in Eastern bloc.

2 March.   King Hussein of Jordan, facing pressure from Arab radicals, dismisses British General Glubb, Commander of the armed forces.

26 March.   Last French troops leave South Vietnam.

6 April.   Wladislaw Gomulka released from imprisonment (arrested 31 October 1951) in Poland; rehabilitated 5 August.

18 April.   Dissolution of the Cominform.

18–28 April.   Khruschev and Bulganin visit Britain to solidify detente.

29 April.   British announce disappearance of a frogman, Commander Crabb; later admitted to have been spying on Soviet ships during Khruschev visit.

16 May.   Nasser of Egypt recognises Communist China.

1 June.   Molotov replaced as Soviet foreign minister on eve of three-week visit by Tito to USSR.

13 June.   Under 1954 agreement, last British soldiers leave Suez Canal base.

27 June.   In Hungary, the Petofti group of intellectuals openly attacks the government.

28 June.   'Poznan Rising' of workers in Poland; put down by Polish army.

18 July.   Matyas Rakosi, leader of Hungarian Communists, resigns; succeeded by Ernoe Geroe.

18–19 July.   Tito, Nehru of India and Nasser of Egypt meet at Brioni, Yugoslavia, and issue a declaration on 'non-alignment'.

18 July.   US withdraws from financing Egypt's Aswan Dam.

26 July.   Nasser nationalises the Suez Canal Company, mainly British- and French-owned.

16–23 August. Suez Canal users meet in London and agree to send Menzies Committee for talks with Nasser.

17 August. West German Constitutional Court bans Communist Party.

4–9 September. Menzies Committee fails to reach agreement with Nasser over Suez.

19–21 September. Eighteen-nation conference in London agrees to set up 'Suez Canal Users' Association' despite opposition of Egypt and Eastern bloc.

6 October. Reburial of Laszlo Rajk, executed in Stalinist purges, fuels nationalist feeling in Hungary.

13 October. UN talks on Suez crisis fail after Soviet veto.

19 October. USSR and Japan terminate the state of war since 1945 and reopen diplomatic relations.

19–20 October. Visit by Khruschev and other Soviet leaders to Poland confirms Gomulka's appointment as Communist leader in bid to control discontent.

21–24 October. In secret talks at Sèvres, France, Britain and Israel plan military operations against Egypt.

22–23 October. Demonstrators in Hungary demand democratic reforms.

24 October. Reformist Imre Nagy made Hungarian prime minister; Janos Kadar becomes Communist Party head on 25 October.

29 October. Israelis invade Egypt; British vessels sail from Malta for Egypt.

30 October. Britain and France veto UN resolution calling for Israeli withdrawal from Egypt; Britain and France call on Egypt and Israel to end fighting and allow Anglo-French forces into Suez Canal area.

31 October. Britain and France begin to bomb Egypt; Eisenhower publicly criticises them.

1–2 November. Nagy withdraws Hungary from Warsaw Pact and declares in favour of neutrality; Soviets begin military operations against Hungary.

2 November. Special UN General Assembly meeting calls for cease-fire in Middle East; USSR vetoes UN discussion on Hungary.

4 November. Red Army invades Budapest and installs Kadar as new prime minister; Israel completes conquest of Sinai.

5 November. First Anglo-French forces land in Egypt.

6 November. Eisenhower easily defeats Àdlai Stevenson in US election; Britain and France accept cease-fire in Middle East.

7 November. UN agrees to set up expeditionary force (UNEF) to go to Sinai; arrives 21 November.

13 November. Russian Marshal Rokossovsky resigns as Polish defence minister, under Polish pressure.

5–22 December. Anglo-French forces withdraw from Egypt.

1957

1–4 January. Eastern bloc leaders meet in Budapest to discuss post-Hungary situation; meeting confirms new repressive line of Soviet policy.

5 January. 'Eisenhower Doctrine' against Communism in Middle East announced to Congress; approved on 9 March.

19 January. Arab leaders, meeting in Cairo, are critical of Eisenhower Doctrine.

11 February. USSR proposes joint declaration with US, Britain and France on Middle East, to include ban on arms sales and end of Baghdad Pact; rejected by Western powers on 11 March but repeated by USSR later (19 April, 13 September).

25 March. Treaties of Rome (effective 1 January), between France, West Germany, Italy and Benelux states, create European Economic Community (EEC) and an atomic energy authority (EURATOM).

3 April. Jordanian government of Suleyman Nabulsi decides to establish diplomatic relations with USSR; decision is opposed by King Hussein.

10 April. King Hussein asks Nabulsi government to resign; disorder follows.

20 April. Bulganin letter to Britain's Macmillan revives interest in 1955 'Eden Plan' for a limited disarmament zone in central Europe.

25 April. US sends Sixth Fleet to Eastern Mediterranean due to Jordanian crisis; Hussein enforces martial law on Jordan.

29 April. USSR protests over US military moves in Eastern Mediterranean.

10 May. Soviets call on US and Britain to agree to mutual suspension of nuclear tests.

25–26 May. Hussein asks Syrians to withdraw troops (sent in October 1956) from Jordan.

16 June. Jordanian Embassy in Cairo closed on Egyptian demand.

3 July. Khruschev foils the 'Anti-Party' Plot of ex-Stalinists who tried to oust him as leader: Molotov, Malenkov and Shepilov are among those removed from high office (Molotov becoming Ambassador to Mongolia on 30 August).

27–29 July. East German proposal for a 'confederal' relationship with West Germany rejected by Adenauer and Western powers, but (on 8 August) supported by USSR.

1 August. US and Canada begin to operate 'distant early warning' (DEW) system against nuclear attack.

1–2 August. Khruschev and Tito meet in Romania, following strains in Soviet–Yugoslav relations after 1956 Hungarian crisis.

26 August. USSR announces test of first inter-continental ballistic missile.

7 September. Dulles criticises pro-Soviet policy of Syria, which was negotiating aid agreement with USSR.

10–11 September. USSR warns Turkey against any attack on Syria following increasing Turco-Syrian tensions.

19 September.   First US underground nuclear test in Nevada.

2 October.   Poland's 'Rapacki Plan' put to UN Assembly advocating nuclear weapon-free zone in central Europe, including East and West Germany.

4 October.   Soviets launch first space satellite, *Sputnik*.

12 October.   Khruschev accuses US and Turkey of conspiring to attack Syria.

16 October.   Syria complains to UN over Turkish threat; US warns USSR against attacking Turkey.

17 October.   Turkey denies any wish for war with Syria.

19 October.   Under 'Hallstein Doctrine', West Germany breaks relations with Yugoslavia after latter recognised East Germany.

29 October.   Khruschev attends a Turkish Embassy reception; end of Turco-Syrian war crisis.

3 November.   Soviets launch dog, Laika, into space on *Sputnik II*.

14–16 November.   Major meeting of Communist parties in Moscow continues anti-liberal line, and shows desire of local Communist leaders for equality with Moscow.

10 December.   Bulganin proposes suspension of nuclear tests and holding of an East–West Summit.

16–19 December.   First NATO heads of government meeting, in Paris, includes discussion of US nuclear missile bases in Europe.

1958

10 January.   US successfully tests an intercontinental ballistic missile.

12 January.   US accepts idea of Summit with USSR. Later (15 February) insists that foreign ministers meet first.

31 January.   US successfully launches space-craft, *Explorer I*, after earlier failures.

8 February.   French air force attacks Tunisian village of Sakhiet, suspected as Algerian nationalist base; leads to international outcry.

14 February.   Poland publishes Rapacki Plan in full.

27 March.   Khruschev replaces Bulganin as Soviet prime minister.

31 March.   USSR begins unilateral moratorium on nuclear tests.

28 April.   US proposes talks on nuclear test control. USSR agrees on 9 May.

3 May.   US formally rejects Rapacki Plan.

12 May.   US and Canada set up a joint North American Air Defence Command (NORAD).

13 May.   Vice-President Nixon attacked by a mob in Caracas, Venezuela. Highlights anti-Americanism in South America.

13 May.   Demonstrations by French Algerians in Algiers lead to 'Committee of Public Safety' being set up.

29 May.   General de Gaulle asked to form new government in France to deal with Algeria.

31 May.   Western powers propose agenda for a Summit, including German reunification.

11 June.   Khruschev publicly questions whether Western powers really want a Summit.

16 June.   Imre Nagy, former Hungarian leader, hanged.

1 July.   US, USSR and Britain begin talks in Geneva on nuclear test ban. Talks continue, intermittently, until 1963.

2 July.   US amends Atomic Energy Act to allow greater co-operation with allies.

14 July.   Iraqi monarchy overthrown and King Feisal killed; General Kassem in power.

15 July.   Iraqi premier, Nuri el-Said, killed by a mob; thousands of US marines land in Lebanon to support government of President Chamoun.

17 July.   Two thousand British paratroops arrive in Jordan to support King Hussein against radicals.

19 July.   Iraq signs defence pact with Egypt; Khruschev proposes Summit meeting to discuss Middle East.

24 July.   Soviet troops announced to be leaving Romania.

28 July.   US promises defence agreements with Iran, Turkey and Pakistan (members of Baghdad Pact).

29 July.   National Aeronautics and Space Administration (NASA) founded in US to provide for civilian space programme.

31 July–3 August.   Khruschev meets Mao in Beijing: they call for a Summit with West and end of Western intervention in Middle East.

6 August.   Beginning of new Quemoy–Matsu crisis after Taiwanese government declares state of emergency on islands.

8 August.   US–Soviet agreement finally allows UN General Assembly to discuss Middle East crisis.

24 August.   Dulles warns China against invasion of Quemoy and Matsus.

5 September.   East German government proposes talks on German peace treaty. Western powers refuse to reply, not recognising East Germany.

6 September.   China proposes talks on Quemoy–Matsu.

24 September.   De Gaulle proposes to US and Britain that France should help to direct NATO in a triumvirate; rejected by Eisenhower and Macmillan.

30 September.   Dulles statement supports peaceful resolution of Quemoy–Matsu crisis.

2 October.   Soviets say they will resume nuclear tests.

6 October.   Chinese allow nationalists to resupply Quemoy and Matsus; crisis eases.

25 October.   US marines leave Lebanon.

31 October. New talks on test ban lead to moratorium on tests by US and USSR.
2 November. British paratroops leave Jordan.

6. Khruschev's Cold War, 1958–62

10 November 1958. Start of second Berlin crisis. Khruschev says the West should leave Berlin and that USSR plans to hand East Berlin to East Germany.
21 November. US promises to maintain its position in West Berlin.
27 November. Soviet note to US, Britain and France demands resolution of Berlin situation within six months and threatens to transfer Soviet sector to East Germany.
14 December. US, British and French foreign ministers in Paris reject Soviet note on Berlin; Western notes sent to Moscow on 31 December.

1959
2 January. Cuban dictator, Batista, overthrown by Fidel Castro.
4–23 January. Soviet Politbureau member, Anastas Mikoyan, arrives on 'holiday' in US to reduce tensions over Berlin.
10 January. USSR proposes German peace conference in two months.
16 February. Western powers respond to latest Soviet note with proposal for four-power foreign ministers' conference.
21 February–3 March. British premier Macmillan visits USSR, despite criticism.
1 March. Soviets still want a Summit but accept foreign ministers' conference with US, Britain and France.
5 March. US concludes defence agreements with Turkey, Iran and Pakistan.
26 March. Western powers propose four-power foreign ministers' meeting should be on 11 May in Geneva. Soviets agree on 30 March.
31 March. Dalai Lama, religious leader of Tibet, flees to India after Chinese repression of Tibetan nationalist rising (since 10 March).
15 April. Resignation of Dulles (died on 24 April).
21 April. Soviets protest over basing of nuclear weapons in West Germany.
11 May–20 June. US, Soviet, British and French ministers hold first session of Geneva talks on Germany.
9 June. USS *George Washington*, first US submarine armed with nuclear missiles (Polaris), launched.
8 July. Two US soldiers killed by Communists at Bien Hoa in South Vietnam as North Vietnamese begin to aid local Communist guerrillas.
13 July–5 August. More four-power talks on Germany in Geneva fail to make progress.

24 July.   The 'Kitchen Debate': Khruschev and Vice-President Nixon meet in exhibition centre in Moscow and exchange views on US and Soviet ways of life.

28 July.   Arrest of Communist leaders in Laos provokes widespread unrest.

3 August.   Eisenhower invites Khruschev to US in surprise move.

21 August.   Baghdad Pact becomes Central Treaty Organisation (CENTO).

15–27 September.   Khruschev's visit to US includes UN speech (on 18 September) and talks with Eisenhower (on 15 and 25–27 September).

30 September–4 October.   Khruschev visits China for tenth anniversary of Mao's regime, but no communiqué is issued: Chinese criticise Khruschev's desire for coexistence with West.

20–21 October.   Nine Indians killed in Chinese–Indian border clash.

1 December.   US, USSR and other nations sign agreement on peaceful use of Antarctica. First major post-war disarmament agreement.

3–23 December.   Eisenhower world tour includes first visit by US President to Asia.

19–21 December.   Eisenhower, Macmillan, de Gaulle and Adenauer, in Paris, invite Khruschev to a Summit in 1960.

1960

14 January.   Khruschev announces major reductions in Soviet armed forces.

19 January.   US and Japan sign security treaty to last at least ten years.

1 February.   Chinese fail to attend a Communist meeting in Moscow.

10 February–5 March.   Khruschev visits India and other South Asian countries.

13 February.   French test their first atom bomb in the Sahara.

23 March–2 April.   Khruschev visits Paris.

1 May.   Gary Powers' U-2 spy-plane shot down over Ural mountains.

5 May.   Soviets announce U-2 shot down; US denies it was spying.

8 May.   USSR and Cuba establish full diplomatic relations.

11 May.   Eisenhower admits Gary Powers was spying.

14 May.   Khruschev arrives for Summit meeting in Paris.

16 May.   The Summit is abandoned.

27 June.   Eastern bloc states walk out of UN disarmament talks.

30 June.   Congo given its independence by Belgium.

5–8 July.   The Congolese army mutinies; Belgium despatches troops to Congo which appeals to UN.

11 July.   Katanga province under Moise Tshombe declares independence from Congo.

13–14 July.   UN Security Council decides to send troops to Congo.

14 July.   US reaffirms Monroe Doctrine after Khruschev (on 9 July) warned US against intervention in Cuba.

31 July. End of 'emergency' in Malaya against Communist guerrillas.

9–30 August. Coup in Laos results in neutralist Prince Souvanna Phouma replacing pro-US government.

19 August. USSR sentences Gary Powers to imprisonment.

2 September. Soviets begin to supply Congolese premier, Patrice Lumumba, with aircraft.

5–6 September. Lumumba and Congolese President Kasavubu dismiss each other from their posts!

19 September–30 October. Khruschev attends UN, makes a number of speeches, thumps his desk during a speech by Macmillan (29 September) and hits the desk with a shoe when the Philippine delegate speaks (12 October).

18 October. Soviet newspaper *Pravda* makes first major criticisms of China.

19 October. US recalls Ambassador to Cuba and launches embargo on trade.

8 November. John F. Kennedy defeats Nixon in presidential election.

21 November. General Norstad suggests NATO nuclear force.

1 December. Pro-Soviet Lumumba captured by Congolese army and later killed.

7–8 December. Communist meeting in Moscow fails to heal Sino-Soviet split.

9–13 December. Neutralist Souvanna Phouma replaced by pro-US Prince Boun Oum in Laos. USSR accuses US of undermining Laotian neutrality.

14 December. Establishment of Organisation of Economic Co-operation and Development (OECD) by US, Canada and West Europeans.

20 December. Vietnamese Communists establish 'National Liberation Front', known as 'Vietcong', in South Vietnam.

1961

3 January. US breaks diplomatic relations with Cuba and induces other Latin American states to follow.

6 January. Khruschev speech supports 'wars of national liberation'.

20 January. Kennedy's Inaugural Speech says US will 'pay any price, bear any burden, meet any hardship, support any friend, oppose any foe, to ensure the survival and the success of Liberty'.

8 February. Ex-premier Lumumba murdered in the Congo.

22 February. Khruschev criticises policy of UN Secretary-General Hammarskjöld in the Congo.

1 March. Kennedy launches 'Peace Corps' of aid workers to assist Third World.

13 March. Kennedy launches 'Alliance for Progress' to provide development aid to Latin America (established at Punta del Este conference in August).

12 April.   Yuri Gagarin becomes first person in space.

17–20 April.   Bay of Pigs invasion, by CIA-backed Cuban exiles, ends in failure.

3 May.   Cease-fire between pro-US and pro-Communist forces in Laos, followed (on 12 May) by talks in Geneva.

5 May.   Alan Shepard becomes first American in space.

3–4 June.   Vienna Summit between Kennedy and Khruschev; Khruschev demands demilitarisation of Berlin.

8 July.   Khruschev cancels planned reductions of Soviet armed forces.

17 July.   Western powers reject Khruschev's proposals on Berlin.

23 July.   East Germans try to stem flood of refugees to West Berlin through new travel restrictions.

25 July.   Kennedy television speech declares his support for West Berlin and announces new arms spending.

31 July.   Macmillan announces British application to join EEC.

3 August.   Soviet note threatens to sign separate peace treaty with East Germany.

5–6 August.   US, British and French foreign ministers, in Paris, reject latest Soviet note.

19–22 August.   Berlin Wall built, leaving only a few crossing points between East and West Berlin.

31 August.   Resumption of Soviet nuclear tests (first since 1958).

1–6 September.   Non-aligned leaders Tito (Yugoslavia), Nehru (India) and Nasser (Egypt) meet in Belgrade.

3 September.   US and Britain propose ban on atmospheric nuclear tests. Rejected on 9 September by USSR.

15 September.   US resumes nuclear tests underground.

17 September.   UN Secretary-General Hammarskjöld killed in air crash over Congo while trying to resolve question of Katangan secession.

6 October.   Kennedy and Gromyko meet in the While House, but cannot agree on Berlin.

17–31 October.   Twenty-Second Soviet Communist Party Congress sees clear differences between USSR and its satellites on one side, and China and Albania on the other.

19 October.   Emergency declared against Vietcong in South Vietnam.

27–29 October.   US and Soviet tanks face each other 'nose-to-nose' at Checkpoint Charlie, Berlin.

10 November.   After rising tension USSR closes its embassy in Albania.

20 November.   Test-ban talks reopen in Geneva.

5–21 December.   UN forces invade Katanga to end its seccession from the Congo.

17–19 December.   India forcibly annexes Portuguese enclave of Goa after months of tension. USSR vetoes UN cease-fire call.

1962

19 January.   Coalition government formed in Laos, but the country remains unstable.

31 January.   OAS excludes Cuba from its activities.

8 February.   US Military Assistance Command established in Vietnam.

20 February.   John Glenn becomes first American to orbit Earth.

2 March.   Kennedy says US will renew atmospheric tests unless USSR signs test ban; threat carried out on 25 April.

19 March.   Cease-fire in war between French and Algerian National Liberation Front.

5 May.   US Defence Secretary McNamara, in Athens, makes his first public speech on a 'counterforce strategy' for nuclear weapons.

13 May.   Kennedy sends US marines to Thailand as a precaution against trouble in Laos (withdrawn by 7 October).

24 June.   New cease-fire agreed in Laos.

3 July.   Algeria wins its independence from France.

23 July.   Agreement on Laotian neutrality signed in Geneva.

31 August.   Republican Senator Keating claims that Soviets are using Cuba as a military base.

4 September.   Kennedy warns USSR not to deploy surface-to-surface missiles on Cuba.

8 September.   Chinese troops begin to cross the Indian border near Tibet.

11 September.   Moscow denies any intention to base nuclear missiles outside USSR; further reassurances are given later.

10 October.   Full-scale Chinese invasion of India.

7. The Cuban Missile Crisis

1962

14 October.   An American U-2 spy-plane photographs launch-sites for nuclear missiles on Cuba.

16 October.   President Kennedy is told of the discovery and forms an Executive Committee of the NSC (Ex Comm) to discuss US response. Ex Comm includes Secretary of State Rusk, Defense Secretary McNamara, CIA chief McCone and others. Opinions differ as to how to deal with the Soviets, but preference is for an air strike against the missiles.

18 October.   Kennedy meets Gromyko and warns him offensive missiles must not be installed on Cuba. Gromyko appears not to know about missile bases. US forces are prepared for possible military action.

20 October.   Meeting of Kennedy and Ex Comm. Adlai Stevenson, Ambassador to UN, suggests US withdraw missiles from Turkey and Italy as a *quid pro quo* for Soviet withdrawal from Cuba, but others reject this. Balance is now in favour of a blockade of Cuba to prevent arrival of missiles. Following this, US allies are informed of the situation and more US forces prepared.

22 October. Congressional leaders and Soviet Ambassador Dobrynin are forewarned of a TV announcement by Kennedy. The speech publicly reveals the existence of missile bases and announces a 'quarantine' of Cuba. US forces are put on a high 'Defence Condition' (DEFCON-3).

24 October. US forces put on DEFCON-2 (one short of war), their highest-ever alert, and steps are taken to ensure the Soviets know of this. Soviet vessels on their way to Cuba approach the US blockade but then stop. UN Secretary-General, U Thant, calls for talks but Kennedy says Soviet missiles must be withdrawn.

26 October. After earlier fruitless exchanges, a message from Khruschev suggests the Soviets could withdraw missiles if US lifts the blockade and guarantees Cuba won't be invaded.

27 October. A new Soviet message wants the US to withdraw missiles from Turkey if it is to end the blockade – a step which would humiliate Turkey. A U-2 is shot down over Cuba. Pressure on Kennedy for military action is intense. But someone (the president's brother, Robert, according to common mythology; Llewellyn Thompson according to the record) suggests agreeing to the terms of Khruschev's 26 October message, and ignoring the second one. The president agrees, but also gives secret assurances to the Soviets that US missiles could soon leave Turkey.

28 October. Khruschev agrees to withdraw missiles from Cuba in return for a US guarantee of Cuban security and the end of the blockade. The move upsets the Cubans, who surround Soviet bases for the next four days.

8. Vietnam and early signs of detente, 1962–68

1962

6 November. US says Soviet nuclear bombers, as well as missiles, must leave Cuba.

20 November. Khruschev says Soviet bombers will leave Cuba but Castro will not allow US verification; US pledge, not to invade Cuba, is therefore not formalised (until 1970).

21 November. China announces withdrawal of its forces from India.

18–21 December. Kennedy meets Macmillan at Nassau and agrees to supply Polaris missiles to Britain, highlighting continued British reliance on US.

23–24 December. In exchange for food and medicine, Cuba exchanges about 1,100 prisoners taken at Bay of Pigs.

28 December.   Renewal of fighting in the Congo between UN forces and Katanga secessionists after breakdown of talks.

1963

14 January.   Moise Tshombe admits defeat of Katangan secession and goes into exile.

14 January.   De Gaulle vetoes Britain's 1961 application to join European Communities, claiming Britain is too close to US.

22 January.   De Gaulle makes a co-operation treaty with Adenauer in Paris.

8 March.   Chinese *People's Daily* questions validity of border with USSR.

10 June.   US, USSR and Britain agree to new test-ban talks in Moscow.

10 June.   Kennedy makes a speech at American University, Washington aimed at reducing Cold War tensions, denying any desire for a *Pax Americana*.

11 June.   Quang Duc, a Buddhist priest, burns himself to death in Saigon in protest against Diem government; other such burnings follow.

20 June.   US and USSR agree to establish 'hot line' between Kremlin and White House.

26 June.   Kennedy, at Berlin Wall, declares 'Ich bin ein Berliner.'

15 July–5 August.   Test-ban talks in Moscow successfully result in treaty between US, USSR and Britain.

2 September.   Kennedy publicly criticises Diem regime.

16 September.   President Sukarno of Indonesia launches a 'confrontation' with neighbouring Malaysia; sporadic border clashes continue until August 1966.

1–2 November.   Diem and his brother Nhu are killed in a coup, after which General Van Minh becomes head of state.

22 November.   Kennedy assassinated in Dallas.

17 December.   Speech by new president, Johnson, calls for an end to the Cold War.

1964

12 January.   USSR signs agreement to buy wheat from US for first time.

20 January.   De Gaulle recognises Communist China.

30 January.   General Nguyen Khanh takes power in South Vietnam; Johnson declares his support on 1 February.

12 February.   Fighting breaks out on wide scale between Greek and Turkish communities in Cyprus.

19 March.   UN forces fly to Cyprus to maintain the peace.

3 April.   Malenkov and Molotov are expelled from the Soviet Communist Party.

9–15 May.   Khruschev visits Egypt and makes Nasser a 'Hero of the Soviet Union'.

18 May. Johnson asks Congress to increase aid to South Vietnam.

30 June. UN forces (present since 1960) leave the Congo.

2 August. USS *Maddox* attacked by North Vietnamese torpedo boats in Gulf of Tonkin.

4 August. Supposed second attack on US vessels.

5 August. US aircraft begin to bomb targets in North Vietnam.

7 August. In 'Gulf of Tonkin Resolution' Congress gives Johnson a 'blank cheque' to deal with the Vietnam situation.

9–10 August. UN calls for, and obtains, a cease-fire in Cyprus after Turkish aircraft bomb Greek Cypriots.

21–25 August. Demonstrations in South Vietnam force General Khanh to share power.

14 October. Khruschev is overthrown and replaced by Brezhnev and Kosygin.

16 October. China explodes its first atomic bomb.

20 October. New civilian government formed in South Vietnam but instability continues.

3 November. Johnson defeats Barry Goldwater in US election.

26 November. Soviets condemn US air attacks on North Vietnam.

24 December. Communist Vietcong bomb a US base in Saigon.

1965

4 January. USSR publicises letter to North Vietnam promising it support against US pressure.

20 January. Warsaw Pact accepts Polish proposal for an East–West European Security Conference to exclude US and Canada: marks the start of a determined Eastern bloc campaign for such a conference.

20 January. Johnson's inaugural address emphasises need for fairer America ('Great Society') but also favours detente with USSR.

27 January. General Khanh again seizes power in South Vietnam.

5–10 February. Soviet premier Kosygin visits North Vietnam, China (meets Zhou Enlai) and North Korea.

7 February. After Vietcong attacks US personnel, US begins to bomb North Vietnam; 'Operation Rolling Thunder' launched on 24 February.

20 February. General Khanh overthrown by South Vietnamese army officers.

8 March. First US ground combat troops, Marines, land at Da Nang in South Vietnam.

April. Chinese launch 'Cultural Revolution' to reinvigorate Communist revolution.

7 April. Johnson speech at Johns Hopkins University sets out terms for peace in Vietnam.

8 April. North Vietnamese call for US withdrawal.

9 April. Indo-Pakistan border clashes (since February) reach new intensity with Pakistani artillery bombardment in Rann of Kutch area.

25 April. Right-wing government of Donald Reid Cabral overthrown in Dominica. Unrest follows.

28 April. Johnson decides to use force in Dominica to prevent a Castro-style regime.

30 April. US marines land in Dominica.

2 May. 'Johnson Doctrine' inaugurated against Communism in Latin America.

14 May. New junta established in Dominica under General Imbert.

11 June. Air Vice-Marshal Nguyen Cao Ky becomes premier of South Vietnam.

28 July. Johnson approves increase of troops in Vietnam to 125,000.

5 August. Indo-Pakistani border clashes intensify again in disputed region of Kashmir.

6 September. Indians launch invasion of West Pakistan.

22 September. Cease-fire between India and Pakistan; tensions continue until January 1966.

30 September. Failed bid to overthrow President Sukarno of Indonesia leads army, in October, to launch bloody purge against Chinese-backed Communists.

15–16 October. First major anti-Vietnam War rallies in US.

24 December. First Christmas truce in Vietnam. US suspend bombing.

1966

31 January. US resumes bombing of North Vietnam.

7–8 February. Johnson meets South Vietnamese leaders in Honolulu.

10–14 February. Trial in USSR of writers Andrei Sinyavsky and Yuli Daniel (arrested in September) results in imprisonment. Start of new KGB crackdown on dissidents.

10 March. De Gaulle announces France will leave NATO integrated command.

11–12 March. Pro-US General Suharto takes power in Indonesia from Sukarno and bans Communists.

2 April. South Vietnamese troops join in Buddhist anti-government demonstrations, underway since March.

7 April. Communist Party leader, Nicolae Ceauşescu, declares Romania to be an independent state within Communist bloc.

15–23 May. South Vietnamese troops take Da Nang from protesting Buddhists.

16 June. South Vietnamese government takes old imperial city of Hue from Buddhists.

20 June–1 July. De Gaulle visits USSR.

29 June.   US bomb areas near Hanoi and Haiphong in North Vietnam.

4–8 July.   Warsaw Pact ministers call for European security arrangement to replace Warsaw Pact and NATO.

5 and 9 July.   China and USSR condemn American bombing in Vietnam.

12 July.   Johnson again puts forward a peace plan for Vietnam.

18 August.   Mao Zedong intensifies 'Cultural Revolution' with encouragement to young Red Guards to attack traditionalist and bourgeois elements.

1 September.   De Gaulle criticises US policy in Vietnam on visit to Cambodia.

7 October.   Johnson expresses hope for detente with USSR despite Vietnam.

13 October.   Johnson rejects idea of 'bombing halt' in Vietnam.

26 October.   NATO decides to move its headquarters from Paris to Brussels.

13 December.   US bomb outskirts of Hanoi.

1967

26 January–12 February.   Chinese demonstrators besiege Soviet Embassy in Peking.

27 January.   US, USSR and Britain sign treaty banning nuclear weapons from outer space and the planets.

28 January.   North Vietnam says US bombing must stop before peace can be considered.

31 January.   Romania breaches Soviet bloc by recognising West Germany.

2 February.   Johnson offers bombing halt if Communists end infiltration into South Vietnam.

14 February.   Ttatelco Pact makes Latin America a 'nuclear-free zone'.

6 March.   Stalin's daughter, Svetlana, defects to the West.

19–21 March.   Johnson meets South Vietnamese leaders and US commanders on Guam; decides to maintain military pressure on the North.

20 April.   US bomb the port of Haiphong for the first time.

21 April.   A group of Colonels seizes power in Greece, cancels the general election and establishes a repressive regime. George Papadopoulos predominant.

13 May.   China's Red Guards extend their anti-traditionalist campaign to an invasion of the foreign ministry, whose files are destroyed.

5–10 June.   Mounting tension with the Arabs leads Israel to launch the lightning 'Six-Day War': territory occupied from Egypt (Sinai), Jordan (West Bank) and Syria (Golan Heights).

17 June.   Chinese hydrogen bomb exploded.

23–25 June.   Johnson and Kosygin meet in Glassboro' 'Mini-Summit'.

22 August.   Chinese demonstrators burn the British Embassy in Beijing after differences on Hong Kong.

29 August–1 September. Arabs' Khartoum Summit agrees to end oil sales boycott begun 6 June against US and Britain and reject any recognition of Israel.

3 September. General Nguyen Van Thieu becomes South Vietnamese president.

18 September. Defense Secretary McNamara, in San Francisco, announces US to build 'Sentinel' anti-Ballistic Missile (ABM) system, primarily against China.

29 September. Johnson speech in San Antonio says US is ready to end Vietnam bombing if peace is possible.

21 October. Major demonstrations in US cities against Vietnam War.

22 November. UN Resolution 242 calls on Israel to leave occupied areas and on Arabs to respect Israel's existence.

14 December. NATO foreign ministers accept report by Belgium's Pierre Harmel that, alongside its security role, the alliance should work for detente.

14 December. US Defense Department announces decision to test 'Multiple Independent Re-entry Vehicle' (MIRV), a multi-warhead missile.

1968

5 January. Alexander Dubcek replaces conservative Novotny as leader of Czechoslovakian Communists.

21 January. North Korean group tries to attack South Korean president in Seoul.

23 January. North Koreans seize USS *Pueblo*, an intelligence gathering ship.

30–31 January. Vietcong and North Vietnamese seize control of South Vietnamese cities on Tet holiday.

16 February. Robert Kennedy announces he will challenge Johnson for Democratic nomination.

25 February. US and South Vietnamese troops recapture Hue, ending 'Tet offensive'.

22 March. General Westmoreland relieved as US commander in Vietnam; Johnson decides to avoid escalation of the war after Tet.

31 March. Johnson announces partial bombing halt in Vietnam and pulls out of presidential election campaign.

4 April. Assassination of black civil rights leader Martin Luther King leads to riots in US cities.

9 April. Communist Party in Czechoslovakia promises liberal reforms.

11 April. Assassination attempt on student leader Rudi Dutschke leads to riots in West Germany.

3 May. Student unrest begins in Paris, later spreading to other groups around France and lasting into June.

8 May. 'Group of Five' (USSR, Poland, East Germany, Hungary, Bulgaria) meet in Moscow to discuss Dubcek's liberalisation in Czechoslovakia.

13 May. Peace talks begin in Paris between US and North Vietnam, but fail to progress.

2–9 June. Student unrest in Yugoslavia leads Tito to offer university reforms.

5 June. Assassination of Robert Kennedy in Los Angeles adds to upheaval in US.

27 June. Czechoslovakian government abolishes censorship.

30 June. De Gaulle reasserts authority in France with big election win.

1 July. US, USSR and Britain sign Non-proliferation Treaty to stop spread of nuclear weapons; US and USSR announce they will begin Strategic Arms Limitation Talks (SALT).

14 July. 'Group of Five' Communist states meet in Warsaw and demand meeting with Czechoslovakia.

29 July–1 August. Soviet and Czechoslovak leaders meet.

2–3 August. 'Group of Five' leaders meet Czechoslovakians at Bratislava and seem co-operative.

9 and 15 August. Tito, and subsequently Ceauşescu, visit Czechoslovakia to demonstrate support for Dubcek.

20 August. 'Group of Five' launch invasion of Czechoslovakia to restore hard-line Communism.

23–26 August. Czechoslovakian leaders forced to visit Moscow.

12 September. Albania leaves Warsaw Pact.

1 November. Johnson begins complete bombing halt in Vietnam.

5 November. Richard Nixon defeats Hubert Humphrey in US election.

12 November. In Poland Brezhnev enunciates 'Brezhnev Doctrine' of limited sovereignty for Communist states.

23 December. Crew of USS *Pueblo*, captured in January, released by North Koreans.

9. The 'Era of Negotiations', 1969–75

1969

16 January. Student Jan Palach burns himself to death in Prague in protest at Communist suppression.

20 January. Nixon's inauguration speech looks forward to 'an era of negotiations' in relations with USSR.

2 March. Chinese–Soviet border clash begins at Damansky island on River Ussuri; intermittent border clashes continue until August.

17 March. Warsaw Pact makes new proposals for a European security conference.

18 March.   US government secretly begins to bomb Communist sanctuaries in Cambodia.

15 April.   US EC-121 spy-plane shot down by North Korea.

17 April.   Dubcek forced to resign as Czechoslovakian Communist leader; replaced by Gustav Husak.

14 May.   Nixon proposes that both US and North Vietnamese should leave South Vietnam, to be followed by national elections.

8 June.   Nixon meets President Thieu on Midway and says US to withdraw 25,000 troops from Vietnam.

19 June.   Nixon proposes SALT talks (called off over Czech crisis in August) should now begin.

10 July.   Soviets agree to SALT talks.

21 July.   Neil Armstrong of Apollo 11 space-craft becomes first person to walk on the moon.

25 July.   Nixon explains 'Vietnamisation' (handing war over to South Vietnam) under 'Guam Doctrine'.

2–3 August.   Nixon upsets USSR with visit to Romania, as part of European tour.

4 August.   US National Security Adviser, Kissinger, begins secret talks with North Vietnamese in Paris.

13 August.   More Chinese–Soviet border clashes in Sinkiang.

3 September.   Ho Chi Minh dies.

11 September.   On returning from Ho's funeral, Kosygin visits Beijing, paving way to easier relations.

19 October.   Chinese–Soviet talks open on border disputes.

3 November.   Nixon confirms US will withdraw forces from Vietnam and appeals for support from 'silent majority'.

16 November.   My Lai Massacre of South Vietnamese civilians (16 March 1968) by US troops revealed to public.

17 November.   US team under Gerard Smith and Soviets under Vladimir Semenov begin SALT talks in Helsinki. Later alternate between Helsinki and Geneva.

15 December.   Nixon announces withdrawal of another 50,000 troops from Vietnam.

1970

6 January.   *Pravda* accuses China of preparing war against USSR as Sino-Soviet relations worsen once more.

20 January.   US–Chinese links reopened between their ambassadors in Warsaw.

10 March.   US announces it will deploy a missile with several independently-targettable warheads in June.

17 March.   US uses its veto for the first time in the UN Security Council.

18 March.   Neutralist Prince Sihanouk of Cambodia overthrown by pro-American General Lon Nol.

19 March.   West and East German premiers, Willy Brandt and Willi Stoph, meet in Erfurt: first such meeting since the countries were founded.

26 March.   US, USSR, Britain and France begin talks on future status of Berlin.

20 April.   Nixon announces another 150,000 US troops to leave Vietnam.

30 April.   Nixon announces US–South Vietnamese invasion of Cambodia to attack Communist 'sanctuaries'.

2 May.   US resumes large-scale bombing of North Vietnam for first time under Nixon.

4 May. Four students shot by National Guardsmen at Kent State University, Ohio, in anti-Vietnam protests.

21–22 June.   Warsaw Pact ministers in Budapest again call for a European Security Conference and concede the US and Canada can take part.

25 June.   State Department launches 'Rogers Plan' for Arab–Israeli ceasefire and peace talks in Middle East.

29 June.   US and South Vietnamese forces withdraw from Cambodia.

7 August.   Cease-fire agreed in Arab–Israeli conflict, followed by ineffective peace talks under UN auspices between Israel, Egypt and Jordan.

12 August.   Soviet–West German Treaty of Moscow says European borders can only be changed by peaceful means.

1 September.   Assassination attempt on King Hussein of Jordan leads to Jordanian crackdown against Palestinian guerrilla groups.

5 September.   Salvador Allende elected President of Chile: first democratically elected Marxist leader.

6–12 September.   Palestinian groups hijack four aircraft, three of which are flown to Jordan and blown up. Hostages released.

19–23 September.   Syrian tanks launch brief incursion into Jordan in support of Palestinians.

25 September.   Kissinger warns USSR not to base nuclear forces in Cuba, after US discover work on a nuclear submarine base at Cienfuegos.

27 September.   King Hussein, Yasser Arafat (Palestinian leader) and other Arab leaders agree to end Jordanian civil war.

28 September.   Sudden death of President Nasser of Egypt.

6 October.   Soviet Ambassador Dobrynin assures US that no Soviet submarine base will be built on Cuba.

7 October.   Nixon proposes a 'cease-fire in place' in South Vietnam, which would allow North Vietnamese forces to remain after settlement. Rejected by Hanoi.

8 October.   Nobel literature prize awarded to Soviet dissident Alexander Solzhenitsyn.

7 December.   West German–Polish Treaty of Warsaw recognises Oder–Neisse border. As a sign of reconciliation Brandt kneels at the memorial to victims of the Warsaw ghetto.

14 December.   Rioting in Gdansk, Poland, after price increases, later spreads to other Baltic ports.

20 December.   Gomulka is replaced as Polish Communist leader by Edward Gierek.

1971

8 February–24 March.   South Vietnamese forces launch incursion into Laos to disrupt Communist supplies.

11 February.   US, USSR and others sign treaty banning nuclear missiles from sea-bed.

25 March.   Bangladeshi leader, Mujibur Rahman, arrested by Pakistan government; Pakistan army then suppresses discontent in East Pakistan.

29 March.   Lieutenant William Calley found guilty of 1968 My Lai Massacre.

30 March–9 April.   Soviet Communist Party Congress sees party General Secretary Brezhnev emerge as predominant leader.

6 April.   'Ping-pong diplomacy': US table tennis team invited to China (arriving on 10 April).

7 April.   Nixon announces another 100,000 troops to leave Vietnam.

2 and 13 May.   President Sadat of Egypt sacks pro-Soviet ministers.

3 May.   Ulbricht replaced as East German leader by Erich Honecker who is better disposed to detente.

20 May.   Kissinger and Soviet Ambassador Dobrynin, working in the so-called 'backchannel', reach a SALT 'breakthrough': will conclude an anti-ballistic missile treaty (which USSR want) *and* a limit on offensive missiles (which US want).

27 May.   Fifteen-year Soviet–Egyptian friendship treaty signed.

10 June.   End of US trade embargo (begun 1950) against China.

13 June.   *New York Times* publishes 'Pentagon Papers' – government documents on Vietnam War leaked by Daniel Ellsberg.

13–19 June.   More fighting in Jordan leads to Palestinian withdrawal; Iraq and Syria later protest by breaking relations with Jordan.

10–12 July.   Comecon summit launches 'Complex Programme' for greater economic integration in Eastern bloc.

15 July.   Following secret visit by Kissinger to Beijing, Nixon announces that he too will visit China in 1972; the sudden Sino-American *rapprochement* astonishes many.

9 August.   Twenty-four year Soviet–Indian friendship treaty signed.

15 August.   The 'Nixon shock': US ends convertibility of dollars into gold and introduces trade restrictions. Fatally undermines post-war Western currency system whereby all currencies are fixed against the dollar.

September.   Chinese leader Lin Biao killed in air crash whilst trying to flee to the USSR after disagreement with Mao Zedong.

3 September.   US, USSR, Britain and France sign agreement on Berlin which paves way to East–West German agreement, and to a European Security Conference.

28 September.   Cardinal Mindsentzy allowed to leave Hungary after living in US embassy in Budapest since 1956 rising.

3 October.   Thieu is only candidate in South Vietnamese presidential elections.

12 October.   Nixon announces US–Soviet Summit in Moscow in 1972.

20 October.   Nobel Peace Prize awarded to Brandt for *Ostpolitik*.

25 October.   UN votes to give seat of Taiwan to Communist China.

12 November.   Nixon announces 45,000 more troops to leave Vietnam.

22 November.   Indian forces mass on Pakistan border.

30 November.   Warsaw Pact foreign ministers again call for European security conference.

6 December.   India recognises Bangladesh (East Pakistan) as independent; war with Pakistan intensifies.

9–10 December.   NATO foreign ministers in Brussels agree to European Security Conference.

12 December.   'Hot line' used for first time under Nixon due to fear of Soviet (pro-Indian) or Chinese (pro-Pakistan) intervention in war over Bangladesh; US fleet sent to Bay of Bengal.

16 December.   Pakistanis and Indians agree to cease-fire, after latter occupy East Pakistan.

17 December.   West and East Germans sign agreement on transit in Berlin.

17–18 December.   Western countries discuss world economic situation and agree dollar should be devalued.

20 December.   Yahya Khan of Pakistan resigns in favour of Ali Bhutto, leader of West Pakistan 'People's Party'.

1972

22 January.   Britain, Denmark and Ireland sign Treaty of Accession to European Community.

25 January.   Nixon publicises peace talks between Kissinger and North Vietnamese in Paris, underway since 1969.

14 February.   US eases trade restrictions against China.

21–28 February.   Nixon makes first visit by a US president to China, meets Mao Zedong.

30 March.   North Vietnamese launch spring offensive; largest since 1968.

10 April.   US, USSR and others sign agreement against biological weapons.

15 April.   US bombs areas around Hanoi and Haiphong in response to Communist offensive.

15–16 April.   The 'tundra talks' between US and Soviet delegations in Finland make major progress on an anti-ballistic missile treaty.

20 April.   Kissinger in Moscow to discuss forthcoming summit.

1 May.   North Vietnamese forces take South Vietnamese city of Quang Tri.

8 May.   US begins to mine Haiphong harbour in North Vietnam.

17–19 May.   West German parliament ratifies 1970 treaties of Moscow and Warsaw.

22–26 May.   Nixon makes first visit by a US president to Moscow to meet Brezhnev.

26 May.   West Germany–East Germany traffic treaty signed.

3 June.   US, USSR, Britain and France sign agreement on future of Berlin.

17 June.   US Democratic Party Headquarters at Watergate Hotel broken into by 'the plumbers', who are soon linked by the police to the White House.

8 July.   Three-year US–Soviet grain sales deal signed.

18 July.   President Sadat expels about 17,000 Soviet advisers from Egypt.

1 August.   New round of talks between Kissinger and North Vietnam's Le Duc Tho opens in Paris.

11 August.   Last US combat troops leave Vietnam: remaining troops are all volunteers in support roles.

15 September.   South Vietnamese troops retake Quang Tri.

25–29 September.   Japanese premier Kakuei Tanaka visits China and agrees to re-establish diplomatic relations.

4 October.   President Thieu of South Vietnam tells US he opposes the peace deal worked out by Kissinger and Le Duc Tho.

18 October.   US-Soviet trade agreement signed.

26 October.   North Vietnamese publicise the draft agreement between Kissinger and Le Duc Tho; Kissinger declares 'peace is at hand'.

7 November.   Nixon overwhelms Senator George McGovern in presidential election.

20 November.   Kissinger presents revised peace agreement to North Vietnamese, who reject the changes.

22 November–10 December.   Preparatory conference on European Security held in Helsinki: thirty-four countries present.

4 December.   More Kissinger–Le Duc Tho talks in Paris.

12 December.   Thieu formally rejects the latest Kissinger–Le Duc Tho proposals.

18–30 December.   US launches 'Christmas bombing' of North Vietnam. Round-the-clock raids to drive the North back to the peace talks.

21 December.   West and East Germany sign the 'Basic Treaty' on mutual relations.

1973

8–23 January.   More Kissinger–Le Duc Tho talks in Paris.

8 January.   Trial of Watergate burglars opens in US.

15 January.   End of US military activity against North Vietnam; US bombers continue to be used against Communists in Cambodia and Laos.

27 January.   Vietnam peace agreement signed in Paris; end of US military draft announced.

12 February.   First US prisoners of war released by North Vietnam.

22 February.   Following Kissinger visit to Beijing, US and China are to open 'liaison offices' in each other's capitals.

16 March.   Western finance ministers in Paris agree to a system of 'floating' exchange rates after breakdown of dollar-based system.

29 March.   Last US troops leave South Vietnam.

23 April.   Kissinger speech in New York proposes a new Atlantic Charter to revive NATO.

27 April.   In first major reshuffle since 1964 Gromyko (foreign affairs), Grechko (defence), and Andropov (KGB) are made full members of Politbureau, strengthening Brezhnev's hold on power.

30 April.   Revelations in Watergate case lead to resignations of some White House staff and force Nixon to promise a full investigation.

17 May.   In US, Senate Committee begins inquiry into Watergate.

18–22 May.   Brezhnev makes first visit by a Soviet Communist Party leader to West Germany, makes ten-year agreement on economic co-operation.

18–24 June.   Second Brezhnev–Nixon Summit in Washington, Camp David.

25 June.   John Dean, formerly on White House staff, testifies that Nixon tried to 'cover up' the Watergate burglary.

29 June.   US Congress insists on end to all bombing in Indo-China (underway in support of Cambodian government) on 15 August.

3 July.   Thirty-five countries (including US and Canada) begin Helsinki Conference on European Security.

25 July.   Senator Mike Mansfield proposes US cut its overseas ground forces by half; a 40 per cent cut was agreed by the Senate but defeated in a later vote. (Mansfield had regularly proposed such reductions since 1966.)

11–12 September.   Overthrow of President Allende of Chile; replaced by pro-US military government under General Pinochet.

6 October.   Middle East War breaks out: Egyptian attacks across Suez Canal on Jewish holiday of Yom Kippur; Syrian attacks on Golan Heights.

7 October.   Arab states cut back oil production.

10 October.   US Vice-President Spiro Agnew resigns after tax-evasion charges; succeeded by Gerald Ford on 6 December.

13 October.   Kosygin visits Cairo.

15–16 October.   Israeli forces recross the Suez Canal.

16 October.   Nobel Peace Prize awarded to Kissinger and Le Duc Tho for Vietnam settlement.

18 October.   Arabs launch oil embargo against US and increase oil prices.

22-23 October.   Israeli-Egyptian cease-fire quickly breaks down; Israelis threaten to surround Egyptian Third Army around Port Said.

23 October.   US House of Representatives begins to study possible impeachment of Nixon.

24-25 October.   US forces worldwide put on high 'defense condition' after Soviet threat to send troops to Middle East: new Israeli-Egyptian cease-fire agreed.

30 October.   NATO and Warsaw Pact states begin talks on conventional arms reductions in Vienna. The talks continue for years, making little progress.

7 November.   Kissinger in Cairo to discuss post-ceasefire arrangements between Israel and Egypt; US-Egyptian diplomatic relations (broken in 1967) restored.

7 November.   War Powers Act by Congress limits presidential ability to wage war.

11 November.   Israeli-Egyptian agreement signed to consolidate cease-fire.

11 December.   West German-Czech Treaty signed by Brandt in Prague.

21-22 December.   US, USSR, Israel, Egypt and Jordan attend conference in Geneva; agreement on talks to disengage Israeli and Egyptian forces.

23 December.   Middle East oil-producers more than double price of oil from 1 January.

1974

18 January.   Conciliation efforts by Kissinger result in Israeli-Egyptian agreement on disengagement.

11 February.   Leading Western industrial nations meet in Washington to discuss energy crisis.

13 February.   Writer Alexander Solzhenitsyn exiled from USSR.

4 March.   European Community approach to Arab oil-producers leads to complaints from US; reflects US-European division on Middle East.

18 April.   In Watergate case Nixon is subpoenaed to produce more evidence.

25 April.   Portuguese dictatorship of Marcel Caetano overthrown by army in 'Carnation Revolution'; General Spinola becomes provisional president in May.

8 May.   Resignation of Brandt as Chancellor after one of his staff is exposed as a spy.

9 May.   US House of Representatives Committee begins impeachment hearings against Nixon.

18 May.   Explosion of first Indian nuclear bomb: world's sixth nuclear power.

31 May.   Kissinger's 'shuttle diplomacy' (visits between Israel and Arab states) finally results in Israeli–Syrian cease-fire agreement after Yom Kippur War (1973).

10–19 June.   Nixon visit to Middle East, including Egypt and Syria, confirms US importance in post-1973 regional settlement.

19 June.   'Ottawa Declaration' by NATO (result of Kissinger's 1973 call for a new Atlantic Charter) declares principles on which Atlantic Alliance is based.

27 June–3 July.   Nixon in USSR for third Summit with Brezhnev.

16 July.   President Makarios of Cyprus overthrown by National Guardsmen favouring 'Enosis', or union with Greece.

20–22 July.   Turkish forces invade Cyprus and establish a Turkish enclave in the North.

23–24 July.   Following the Cyprus humiliation, the Greek military regime in Athens surrenders power to Constantine Karamanlis, democratic leader who had been in exile.

24 July.   Nixon is ordered by Supreme Court to surrender more material as evidence in Watergate case.

29 July.   House of Representatives Committee recommends impeachment of Nixon.

8 August.   After admitting (5 August) to withholding evidence in the Watergate case, Nixon resigns.

14–16 August.   Further fighting in Cyprus leads to more Turkish advances; Greece leaves NATO integrated command in protest.

8 September.   President Ford pardons Nixon over Watergate.

12 September.   After growing unrest Emperor Haile Selassie of Ethiopia is overthrown by army officers who establish a pro-Soviet regime.

19 September.   Kissinger tells Senate Foreign Relations Committee that detente should not depend on domestic reforms in USSR.

23–24 November.   Ford–Brezhnev Summit at Vladivostok lays basis for SALT II Treaty.

1975

3 January.   Ford signs Trade Reform Act which extends US–Soviet trade only on condition (known as the Jackson–Vanik Amendment) that Soviets allow greater Jewish emigration.

4 January.   Rockefeller Commission established to investigate illegal domestic activities of the CIA.

7 January.   Communist advances in Vietnam escalate with capture of Phuoc Lang province.

10 January.   Alvor Accord signed in Portugal which establishes coalition government of resistance movements in Angola and promises independence on 11 November.

14 January. US and Soviets cancel 1972 trade deal after USSR rejects Jackson–Vanik Amendment.

15 March. President Thieu of South Vietnam decides to abandon northern provinces; fall of Hue on 25th and Da Nang on 30 March.

23 March. First major clash between MPLA and FNLA forces in Angola.

16 April. Cambodian government falls to Communist Khmer Rouge, who begin to execute all their opponents.

21 April. President Thieu resigns; flees Saigon on 25 April.

25 April. Socialists emerge a strong first in Portuguese elections; Communists gain only 12.5 per cent of vote.

30 April. Saigon is surrendered to Communist forces; end of Vietnam War.

9 May. Pro-American ministers are forced to resign from coalition government in Laos.

12 May. US merchant ship *Mayaguez* is captured by Cambodians.

14–15 May. US Marines and aircraft attack targets in Cambodia; the crew of the *Mayaguez* are released.

5 June. Suez Canal reopened for first time since 1967.

10 June. Rockefeller Commission reports that CIA *did* spy on US citizens.

25 June. Mozambique gains independence from Portugal with a Marxist (FRELIMO) government under Samora Machel.

17–19 July. Joint US–Soviet space mission, agreed in 1972, takes place.

30 July–August. Helsinki Summit of Europeans, US and Canada; Helsinki Accords signed.

10. The decline of detente, 1975–79

18 August 1975. US shipworkers begin a boycott of Soviet grain exports in protest over food prices.

19 August. Ford warns USSR not to interfere in Portuguese politics.

23 August. Communist Pathet Lao take Vientiane (declare Communist Republic on 2 December).

9 October. Soviet scientist and dissident Andrei Sakharov is awarded the Nobel Peace Prize.

19–22 October. Chinese criticise US–Soviet detente during Kissinger visit to China.

20 October. US and USSR sign new trade deal.

3 November. The 'Halloween Massacre': major reorganisation of international policy posts by Ford.

11 November. Angolan independence sees rival governments created by Marxist MPLA and its opponents, the pro-Chinese FNLA and pro-Western UNITA.

15 November. Italian, French and Spanish Communists sign a joint declaration in favour of 'Eurocommunism'.

20 November.   America announces 3,000 Cuban troops have arrived (since September) to aid the MPLA in Angola.

20 November.   Death of Spain's General Franco; his successor King Juan Carlos moves towards greater democracy.

21 November.   Senate Report reveals past CIA assassination plots against foreign leaders.

25–26 November.   Conservative army officers assert their power over the Left in Portugal.

1–5 December.   Ford meets Mao Zedong in China; the Chinese again criticise US–Soviet detente.

19 December.   The Senate ends funding for pro-Western forces in Angola.

1976

20 January.   South African troops are admitted to be aiding UNITA forces in southern Angola.

21–22 January.   US–Soviet talks in Moscow fail to make progress on Angola or a SALT II Treaty; last real chance for a SALT II Treaty before the US election.

11 February.   Organisation of African Unity accepts MPLA as Angolan government; MPLA and Cuban troops now control most of the country.

26 February.   Portuguese military leaders agree to hand power to politicians.

March.   Ford no longer uses the word 'detente' in his re-election campaign, because detente is so unpopular.

15 March.   Egypt abrogates its 1971 Treaty with USSR.

13 April.   Kissinger says US will not welcome a Communist role in the Italian government.

28 May.   US–Soviet agreement to limit the size of certain underground nuclear tests.

21 June.   Communist gains in Italian general elections, close behind Christian Democrats.

2 July.   Vietnam reunited into a single state.

23 July.   Socialist Mario Soares becomes first constitutional Portuguese premier since 1974 revolution.

18 August.   Two US servicemen killed in incident on North Korean border.

9 September.   Death of Mao Zedong.

2 November.   Carter defeats Ford in presidential election after criticising his opponent's detente policy and emphasising human rights.

1977

18 January.   Brezhnev speech says detente must triumph over Cold War and denies that USSR seeks first-strike capability.

20 January.   Carter's inauguration speech emphasises human rights and need for a 'new start' for America.

17 February.   Carter writes to the Soviet dissident Sakharov promising support for human rights in the USSR.

27–30 February.   Secretary of State Vance in Moscow; Gromyko says USSR cannot accept major revision of the 1974 Vladivostok deal on SALT II, and rejects US interference in Soviet politics.

9–11 May.   NATO Summit agrees to increase defence spending by 3 per cent per annum to match Soviet arms build-up.

16–18 May.   After three months of deadlock, Vance–Gromyko talks in Geneva resume movement on SALT II on lines of Vladivostok Conference.

3 June.   US agrees to reopen diplomatic links with Cuba.

30 June.   Carter announces cancellation of B-1 strategic bomber project.

5 July.   In Pakistan, General Zia ul-Haq leads military coup which topples President Ali Bhutto, who is later arrested.

12 July.   Carter asks Congress to fund development of a neutron bomb.

7 September.   Carter and President Torrijos of Panama sign two treaties which will transfer the Panama Canal to Panamanian control by 2,000 but imply a US right to defend the Canal.

14 September.   After fighting since July, Somali forces capture the town of Jijiga in the Ethiopian region of Ogaden (claimed by Somalia); both countries are linked to the Eastern bloc.

1 October.   Joint US–Soviet communiqué on the Middle East upsets Israel by mentioning Palestinian rights.

4 October–9 March 1989.   Belgrade Conference of CSCE held: 'follow up' to 1975 Helsinki Agreements.

18 October.   Sentences are passed in Czechoslovakia on members of the 'Charter 77' dissident group, including Vaclav Havel.

9 November.   To break deadlock in Middle East peace process, President Sadat of Egypt says he would be ready to talk to the Israeli parliament (Knesset).

13 November.   Somalia abrogates its 1974 Friendship Treaty with USSR and expels Cuban advisers, after Soviet and Cuban support for Ethiopia in the Ogaden War.

14 November.   Israeli premier Begin invites Sadat to Israel.

19–21 November.   Sadat makes the first visit to Israel by an Egyptian leader and addresses the parliament (Knesset).

26 November.   Sadat invites US, USSR, Israel and Arab states to a conference in Cairo on 14 December; only US, Israel and UN agree to attend.

25–26 December.   Sadat and Begin meet again, in Egypt.

31 December.   Following serious border clashes during the month, Cambodia breaks off diplomatic relations with Vietnam: Vietnam occupies border areas of Cambodia.

1978

28 February. US warns USSR not to interfere in the intensifying Ethiopian–Somali conflict.

4 March. Dutch foreign minister resigns in opposition to deployment of neutron bomb by US.

5 March. Ethiopian forces, supported by Cubans, retake Jijiga in Ogaden.

9–24 March. Somalis withdraw all their forces from the Ogaden.

5 April. West German Chancellor Schmidt says he accepts production of the neutron bomb.

7 April. Carter defers production of the neutron bomb.

20–22 April. Vance visits Moscow and makes some progress on SALT II.

27–28 April. Overthrow and execution of President Daud of Afghanistan; Marxist regime created under Mohammed Taraki on 30 April.

11–12 May. China and USSR issue different accounts of a border clash on the River Ussuri.

16 May. Cuban troops begin to aid Ethiopian forces in the war against Eritrean secessionists (begun 1961).

18 May. Yuri Orlov, head of Helsinki Monitoring Group, imprisoned in USSR.

19–20 May. French and Belgian troops, with US transport, rescue Europeans caught in fighting between Zaïrean troops and secessionists in Shaba (formerly Katanga); Soviets and Cubans deny that they support the secessionists.

20–22 May. US National Security Adviser, Brzezinski, visits China to pave way for establishment of full diplomatic relations.

24 May. China accuses Vietnam of mistreating its Chinese minority.

30 May. Carter attacks Cuban involvement in Africa.

7 June. Carter speech warns USSR it must choose between confrontation and detente.

7 July. China suspends all aid to Albania, which is now isolated from all other Communist states: Albania critical of Chinese links to the US after 1972.

12–13 July. Latest Vance–Gromyko talks, in Geneva, fail to progress on SALT II.

13 July. USSR imprisons dissidents Anatoly Scharansky and Alexander Ginsburg.

12 August. China and Japan sign ten-year friendship treaty; criticised by USSR.

6–17 September. Carter, Sadat and Begin meet at Camp David and reach accord on a framework for peace: Israel to leave Sinai in return for recognition.

16 October. Polish Karol Wojtyla elected Pope John Paul II.

3 November. USSR and Vietnam sign a twenty-five-year Friendship Treaty, including a commitment to 'consult' if either is attacked; condemned by China.

6 November. Shah of Iran declares martial law after unrest (sporadic since February) reaches new heights.

December. 'Boat people' begin to flee Vietnam to escape political and economic oppression.

5 December. USSR and Afghanistan sign a new Friendship Treaty.

15 December. Carter announces that US and China will normalise relations on 1 January; condemned by Soviets.

18 December. General strike declared in Iran amid continuing unrest.

21–22 December. Vance–Gromyko talks in Geneva again fail to progress on SALT II.

25 December. Vietnam launches full-scale invasion of Cambodia, after occupying border areas for a year.

1979

6 January. Carter meets British, French and West German leaders in Guadeloupe; they recommit themselves to detente and a strong NATO defence.

7 January. Vietnamese troops drive Pol Pot from Cambodia and install a puppet government; full extent of Khmer Rouge genocide in Cambodia begins to be revealed.

16 January. Faced by nation-wide unrest, the Shah leaves Iran.

28 January–5 February. Deng Xiaoping becomes first major Chinese leader to visit US; signs cultural and technological agreements.

1 February. The Ayatollah Khomeini returns to Iran and begins to establish a theocratic regime.

14 February. An Iranian mob occupies the US Embassy in Iran for two hours.

14 February. US Ambassador Adolph Dubs is killed by Afghan security forces who were trying to rescue him from kidnappers; US criticises the Afghans.

17 February. China invades Vietnam with over 200,000 troops, and occupies border areas.

5–15 March. Chinese troops withdraw from Vietnam.

26 March. Israeli–Egyptian peace treaty signed on lines of Camp David Accords.

31 March. Arab League states break their ties with Egypt.

3 April. China refuses to renew 1950 friendship treaty with USSR.

4 April. General Zia executes ex-President Bhutto of Pakistan, leading US to suspend aid.

15 April. Iran raises oil prices, threatening a new round of inflation in the West.

28 May.   Greece joins the European Community.

2 June.   John Paul II makes first Papal visit to a Communist country, Poland.

4 June.   After growing discontent since 1978 a general strike is called against the regime of Anastasio Somoza in Nicaragua.

7 June.   Carter approves MX missile development; announces on 7 September that it will be on an underground rail system.

15–18 June.   Carter–Brezhnev Summit in Vienna sees signature of SALT II.

7 July.   US gives 'most favoured nation' status to China in new trade deal.

16 July.   Saddam Hussein takes power in Iraq.

17 July.   Left-wing Sandinistas topple President Somoza of Nicaragua.

31 August.   State Department says there are over 2,000 Soviet combat troops in Cuba.

5 September.   Vance criticises presence of Soviet troops in Cuba.

10 September.   Soviets deny there has been any change in the status of their forces in Cuba since 1962.

16 September.   President Taraki of Afghanistan is overthrown by his fellow-Marxist, Hafizullah Amin.

6 October.   Brezhnev, in East Berlin, says Soviets will reduce their medium-range missiles in western USSR if NATO avoids new missile deployments.

15 October.   President Carlos Romero of El Salvador overthrown by the military; growing divisions between Right and Left follow.

22 October.   The deposed Shah arrives in the US for medical treatment; antagonises Iran.

30 October.   Iraq demands changes in 1975 border agreement with Iran.

4 November.   Iranian students occupy the US Embassy in Tehran and take the diplomats hostage; Carter suspends oil purchases from Iran on 12 November.

21 November.   US Embassy in Pakistan attacked by a mob; low point in US–Pakistani relations.

10 December.   NATO meeting in Brussels agrees to deploy Cruise and Pershing missiles, but also offers talks on limiting such weapons.

25–27 December.   Soviet troops invade Afghanistan; President Amin is executed and replaced by Babrak Karmal.

11. The 'New' Cold War, 1980–85

1980

1 January.   Carter admits in the *New York Times* that events in Afghanistan have made 'a dramatic change in my own opinion of what the Soviets' ultimate goals are'.

4 January. Carter introduces measures following Soviet invasion of Afghanistan, including trade restrictions, suspension of SALT II ratification and greater aid to Pakistan.

5 January. State Department says US will adhere to SALT II Treaty, despite non-ratification.

23 January. Carter's State of the Union address enunciates 'Carter Doctrine' on defence of the Persian Gulf.

29 January. Thirty-six Islamic states meet in Islamabad, Pakistan, to condemn Soviet action in Afghanistan.

18 February. Gromyko says USSR will maintain arms control talks only if NATO abandons its decision to modernise its intermediate nuclear forces (INF).

21–22 February. Protests in Kabul lead Afghan government to declare martial law.

4 March. In Rhodesia (now Zimbabwe) Robert Mugabe's Marxists win a majority in elections; this follows 1979 London Agreement on independence, after fourteen years of illegal White rule.

30 March. Left–Right violence claims over twenty lives in El Salvador during the funeral of Archbishop Oscar Romero, an advocate of reform who had earlier been assassinated by Rightists.

7 April. US breaks diplomatic relations with Iran in continuing hostages crisis.

22 April. US Olympic Committee votes to boycott Moscow Games because of Afghanistan situation.

25 April. US attempt to rescue the Tehran hostages is abandoned prematurely.

28 April. Vance resigns over the hostage rescue mission.

4 May. Death of Yugoslav leader Tito, succeeded by a collective leadership with rotating presidency.

27 July. Death of the exiled Shah of Iran.

14 August. Price increases lead workers at Lenin shipyard in Gdansk, Poland, to demand an independent trade union.

4 September. After months of border tensions, Iranian artillery shell Iraqi positions.

5 September. Unrest in Poland leads Edvard Gierek to resign leadership of Communist Party; new leader is Stanislaw Kania.

8 September. Carter authorises expansion of nuclear arsenal and says he wants INF talks without conditions.

22 September. Gdansk shipworkers launch Solidarity trade union under Lech Walesa.

22 September. Iraq (after denouncing 1975 border treaty five days earlier) invades Iran; Iraqi forces take Khorramshahr on 24 September.

11 November. Madrid Conference of CSCE opens: further 'follow-up' to 1975 Helsinki Agreements.

16–17 November. US and USSR hold exploratory talks on strategic arms limitation in Geneva.

4 November. Ronald Reagan easily defeats Carter in US election.

10 November. Polish Supreme Court legalises Solidarity trade union, which now has ten million members; return to relative peace in Polish industry.

1981

11 January. El Salvador government under José Napoleon Duarte declares martial law to end Right–Left violence.

18 January. Iran agrees to release US hostages in return for freeing of Iranian assets; hostages leave Iran on 20 January.

20 January. Reagan's inauguration speech includes commitment to strong foreign policy.

9 February. General Wojtech Jaruzelski becomes Polish premier (replacing Gierek), following failure of Communist Party to control discontent.

9 March. Reagan announces a new effort to arm the Mujahedin resistance in Afghanistan.

27 March. Another major strike in Poland, as Soviet troops carry out manoeuvres on the border.

24 April. Reagan lifts grain embargo against USSR which is harming US farmers.

3 May. US says it has no legal commitment to abide by SALT treaties.

25 May. Brezhnev sends a letter to Reagan criticising US policy in Europe and Middle East.

17 June. US agrees first arms sales to Communist China; offends USSR.

6 August. Reagan announces stockpiling of neutron bomb by US.

7 August. New wave of strikes by Solidarity in Poland.

2 September. Reagan speech in Chicago says any nuclear arms agreement must be verifiable or there will be an arms race which US will win.

22 September. Gromyko, at UN, proposes universal renunciation of nuclear 'first use'; rejected by NATO which relies on nuclear arms to balance Red Army.

23 September. Gromyko and Secretary of State Haig agree to begin talks on INF (intermediate nuclear) weapons.

2 October. Reagan announces new arms development programme, including revival of strategic bomber project cancelled by Carter.

6 October. Assassination of Egypt's Anwar Sadat at a military review.

16 October. Reagan says Soviets plan to fight and win a nuclear war; Brezhnev denies this on 20 October, and calls for 'no first use' commitment.

18 October. In Poland General Jaruzelski succeeds Kania as leader of the Communist Party.

10 November. Reagan says a nuclear war in Europe need not lead to a strategic exchange; criticised by West Europeans and Eastern bloc.

18 November.   Reagan launches new agenda on disarmament including the complete destruction of INF weapons; first time the 'zero option' is seriously proposed.
30 November.   US–Soviet talks on INF begin in Geneva.
13 December.   Jaruzelski surprises Solidarity in Poland by declaring martial law to forestall Soviet intervention.

1982
17–18 January.   Articles by Henry Kissinger in *New York Times* criticise weak US response to events in Poland.
26–27 January.   Haig–Gromyko talks in Geneva are overshadowed by events in Poland; but US government says it won't 'link' Polish issue to nuclear arms talks.
1 February.   Reagan announces aid to the El Salvador government which is involved in fighting left-wing guerrillas.
3 February.   Brezhnev says the international situation is the worst since 1945 and proposes INF cuts by two-thirds; rejected by Reagan on 4 February.
9–10 February.   US rejects a new Soviet plan on arms reductions in Europe because SS-20s would remain in Asia.
2 April.   Argentinian forces invade the Falkland Islands, a British colony in the South Atlantic.
6 April.   Haig speech redefines US nuclear strategy at Georgetown University.
9 May.   Reagan speech at Eureka College proposes new strategic arms reduction talks (START) should begin in June and says US will aid those in the third world who are fighting Communism (this becomes the 'Reagan Doctrine').
24 May.   Iranians recapture Khorramshahr from Iraqis.
30 May.   Reagan promises US will adhere to SALT II as long as USSR does.
3 June.   Assassination attempt on Israeli ambassador to London, Shlomo Argou.
6 June.   Israel launches full-scale invasion of neighbouring Lebanon to root out Palestinian bases; rapid advance to Beirut.
14 June.   British forces complete their reconquest of the Falkland Islands.
29 June.   US and USSR begin new strategic arms control talks (START) in Geneva.
14 July.   Iranian forces cross into Iraq in continuing conflict.
21 August.   Palestinian Liberation Organisation begins withdrawal from Lebanon under Israeli pressure.
17 September.   Christian militiamen massacre Palestinian refugees in Beirut.

27 September. US forces, backed by France and Italy, then Britain, are sent to Beirut as a peace-keeping force.

8 October. Solidarity union banned in Poland.

27 October. Brezhnev accuses Reagan of wanting nuclear war.

November. Reagan abandons pressure on European allies (since early 1981) to cease co-operation with Moscow on an oil–gas pipeline from Siberia.

12 November. Lech Walesa released in Poland after Solidarity fails to win support for a new strike.

22 November. New Soviet leader Andropov calls for a 'freeze' in nuclear arsenals; a speech by Reagan coincidentally announces the 'MX' missile programme will go ahead.

6 December. USSR attacks MX missile as breaching SALT Treaties.

12 December. In Poland Jaruzelski announces partial suspension of martial law as of 1 January.

1983

9 March. Speech by Reagan describes the USSR as an 'evil Empire'.

23 March. Speech by Reagan announces the 'Star Wars' Strategic Defense Initiative (SDI).

24 March. Soviets say SDI violates the 1972 ABM treaty.

30 March. Reagan offers to end deployment of Cruise and Pershing missiles if Soviets dismantle their intermediate-range weapons.

April. Scowcroft Commission (established January) reports nuclear forces are adequate to defend US, despite earlier Republican claims of a 'window of vulnerability'.

2 April. Gromyko rejects Reagan's latest INF offer and demands British and French weapons be included in arms talks.

27 April. Reagan tells Congress US must resist 'externally supported aggression' in Central America.

21 July. Martial law ended in Poland.

25 August. Five-year US–Soviet grain agreement shows efforts of George Schultz to improve relations.

1 September. South Korean airliner, KAL 007, shot down by Soviets, provoking international outcry.

8 September. CSCE Review Conference opens in Madrid with deep East–West divisions.

5 October. Lech Walesa awarded Nobel Peace Prize.

9 October. Several South Korean ministers killed by a bomb in Rangoon, Burma. East Asian states respond with sanctions against North Korea.

22 October. Large-scale demonstrations in Western Europe against deployment of Cruise missiles.

23 October. Almost 300 (including 241 US Marines) killed in 'suicide bomb' attacks on US and French forces in Beirut.

25 October. US forces and Caribbean contingents invade Grenada following seizure of power there by a Revolutionary Military Council.

26 October. Andropov warns Cruise deployment will mean end of INF talks.

15 November. Cruise deployment begins in Britain.

22 November. West German parliament votes to deploy Cruise and Pershing.

23 November. Soviets leave INF talks.

8 December. START talks adjourned without setting a date for subsequent meetings.

15 December. MBFR (conventional arms in Europe) talks ended without setting a date for subsequent meetings.

1984

11 January. Kissinger Commission on Central America (established July 1983) recommends economic aid to region and military assistance to El Salvador.

7 February. Reagan announces 'redeployment' (actually withdrawal) of forces from Beirut.

9 February. Death of Yuri Andropov.

13 February. Konstantin Chernenko elected General Secretary of the Soviet Communist Party.

16 March. MBFR talks resume in Vienna.

26 April–2 May. Reagan visits China.

8 May. Soviets announce they will not attend the Los Angeles Olympics. Other Eastern bloc states follow.

29 June. Soviets propose talks on demilitarisation of space.

21 July. Amnesty for political prisoners announced in Poland.

4 September. Under Soviet pressure East Germany's Erich Honecker cancels proposed visit to West Germany.

28 September. Reagan meets Gromyko for the first time, in Washington, while latter is visiting UN.

19 October. Kidnap of Father Jerzy Popieluszko in Poland, who is later murdered; rekindles anti-government sentiment.

6 November. Reagan re-elected US President, defeating Walter Mondale.

22 November. Announcement that Gromyko and Schultz will meet in January to discuss disarmament.

1985

7–8 January. Schultz–Gromyko talks in Geneva agree on three sets of talks: START, INF and defensive systems (including those based in space).

4 February. US budget increases arms spending by 6 per cent.

4 February. New Zealand's refusal to grant port facilities to a nuclear-capable US ship creates crisis in ANZUS.

4 March. ANZUS council meeting cancelled indefinitely due to US–New Zealand disagreements.

12. The end of the Cold War, 1985–89

11 March 1985. Mikhail Gorbachev elected General Secretary of Soviet Communist Party.

12 March. US–Soviet arms talks reopen in Geneva.

24 March. US Major Arthur D. Nicholson killed while visiting East Germany.

7 April. Gorbachev 'freezes' Soviet missile deployments, but says they will restart in November unless NATO halts its deployments.

25–26 April. Warsaw Pact Summit renews the Warsaw Treaty for twenty years.

1 May. Reagan announces trade embargo against Nicaragua.

14–15 May. Schultz–Gromyko talks on nuclear disarmament in Vienna prove difficult.

8 and 22 June. First multi-candidate elections in Hungary allow some independents to be elected.

2 July. Veteran Soviet foreign minster Gromyko 'kicked upstairs' to be President. Succeeded by Edward Shevardnadze.

31 July. Shevardnadze meets Schultz for first time, in Helsinki, to commemorate ten years of Helsinki Accords.

6 August. Soviets begin five-month moratorium on nuclear tests, on fortieth anniversary of Hiroshima.

25–27 September. Shevardnadze visits US, to prepare for Reagan–Gorbachev summit.

3 October. Gorbachev proposes that Superpower strategic arsenals should be halved.

6 October. US National Security Adviser McFarlane 'reinterprets' 1972 ABM treaty to allow testing of SDI weapons. Criticised by Allies.

12 November. In Poland, Jaruzelski surrenders premiership and becomes president.

19–21 November. First Reagan–Gorbachev summit in Geneva proves a surprising success, pushing forward arms talks.

1986

15 January. Gorbachev proposes fifteen-year timetable to destroy all nuclear weapons and accepts 'zero option' on INF weapons.

28 January. American space shuttle 'Challenger' explodes on take-off, calling into question 'Star Wars' programme.

30 January. Reagan meets UNITA (Angolan anti-government) leader, Jonas Savimbi.

2 February. At Soviet Communist Congress Gorbachev attacks the 'years of stagnation' under Brezhnev and says Afghanistan is a 'bleeding wound'.

11 February.   Human rights activist Anatoly Scharansky is part of prisoner exchange in Berlin.

25 February.   Mrs Corazon Aquino becomes new Philippine leader after electoral defeat of the oppressive Ferdinand Marcos.

12 March.   Spain votes in referendum to stay in NATO, but without nuclear weapons or participation in military command.

11 April.   Soviets end moratorium on nuclear tests after US explodes device (on 10 April) in Nevada.

15 April.   US aircraft bomb Libya following terrorist attack (on 5 April) on US servicemen in Berlin.

26 April.   Nuclear reactor explodes at Chernobyl near Kiev, spreading radioactivity across northern Europe.

27 May.   Reagan accuses Soviets of breaching SALT II and says US will not be bound by it.

29 May.   Soviets agree to exclude US 'forward base systems' (in Europe) from START talks.

27 June.   New Zealand ends full participation in ANZUS after refusing visits by nuclear-capable US warships.

28 July.   Vladivostok speech by Gorbachev on Far East: will reduce troop levels in Afghanistan and Mongolia, and wants improved relations with China.

12 August.   US suspends obligations to New Zealand under ANZUS.

18 August.   Soviets renew moratorium on nuclear tests.

23 August.   US arrest Gennady Zakharov, a Soviet official, for espionage.

30 August.   Soviets respond by arresting journalist Nicholas Daniloff.

11 September.   Remaining political prisoners released in Poland.

29–30 September.   Soviets release Daniloff; Americans release Zakharov.

11–12 October.   Reykjavik Summit of Reagan and Gorbachev fails to reach agreement on nuclear disarmament.

19 October.   Soviets expel several US diplomats; Americans respond in kind.

3 November.   A newspaper reports that former US National Security Adviser Robert McFarlane secretly visited Tehran on 25 May. Start of 'Irangate' scandal over 'arms for hostages' deal with Iran.

25 November.   National Security Adviser John Poindexter resigns and his aide, Oliver North, is dismissed over 'Irangate'.

28 November.   US deploys new B-52 bomber, breaching SALT II.

23 December.   Dissident Andrei Sakharov is freed from internal exile in Gorki.

1987

1 January.   Afghan leader (since 4 May 1986), Mohammed Najibullah, offers new 'national' government, cease-fire in civil war and return of refugees.

9 February.   First Sino-Soviet border talks since 1979.

26 February.   Report of Commission, under John Tower, on Irangate criticises White House chief of staff Donald Regan (who resigns next day).

28 February.   Soviets agree INF Treaty possible without agreement on Star Wars.

10 April.   Gorbachev speech in Prague talks of a 'common European home'; says Soviets have halted chemical weapons production, and favours agreement on short-range nuclear missiles.

13–15 April.   Schultz, on visit to Moscow, invites Gorbachev to US for Summit.

17 May.   USS *Stark* hit by Iraqi missiles in Gulf; thirty-seven killed. US later accepts it as an accident.

26–27 May.   NATO defence ministers support 'double zero' option to end of INF and short-range nuclear systems.

28 May.   West German Matthias Rust flies light aircraft to Red Square, Moscow, undetected: leading Soviet officers sacked as result.

28–29 May.   Warsaw Pact Summit favours agreements on INF, short-range weapons and conventional arms.

12 June.   In Berlin Reagan calls on Gorbachev to 'tear down' Berlin Wall.

20 July.   UN Resolution 598 calls for Iran–Iraq cease-fire, withdrawal to 1980 border and international commission to decide responsibility for war.

22 July.   Gorbachev says INF systems should be eliminated in Asia as well as Europe.

6–7 August.   Central American leaders endorse Arias Plan (by President of Costa Rica) for cease-fire in Nicaraguan civil war.

26 August.   West Germany (after delays since June) agrees to destroy its old Pershing IA missiles after INF treaty.

15–17 September.   In Washington Schultz and Shevardnadze discuss INF Treaty.

8 October.   US sinks three Iranian gunboats in Gulf.

22–23 October.   Schultz, in Moscow, fails to settle US–Soviet differences on SDI.

30 October.   Shevardnadze, in Washington, agrees to hold Summit in December.

11 November.   Boris Yeltsin sacked as Communist Party boss in Moscow.

23–24 November.   Schultz and Shevardnadze finalise INF Treaty in Geneva.

29 November.   Polish government fails to get 50 per cent of electorate to support its proposed economic reforms.

30 November.   New Afghan constitution ends Communist monopoly of power.

7–10 December. Washington Summit of Reagan and Gorbachev includes INF Treaty (on 8 December).

1988

26 January. Reagan's state of the union address includes support for Contras and SDI.

28–29 January. US, Angolan and Cuban representatives begin meetings to discuss peace in Angola. Further rounds of talks follow during the year including South Africa.

8 February. Gorbachev says USSR ready to leave Afghanistan within ten months after May 1988 if peace agreement reached.

21–22 February. Schultz and Shevardnadze meet in Moscow.

2–3 March. NATO Summit (first since 1982) in Bonn calls for conventional forces agreement.

3 March. Vote by House of Representatives leaves Contras without US funding.

16 March. Reagan sends 3,000 troops to Honduras on Nicaraguan border to stop supposed invasion.

21–23 March. Shevardnadze visit to Washington paves way for new Summit.

23 March. Cease-fire between Nicaraguan government and Contras includes moves to liberalisation in Nicaragua.

April–May. Widespread strikes in Poland over economic situation.

14 April. Geneva Agreement of Afghanistan and Pakistan, guaranteed by US and USSR, paves way to Soviet withdrawal from Afghanistan, beginning 15 May.

20–22 May. Special Communist Conference in Hungary replaces Janos Kadar (leader since 1956) and paves way to radical reform.

29 May–2 June. Friendly Moscow Summit of Reagan and Gorbachev exchanges INF ratifications.

1 June. Vice-President Bush says 'the Cold War is not over'.

28 June–1 July. Special Communist Conference in USSR includes open debate on radical reform and decides to elect a Congress of People's Deputies.

30 June. Vietnam winds down its military command in Kampuchea (formerly Cambodia) as part of military withdrawal. Followed by beginning of informal talks between political factions in Kampuchea.

3 July. USS *Vincennes* shoots down Iranian airliner, killing 290.

11–12 July. Nicaragua expels US ambassador; US responds in kind.

20 July. Ayatollah Khomeini accepts UN Resolution 598 on cease-fire in Gulf.

15 August. Start of new strike wave in Poland.

22 August. Talks on South-West African situation (since January) result in Angolan–South African cease-fire.

31 August.   Talks between Lech Walesa and Polish Interior Minister lead to agreement on negotiations between Solidarity union and government.
1 October.   Gorbachev becomes Soviet President, following resignation of Gromyko.
1 November.   Sino-Soviet talks settle border disputes.
8 November.   George Bush elected US President, defeating Michael Dukakis.
10 November.   Hungarian government approves formation of new political parties.
30 November.   Televised debate between Lech Walesa and a government representative stimulates demand for reform.
1–3 December.   Chinese foreign minister, Qian Qichen, visits Moscow to plan Sino-Soviet summit.
7 December.   Gorbachev speech to UN announces troop withdrawals from Eastern Europe; earthquake in Armenia forces him to return early to USSR after meeting Reagan and Bush.
22 December.   Agreements signed at UN on South-West Africa provide for independence of Namibia and Cuban withdrawal from Angola.

1989
7–11 January.   In Paris 149 countries meet to discuss controls on chemical weapons.
9 January.   Cuban troops begin to leave Angola after fourteen years.
11 January.   Hungary legalises independent political parties.
17–18 January.   Polish Communists agree to open discussions with Solidarity; talks begin on 6 February.
17–19 January.   CSCE ministers meet in Vienna and welcome a new round of conventional arms reduction talks.
20 January.   Bush's inauguration speech promises to maintain good relations with USSR.
1–4 February.   Shevardnadze visits China, to discuss forthcoming Summit, and Pakistan, in last attempt to make peace treaty with Afghan Mujahedin.
4 February.   Western diplomats leave Kabul in anticipation of Mujahedin assault.
9 February.   Bush tells Congress that a major ninety-day review of US policy is underway.
13–14 February.   At a summit of Central American leaders, President Ortega agrees to bring forward the date of elections in Nicaragua.
15 February.   Soviet troops complete their withdrawal from Afghanistan, but the Najibullah regime survives until 1992.
6 March.   'Conventional Forces in Europe' talks open in Vienna between NATO and Warsaw Pact.

7 March. Gorbachev announces 75 per cent reduction in forces in Mongolia.

19 March. Right-wing Alfredo Cristiani elected President of El Salvador.

26 March. First round of elections for Soviet Congress of People's Deputies sees successes for reformists in contested seats; run-off elections held on 9 April.

1 April. Cease-fire between South African and SWAPO forces in Namibia soon disintegrates into new clashes; new agreement is negotiated on 8 April.

5 April. Under Soviet pressure, Vietnam announces that it will withdraw all its forces from Cambodia by 30 September.

5 April. Polish government and Solidarity reach agreement on independent trade unions, economic reform and an elected Assembly.

9 April. Soviet security forces violently suppress unrest in Georgia.

17 April. Bush speech in Michigan (the first result of his policy review) promises aid to Poland and any other East European country which carries out sound economic and political reform.

22 April. About 150,000 demonstrators flood into Tiananmen Square, Beijing, during the funeral of former party leader Hu Yaobang (died on 15th).

25 April. Red Army begins to withdraw from Hungary.

7 May. Elections in Panama defeat President Manuel Noriega who immediately annuls the results.

12 May. Bush's speech at Texas A and M University on policy towards USSR accepts that the Cold War has ended. Also revives Eisenhower's 'open skies' proposal of 1955.

13 May. Students in Tiananmen Square begin hunger-strikes to force a dialogue with the government.

15–18 May. Gorbachev and Deng Xiaoping hold the first Sino-Soviet Summit since 1959.

20 May. Suppression of Turkish minority in Bulgaria; exodus of Turks from the country begins.

21 May. Bush speech in Boston on Western Europe supports European unity and wants good relations.

21 May. Egypt returns to the Arab League after ten years isolation.

25–26 May. Soviet Congress of People's Deputies meets and elects a new Supreme Soviet; few radical successes.

29–30 May. NATO's fortieth anniversary Summit sees disagreements on modernisation of short-range nuclear weapons; West Germany favours 'third zero option' on these but US wants modernisation.

31 May. Bush speech in Mainz, Germany, says the division of Europe must end and the Berlin Wall come down.

4 June. Chinese People's Liberation Army crushes the protests in Tiananmen Square.

4 and 18 June.   Polish elections prove a major success for Solidarity.

16 June.   Tens of thousands attend the reburial of Imre Nagy, hero of 1956, in Hungary.

6 July.   Gorbachev, in Strasbourg, says force should not be used again between European states, even within alliances.

7–8 July.   Bucharest Summit of Warsaw Pact is deeply divided over reform.

9–12 July.   Bush visit to Poland and Hungary emphasises US support for reform, but offers only limited economic aid.

17 July.   Maiden flight of US 'Stealth' (B2) bomber.

19 July.   General Jaruzelski narrowly elected Polish President.

23 August.   Rallies in favour of independence from the USSR, in Lithuania, Latvia and Estonia.

24 August.   End of Communist Party rule in Poland: a non-Communist government to be formed on 12 September under Tadeusz Mazowiecki.

10 September.   Hungary announces that thousands of East Germans 'on holiday' in the country can cross the border to Austria; exodus of East Germans to the West begins.

18 September.   Hungarian government and opposition groups agree to transition to democracy with elections in March.

22–23 September.   Shevardnadze and Baker, in Wyoming, agree to omit 'Strategic Defense Initiative' from START talks.

25–26 September.   At UN, speeches by Bush and Shevardnadze advocate elimination of chemical weapons.

26 September.   Vietnamese troops withdrawn from Cambodia leaving the government to face opposition groups, including the Khmer Rouge.

1 October.   Several thousand East Germans are allowed to leave West German embassies in Warsaw and Prague for the West.

6–7 October.   On fortieth anniversary of East German state, Gorbachev visits the country and criticises the government's failure to reform; mass demonstrations underway against the government.

7–9 October.   Hungarian Communists vote to become new Socialist Party.

17 October.   Hungarian government announces multi-party elections to be held.

18 October.   East German Communist Party leader Honecker resigns; new leader is conservative Egon Krenz.

13. The collapse of Soviet Communism, 1989–91

1989

25 October.   Statement on Soviet–Yugoslav relations effectively ends the Brezhnev Doctrine.

9 November. Reformist Hans Modrow appointed East German prime minister in succession to Willi Stoph; free elections and freedom of travel promised.

9–10 November. The Berlin Wall and the rest of the East German border is opened; clearest symbol of the end of oppression in Eastern Europe.

10 November. In a palace coup, veteran Bulgarian leader Todor Zhivkov is replaced by reformist Petar Mladenov.

11–17 November. New outbreak of violence in El Salvador leaves hundreds dead.

17 November. Mass demonstrations begin in Czechoslovakia against the government.

20 November. Romanian Communists unanimously elect Ceauşescu as president.

24 November. Resignation of the whole Czechoslovakian Politburo but a general strike goes ahead on 27 November.

28 November. Chancellor Kohl of West Germany publicises plan for a German confederation.

2–3 December. Malta Summit of Bush and Gorbachev.

6–8 December. Egon Krenz resigns as East German leader; Gregor Gysi becomes Communist leader; liberal Manfred Gerlach becomes President.

10 December. New coalition government formed in Czechoslovakia under Marian Calfa; resignation of veteran President Husak.

14 December. Death of Andrei Sakharov.

15 December. Attempt to deport Hungarian Protestant, Father Laszlo Tokes, sparks off widespread unrest in Timisoara, Romania.

18 December. European Community signs ten-year trade agreement with USSR.

20 December. US troops launch an invasion of Panama and overthrow the regime of Manuel Noriega.

21 December. Riots break out when Nicolae Ceauşescu tries to address a crowd in Bucharest.

25 December. Execution of Ceauşescu and his wife in Romania, but former Communists remain in 'National Salvation Front' government under new President Ion Iliescu.

28 December. Alexander Dubcek, hero of 1968, elected chairman of the Czechoslovakian parliament.

29 December. Former dissident Vaclav Havel is elected President of Czechoslovakia.

1990

12 January. Gorbachev promises law to allow Soviet republics to secede.

15 January. Bulgaria ends leading role of Communist Party.

18–20 January. Red Army forcibly suppresses unrest in Azerbaijan.

23 January. Soviets agree to military withdrawal from Hungary.

31 January. East German government proposes a reunited, neutralised Germany.

9 February. US and USSR agree in principle on reduction of chemical weapons holdings.

10 February. Chancellor Kohl in Moscow gets agreement in principle on German reunification.

25 February. Soviets agree to military withdrawal from Czechoslovakia.

26 February. Sandinistas defeated in Nicaraguan elections by 'Uno' coalition under Violetta Chamorra.

2 March. In first free elections in USSR, nationalists win large majority in Lithuania.

3 March. Kohl appears to call German–Polish border into question; withdraws remarks on 6 March.

9 March. West and East Germans begin to discuss reunification.

11 March. Chilean President Pinochet gives way to Patricio Aylwin after earlier elections.

11 March. Lithuania declares independence from USSR under President Vytautas Landsbergis.

13 March. Soviet Congress of People's Deputies votes to end leading role of Communist Party.

14 March. Gorbachev becomes Executive President.

18 March. Christian Democratic 'Alliance for Germany' wins 49 per cent in first free elections in East Germany.

20 March. SWAPO leader Sam Nujoma becomes President of Namibia.

25 March. Estonian Communists vote for independence from USSR.

28 March. First free elections in Hungary since 1945. Political Forum leads non-Communist coalition.

30 March. Red Army forcibly rounds up deserters in Lithuania.

17 April. USSR imposes economic blockade on Lithuania.

4 May. Latvia votes for independence from USSR.

18 May. West and East Germany sign accord on monetary union; effective 1 July.

21 May. National Salvation Front wins 70 per cent in first free elections in Romania since before the war.

29 May. Boris Yeltsin elected President of Russian Federation, challenging Gorbachev.

30 May–4 June. Washington Summit of Bush and Gorbachev.

10 June. Communists win first post-war free elections in Bulgaria.

13–15 June. Pro-government mineworkers are used by Romanian government to put down demonstrations in Bucharest.

29 June. Lithuania suspends its independence declaration to allow talks.

5–6 July. NATO Summit in London discusses post-Cold War situation, and reviews force structures and nuclear strategy.

11 July.   Group of Seven states, meeting in Houston, discuss integration of Eastern Europe into world economy.

12 July.   Yeltsin resigns from Communist Party during its twenty-eighth Congress.

2 August.   Iraqi forces invade Kuwait; condemned by UN Security Council; sanctions follow.

8 August.   US troops begin to arrive in Saudi Arabia as Kuwait crisis intensifies.

22 August.   Armenia asserts independence from USSR.

9 September.   Helsinki Summit of Bush and Gorbachev to discuss Kuwait crisis.

12 September.   US, USSR, Britain, France, West and East Germany sign treaty in Moscow to restore sovereignty to a reunited Germany.

20 September.   East and West Germany ratify treaty on reunification.

3 October.   Germany becomes a single state again.

8 November.   German–Polish border confirmed in a new treaty.

17 November.   Soviet parliament votes new powers for Gorbachev.

19 November.   Treaty on Conventional Forces in Europe signed in Paris at CSCE Summit.

2 December.   Kohl elected Chancellor of Germany: Christian Democrats win 55 per cent of the vote.

9 December.   Walesa elected President of Poland in nation-wide elections.

11 December.   Albanian government legalises opposition parties.

12 and 14 December.   US, then European Community (EC), approve food aid to USSR.

17 December.   Gorbachev proposes a period of executive rule in the USSR, partly to deal with the nationalities problem.

20 December.   Shevardnadze announces his resignation as Soviet foreign minister, warning of dangers of dictatorship.

1991

2 January.   President Landsbergis withdraws his 1990 suspension of Lithuania's declaration of independence.

5 January.   Comecon's executive agrees to replace the organisation.

7 January.   Soviet paratroops are sent to the Baltic states and other republics to round up army deserters.

13 January.   Thirteen killed in Lithuania as Soviet forces storm a TV station; Gorbachev, on 14 January, denies authorising this.

16–17 January.   US-led forces begin military action to liberate Kuwait with extensive bombing of Iraqi positions.

20 January.   Three killed in clashes between Soviet forces and Latvian police.

29 January.   Soviet forces are reduced in the Baltic states, after US pressure.

9 February.   Lithuanians vote overwhelmingly in favour of independence in a referendum; Latvia and Estonia follow on 3 March.

12 February.   Soviet premier Pavlov claims there is a Western 'plot' to destabilise the economy.

24–28 February.   US-led forces overwhelm the Iraqi army and liberate Kuwait (Operation Desert Storm).

25 February.   Warsaw Pact agrees to cancel all military agreements, effective 31 March, but to continue 'voluntary' political links.

1 March.   End of the Gulf War.

7 March.   Secretary of State Baker begins a long series of Middle East visits to achieve regional peace.

17 March.   A majority of Soviet people vote to maintain the Soviet Union in a referendum, but six republics boycott the vote.

31 March, 7 and 14 April.   Communists win the first free postwar elections in Albania.

8 April.   Britain proposes 'safe havens' for Kurds in Iraq.

9 April.   Georgia declares independence from USSR.

15–19 May.   Jiang Zemin, General Secretary of Chinese Communists, visits Moscow; first visit at such a level since Mao in 1957; includes a border treaty.

21 May.   Marxist President Mengistu flees Ethiopia as rebel forces close on the capital.

21 May.   The Marxist government of Angola signs a peace settlement with pro-Western Jonas Savimbi in Lisbon, attended by US and Soviet foreign ministers.

28–29 May.   NATO defence ministers agree to form a 'rapid reaction force' as the essence of post-Cold War defences.

12 June.   Boris Yeltsin is easily elected as President of the Russian republic in a popular vote, strengthening his hand against Gorbachev.

13 June.   After discontent since April, a coalition government is established in Albania, ending the Communist monopoly on power since 1944.

17 June.   Prime Minister Pavlov, in Moscow, warns of a Western conspiracy to destabilise the USSR.

17 June.   Poland and Germany sign a Friendship Treaty including the renunciation of force and recognition of the present border.

19 June.   German parliament votes to return the capital to Berlin.

20 June.   Yeltsin visits Washington and makes a good impression on Bush.

23 June.   Pro-Vietnamese premier Hun Sen of Cambodia and opposition leader Prince Sihanouk agree to a permanent cease-fire while political talks proceed.

25 June.   Slovenia and Croatia declare their independence from Yugoslavia.

26 June. The Serb-dominated Yugoslav army begins repression in Slovenia and Croatia.

1 July. Warsaw Pact disbanded.

3 July. Yugoslav federal army agrees to cease-fire in Slovenia, but fighting goes on in Croatia.

4 July. Ex-foreign minister Shevardnadze leaves Communist Party to help found a Soviet opposition group.

10 July. European Community agrees on a peace-keeping mission to Yugoslavia but violence intensifies.

15–17 July. Gorbachev attends a Western (G-7) economic summit in London as an observer but is promised only technical assistance and advice; Gorbachev and Bush announce a START agreement.

30 July. Soviet forces kill six Lithuanian policemen.

29 July–1 August. Moscow Summit of Bush and Gorbachev sees START signature.

3 August. Cease-fire in Yugoslavia soon breaks down with more Serb–Croat clashes.

18–19 August. Gorbachev is replaced by an eight-man Emergency Committee, including Vice-President Gennady Yanayev. The coup is opposed by Boris Yeltsin in Moscow.

20–21 August. Collapse of the coup: return of Gorbachev to Moscow and arrest of coup leaders; Estonia and Latvia declare independence.

21 August. Latvia declares full independence of USSR; most other republics follow.

24 August. Gorbachev resigns as leader of the Communist Party, and party property is seized; Ukraine follows Baltic states in declaring independence (other Republics follow).

29 August. Confirmation of the suspension of the Soviet Communist Party.

11 September. In talks with Baker, Gorbachev says Moscow will end its special relationship with Cuba.

27 September. Bush takes US nuclear bombers off all alert status, announces unilateral cuts in tactical nuclear weapons and proposes new strategic cuts.

11 October. Soviet State Council abolishes the KGB.

30 October–2 November. Middle East peace talks open in Madrid under superpower auspices, including Israeli and Palestinian representatives.

9–11 December. European Community Summit in Maastricht agrees Treaty on European Union including Common Foreign and Security Policy, and plans for single currency.

21 December. Eleven Soviet Republics (all except the Baltic states and Georgia) agree to form a new Commonwealth of Independent States.

25 December. Gorbachev resigns as Soviet President.

26 December.   US recognises Russia and other independent republics of the former USSR.

14. The post-Cold War era, 1992–98

1992
1 January.   Serbia and Croatia approve UN peace-keeping force for Yugoslavia; agreed in principle by Security Council on 21 February; 'Protection Force' established on 7 April.
15 January.   European Community recognises independence of Croatia and Slovenia, but not Bosnia or Macedonia.
1 February.   First US–Russian Summit between Bush and Yeltsin.
1 February.   El Salvador truce ends twelve-year civil war.
29 February–1 March.   Referendum in Bosnia-Herzegovina votes for independence from Yugoslavia.
16 March.   Boris Yeltsin announces creation of Russian army.
27 March.   Bosnian Serbs declare their own republic.
6–7 April.   US and European Community recognise Bosnia-Herzegovina as independent.
16 April.   Najibullah resigns as Afghan President, as Mujahedin forces close on Kabul.
9 May.   Armenians capture last Azerbaijani town in disputed region of Ngorno-Karabakh.
30 May.   Tough UN sanctions on Serbia include a trade ban, withdrawal of Ambassadors and a sports boycott; sanctions tightened further on 16 November.
16–17 June.   Yeltsin, in Washington, tells a joint session of Congress on 17 June that 'Communism is dead' and asks for economic aid.
7 July.   Abkhazia declares itself independent of Georgia.
7 August.   In Mozambique, the Marxist President Joaquim Chissano and the South African-backed Mozambique National Resistance (RENAMO) agree peace terms: formalised by treaty on 4 October.
12 August.   In strife-torn Somalia, faction leader General Aidid agrees on deployment of UN troops to guard food supplies.
13 August.   UN agrees its forces should help protect humanitarian aid efforts in Bosnia.
14 August.   UN Human Rights Commission condemns Serbs for 'ethnic cleansing'.
26–27 August.   London conference of thirty states on former Yugoslavia fails to end fighting.
27 August.   Czechoslovakian leaders agree 'velvet divorce' into Czech and Slovak states (applicable 1 January).

30 September.   UNITA's Jonas Savimbi rejects MPLA win in Angolan elections and restarts civil war.

9 October.   UN declares a 'no-fly zone' over Bosnia, largely to protect Moslems from Serbian air attack.

10 October.   US–Chinese comprehensive trade pact made.

11 October.   Former Soviet foreign minister Eduard Shevardnadze, becomes Georgian head of state.

19 November.   First UN aid convoy in Bosnia reaches city of Tuzla.

20 November.   Macedonia declares independence from Yugoslavia despite refusal of many states to recognise it. (Greece objects to use of name 'Macedonia'.)

4 December.   US troops begin aid mission in Somalia.

8 December.   Serbs close all roads into Sarajevo, the Bosnian capital.

14 December.   Russian Congress of People's Deputies forces premier Yegor Gaidar out of office.

1993

3 January.   Bush and Yeltsin sign START II Treaty.

8 January.   Bosnia's deputy premier, Hakja Turajlic, is murdered by Serbs while under UN protection.

17 January.   US missile attack on Iraq after Saddam Hussein fails to comply with UN sanctions.

1 March.   US begins air drops of medical and food aid to Moslems in Bosnia, despite French criticism.

12 April.   NATO aircraft begin to enforce air-exclusion zone over Bosnia.

25 April.   Russian referendum backs Yeltsin's leadership and his economic reforms.

25–26 April.   Bosnian Moslems reject Vance–Owen peace plan (launched in January) which would have divided Bosnia into three on ethnic lines.

27 April.   Communist Chinese and Taiwanese officials talk for first time in Singapore.

6 May.   UN declares five Moslem-held towns in Bosnia to be 'safe areas' from attack.

19 May.   US recognises Angolan government despite continuing civil war.

5 June.   Forces loyal to General Mohammed Aidid kill twenty-four Pakistani peace-keepers in Somalia.

26 June.   US cruise missile attack on Baghdad after alleged Iraqi assassination attempt on ex-President Bush.

3 July.   Haiti's military leader, General Raoul Cedras, agrees to restore the ousted President Aristide.

3 September.   Permanent peace conference on Bosnia begins to meet in Geneva.

13 September. Israeli premier Yitzhak Rabin and Palestinian leader Yasser Arafat shake hands on White House lawn, four days after agreeing mutual recognition. Plans laid for Israeli withdrawal from parts of West Bank and Gaza.

24 September. Russian deputies barricade themselves in parliament rather than accept dissolution by Yeltsin.

24 September. Sihanouk restored as King of Cambodia.

28 September. Abkhazi rebels take Georgian city of Sukhumi.

29 September. Bosnian Moslems reject Serb–Croat plan to divide Bosnia into three on ethnic lines.

3–4 October. General Aidid's forces kill twelve US servicemen in Somalia as they attack his headquarters; Americans kill hundreds of Somalis in the operation.

15 October. US starts naval blockade of Haiti after murder of justice minister and signs that former President Aristide will not be restored.

7 November. President Clinton says US will use force if North Korea obtains a nuclear weapon.

12 December. Successes for followers of extreme nationalist Vladimir Zhirinovsky in Russian elections.

17 December. US troops begin withdrawal from Somalia.

31 December. In Georgia, rebel leader Zviad Ghamsakhurdia commits suicide.

1994

11 January. NATO's Brussels Summit approves 'Partnership for Peace' allowing military co-operation with ex-Communist states.

12–14 January. Clinton and Yeltsin, meeting in Moscow, agree US and Russia will not target nuclear missiles at each other. They and Ukrainian President Leonid Kravchuk agree on destruction of Ukraine's nuclear arsenal.

20 January. International Atomic Energy Authority announces that North Korea has prevented inspections of suspected nuclear installations.

3 February. Clinton ends nineteen-year US economic embargo against Vietnam.

3 February. Russia and Georgia sign agreement on military co-operation.

5 February. Bosnian Serb mortar attack kills 68 in a Sarajevo market.

Later February. Under threat of NATO air strikes, Serb forces pull back from Sarajevo.

22 February. Aldrich Ames, former head of CIA's anti-Soviet counter-intelligence branch, is arrested for espionage.

28 February. NATO aircraft shoot down four Serbian aeroplanes in the Alliance's first ever act of violence.

18 March. Bosnia's Croats and Moslems agree to form a federation.

23 March.   North Korea threatens to pull out of Non-proliferation Treaty after it is again accused of obstructing nuclear inspectors.

25 March.   US troops complete withdrawal from Somalia but other UN forces take over airport and harbour.

1 April.   Hungary is first ex-Communist state to apply for NATO's 'Partnership for Peace'; soon followed by many others.

29 April.   Nelson Mandela's African National Congress wins first all-race elections following end of apartheid in South Africa.

14 May.   President Izetbegovic of Bosnia rejects latest peace plan which would divide the country into Serb and Moslem–Croat parts after a long truce.

9 June.   US House of Representatives votes to lift arms embargo on Bosnian Moslems.

15–17 June.   Peace mission by ex-US President Jimmy Carter leads to North Korean agreement to terminate its nuclear programme. US then drops pressure for sanctions against North Korea.

6 July.   'Contact Group' (formed by US, Russia, Britain and France on 26 April) proposes a two-way partition of Bosnia with 51 per cent in the Croat–Moslem federation.

10 July.   Voters in Ukraine and Belarus elect Presidents who favour closer links to Russia.

24 August.   Clinton forced to end automatic asylum for Cuban refugees because so many are fleeing.

3 September.   Yeltsin and China's Jiang Zemin agree their countries will no longer target nuclear missiles at each other.

19 September.   US forces invade Haiti to restore ousted President Aristide: no resistance because ex-US President Jimmy Carter persuades the military leader, General Cedras, to resign.

27–28 September.   At Washington Summit with Yeltsin, Clinton says the 1975 Jackson–Vanik amendment (linking US–Soviet trade to Jewish emigration) is no longer applicable.

Early October.   Saddam Hussein masses forces on Iraqi–Kuwait border but pulls back when US responds in kind.

10 November.   US navy stops enforcing UN arms embargo (begun in September 1991) on Yugoslavia: will let others arm Bosnian Moslems, but US itself will not sell them arms.

10 November.   In Angola government forces take Savimbi's headquarters at Huambo, forcing (on 20 November) a new peace agreement.

19 November.   Marxist Joaquim Chissano wins first free elections in Mozambique.

1 December.   Russia refuses to sign agreement on NATO's 'Partnership for Peace' despite earlier saying it would do so.

5–6 December.   CSCE Summit agrees to turn the body into a permanent organisation.

Mid-December. Chechen rebels resist an all-out offensive by 30,000 Russian troops and aircraft against Grozny.

1995

15 January. Russian troops finally capture the Presidential Palace in the Chechen capital, Grozny.

20 February. US troops return to Somalia to protect withdrawal of UN force (completed 3 March).

6 March. Croatia and Bosnia agree anti-Serb military pact.

27 March. UN threatens air attacks on Bosnian Serbs due to continued shelling of towns designated 'safe areas' by the UN.

19 April. Russians capture last Chechen town in rebel hands, but guerrilla war continues.

10 May. Clinton, in Moscow to celebrate V-E Day, meets Yeltsin, who agrees to sign agreement with NATO (done on 31 May).

Late May. Bosnian Serbs take over 300 UN troops hostage following NATO air strikes. All are released within a month.

14–20 June. Chechen rebels hold 2,000 hostages in a Russian hospital north of Chechenia before getting safe conduct home.

11 July. Fall of the 'safe area' of Srbrenica to Bosnian Serbs and massacre of many male inhabitants.

Late July. Britain and France send joint force of 2,000 to Sarajevo as more 'safe areas' attacked. Zepa falls on 25 July.

4–9 August. In a rapid offensive helped by Bosnian Moslems, the Croats capture the Serb-populated region of Krajina which local Serbs had held since 1991.

30 August. NATO begins large-scale bombing of Bosnian Serbs in 'Operation Deliberate Force'.

13 September. As NATO again bombs Bosnian Serb positions, the US helps secure Serb agreement on lifting siege of Sarajevo.

5 October. US peace envoy Richard Holbrooke brokers sixty-day truce in Bosnia.

31 October–21 November. Talks at Dayton airbase in Ohio between Presidents of Bosnia, Serbia and Croatia lead to Bosnian peace agreement (formally signed in Paris on 14 December).

19 November. A former Communist, Alexander Kwasniewski, beats Lech Walesa in Polish Presidential elections.

19 December. Communists emerge as strongest party (22 per cent) in Russian elections.

20 December. 60,000-strong NATO force takes over Bosnian peace-keeping role from UN.

1996

9 January. Chechen rebels take 200 hostages in the Russian town of Kizylar; Chechens later move on to Pervomaiskoye.

18 January.   Russian forces storm Pervomaiskoye to free hostages.

26 February.   Clinton introduces new sanctions after Cuba shoots down two aircraft with exiles on board.

8 March.   China starts test firing ballistic missiles during manoeuvres off Taiwan, ahead of first free Taiwanese Presidential elections (held on 23 March).

12 March.   Clinton signs Helms–Burton Act allowing sanctions against those who trade with Cuba; provokes opposition from other Western states.

29 March.   Russia agrees economic union with Belarus, Kazakhstan and Kyrgyzstan.

5 April.   New Korean crisis after the North says it no longer recognises the demilitarised zone.

21 April.   Chechen leader General Dudayev is killed in a Russian rocket attack.

8 June.   Yeltsin makes General Alexander Lebed (third-placed candidate in election race) his National Security Adviser.

16 June.   Yeltsin tops first round of Russian Presidential elections, but only 3 per cent ahead of Communist Gennadi Zyuganov; Yeltsin wins second round on 3 July.

30 June.   Communists, who had ruled Mongolia since 1921, lose Mongolian elections.

6 August.   Chechens seize control of the capital Grozny in a surprise attack.

11 August.   Yeltsin sends Lebed to negotiate with new rebel leader Aslon Maskhadov on end to fighting in Chechenia: truce on 22 August and peace agreement on 29 August, leading to Russian withdrawal.

3 September.   US missile attacks on Iraq following advances by Saddam Hussein against Kurd rebels in the north.

27 September.   In Afghanistan fundamentalist Taliban militia take Kabul and execute former President Najibullah.

16 October.   Yeltsin dismisses Lebed for plotting mutiny.

5 November.   Following several earlier periods of hospitalisation, Yeltsin has heart by-pass surgery; only resumes duties on 23 December.

18 November.   CIA's Harold Nicolson arrested as a Soviet spy.

24 November.   Clinton meets China's Jiang Zemin during Asia-Pacific meeting in Manila.

December.   Persistent unrest in Belgrade, Serbia following disputed local election results.

1997

27 January.   Aslan Maskhadov, the former rebel leader, elected Chechen President.

1 March.   Albanian President dismisses Albanian government following weeks of protest over pyramid selling schemes; martial law declared on 3 March; elections promised on 9 March.

20–21 March. Clinton–Yeltsin Summit in Helsinki discusses NATO enlargement to Eastern Europe.

15 April. An Italian-led peace-keeping force begins deployment in Albania.

17 April. China and Taiwan resume direct shipping links for first time since 1949.

29 April. The UN-sponsored Chemical Weapons Ban (signed 15 January 1993) comes into force; ratified by more than eighty states: bans development, production and use of chemical weapons, but not signed by Iraq.

16 May. After weeks of civil war, President Mobutu of Zaire flees the country; on 17 May the Democratic Republic of Congo is declared under ex-Marxist guerilla leader, Laurent Kabila.

22 May. Yeltsin replaces his defence minister and Chief of General Staff due to dissatisfaction with the state of Russian armed forces.

23 May. Russia and Belarus sign a Charter of Union.

27 May. Signature of Russia–NATO Founding Act governing relations between them.

Late May. The Taliban offensive in northern Afghanistan is thrown back by General Abdul Dostan and his allies.

20–22 June. The G-7 annual meeting of industrialised states, in Denver, becomes the 'Summit of the Eight' with Russia.

27 June. The Tajikistan government and rebel forces sign a peace agreement in Moscow, ending five years of civil war.

29 June. First round of Albanian elections. Second round on 6 July. Tension is reduced.

1 July. Chinese sovereignty resumed over former British colony of Hong Kong.

8–9 July. NATO's Madrid Summit invites Poland, Hungary and Czech Republic to join.

25 July. In Cambodia the former dictator Pol Pot is sentenced by the Khmer Rouge to life imprisonment after falling out with other leaders.

26 October–3 November. Jiang Zemin visits US, the first Presidential visit since 1985.

29 October. UN arms inspectors suspend operations in Iraq after it threatens to expel American members of the team.

9–11 November. Yeltsin visits China and agrees final settlement of their border dispute, after nearly thirty years of tension.

20 November. Following Russian mediation, Iraq ends its ban on Americans in the UN arms inspection team.

3–4 December. In Ottawa 125 countries sign treaty to end the production and use of anti-personnel mines. Not signed by US, Russia, China or most Middle East states.

9–10 December.   After long preparations, the first round of US–China–North Korea–South Korea talks is held in Geneva to try to get permanent peace in Korea.

14 December.   Iranian President Khatami calls for dialogue with the US.

22 December.   UN Security Council demands Iraq give full access to arms inspectors, following restrictions on their visits.

1998

17 January.   Saddam Hussein says he will only let UN arms inspections continue if sanctions on Iraq are lifted.

21 January.   Pope John Paul II, in Cuba, urges Castro to respect human rights and the US to reconsider its economic embargo.

4 February.   As US and British forces build up in the Gulf, Yeltsin speaks of danger of a Third World War over Iraq.

23 February.   UN Secretary General Kofi Annan agrees a plan with Saddam to defuse the crisis over Iraq.

24 February.   US and Britain accept Annan's peace plan, but maintain their forces in the Gulf.

9 March.   US, Russia and major West European states agree new sanctions on Serbia after a week of repression of the Albanian majority in Kosovo province.

SECTION TWO

Crises and conflicts

1. Poland and Eastern Europe, 1944–48

Of essential importance to the start of the Cold War was the Sovietisation of Eastern Europe after 1944. This was an unstable region between the wars, dominated by Germany during the Second World War.

The Communist take-over took place at a different pace in different countries but followed a similar pattern: anti-Fascist coalition governments were formed, with Soviet encouragement, when a country was liberated; Communists, from the local resistance or from exile in Russia, took key positions in government; industries were nationalised, land was redistributed to the peasants and centralised planning was introduced; conservative institutions, such as the Church, were attacked; liberal-democratic parties were destroyed by the use of 'salami tactics' (the formation of liberal-looking parties by Communist stooges), by the intimidation, exile and murder of political leaders, and finally by rigged elections; socialist parties were forced to unite with the Communists; and in 1948–53, even Communist Party members were imprisoned or killed if they seemed a threat to the centralised, police-state created by puppet leaders loyal to Stalin. The following major events took place in the various states.

Poland

The largest East European state, strategically placed between Germany and Russia, and historically a bone of contention between them, Poland was the essential prize for Stalin. He had claimed half of it under the Ribbentrop–Molotov Pact (q.v.). America, where there was a substantial Polish minority, and Britain, which went to war for Poland in 1939, agreed to alter the Polish border (with losses to Russia and gains for Germany) but were upset in July 1944 when Stalin installed a Communist administration in Lublin to run the country. A Polish government-in-exile existed in London but was dominated by conservatives. Stalin criticised the 'London Poles' and refused to aid the Polish resistance when it launched the Warsaw Rising in August 1944. He recognised the 'Lublin Poles' as the country's government in January. At the Yalta Conference (q.v.) Stalin agreed to allow some London Poles, including the moderate Stanislaus Mikolajcyk, into the government, but promised elections were not held until January 1947, and were rigged. Mikolajcyk fled the country in October 1947, by which time the Communists were securely in power. The Red Army destroyed nationalist guerrilla forces. After September 1948 the principal leader was Boleslaw Bierut.

Romania

In Romania the local Communists joined a 'National Front' of opposition parties in June 1944; in August King Michael threw out the pro-German dictator Ion Antonescu, and in September the new National Front government changed sides in the war. But by then the Red Army was on Romanian soil. Rigged elections were held in September 1946. King Michael was forced to abdicate in December 1947. By 1952 the leading figure was Gheorghe Gheorghieu-Dej.

Bulgaria

Bulgaria also had a 'front' of opposition parties, was invaded by the Red Army in October 1944 and tried to change sides in the war after allying with Hitler. Subsequently Bulgaria was invaded by the Red Army, rigged elections were held in 1945 and in 1946 the monarchy was abolished. The main opposition leader, Nikolai Petkov, was executed in 1947. The Communist leader was George Dimitrov, succeeded, in 1949, by Vulko Chernenko.

Hungary

Hungary was another ally of Hitler whose government tried to change sides when invaded by the Red Army in September 1944. Fighting between the Germans and Soviets took place over several months and devastated the country. The Communists joined a coalition government in 1945. Stalin took little interest in Hungary at first and elections in November gave a majority to the Small Landowners' Party. This party proved divided, however, and in spring 1947 the Communists launched a campaign of intimidation against it. In May the Smallholders' prime minister, Ferenc Nagy, was forced to resign and in August rigged elections were held. The Communist leader was Matyas Rakosi.

Czechoslovakia

Czechoslovakia was, like Poland, an Allied state. Its leader, Eduard Benes, however, was ready to sign a friendship treaty with Stalin in 1943 and, uniquely in Eastern Europe, there was significant local support for Communism. This was partly because Czechoslovakia was an industrial state and partly because of resentment over the Anglo-French betrayal at Munich in 1938. In 1946 the Communists were the largest party (35 per cent) in free elections and their leader, Klement Gottwald, became prime minister. In February 1948 the Communists carried out a coup, backed by their 'Workers' Militia, which completely subverted the government.

2. Greek Civil War, 1944–45 and 1946–49

Greece had been invaded by Italy and Germany in 1940–41 and the royal government had gone into exile in Cairo, where it was protected by the British for whom Greece was of strategic importance. Local resistance to the Germans became dominated by the Communist Greek People's Liberation Army (ELAS) and its political leadership, the National Liberation Front (EAM). In October 1944 British forces arrived in Greece and took control of major cities but the Communists took over much of the countryside and opposed the return of the monarchy. Josef Stalin agreed with Churchill in October 1944 that Greece should be an area of British influence. EAM leaders then agreed to share power in a coalition government but in December fighting occurred between British and Communist forces in Athens. In February 1945 the Varkiza Agreement pacified the Communists, promising social reforms and a plebiscite on the return of the monarchy.

The EAM boycotted elections in March 1946 and were alienated in September when the monarchy was retained in a plebiscite. In October 1946 the Communists launched a civil war, with assistance from Greece's Communist neighbours (Albania, Yugoslavia, Bulgaria). The Truman Doctrine (q.v.) of March 1947 brought US aid to the royal government. This, together with poor Communist military tactics and the 1948 Soviet–Yugoslav split, helped to guarantee a royalist victory in October 1949. During the conflict, 25,000 people were killed.

3. Trieste crisis, May 1945

The region of Venezia Giulia, including Trieste, was part of Italy after 1919 but was claimed by Yugoslavia. On 1 May 1945 British forces, advancing through Italy, arrived in the town at the same time as Yugoslav Communist forces. Initial attempts to negotiate a divided occupation failed. The Soviets supported the Yugoslavs and America backed the British. On 21 May the Yugoslavs backed down and, whilst retaining control of the hinterland, allowed British and US forces to occupy Trieste.

4. Division of Germany, 1945–49

Germany in 1945 faced defeat, economic hardship, the destruction of its government, and substantial human losses. But it lay at the heart of Europe, had enormous economic potential and was a major prize in the East–West struggle. The victorious powers agreed on certain policies, including the 'four Ds': Denazification, Democratisation, Disarmament and Decartelisation (the break-up of the monopolies which had supported Hitler). War-crime trials were held and the country was jointly occupied by America, Britain, the USSR and France ruling through an Allied Control Council (ACC) on the basis of unanimity. However, the occupation powers began to disagree over Germany's future on several issues:

(a) France wished to detach certain Western areas (the Rhineland, Ruhr and Saar) from Germany and rejected all idea of a new centralised government. To achieve its aims France vetoed all attempts at central administration by the ACC.

(b) The USSR seemed determined to cut its zone off from the others, carrying out Soviet-style reforms in agriculture and industry. In April 1946 Social Democrats in the Soviet zone were forced to merge with the Communists in the 'Socialist Unity Party' which was given political authority in the zone.

(c) The Soviets wanted large reparations from Germany to help their reconstruction but the US and Britain feared this would destroy the German economy. The complex deal on reparations agreed at Potsdam (q.v.) proved impossible to carry out. In May 1946 the Deputy Governor, General Lucius Clay, suspended reparations from the US zone.

(d) Regarding Germany's political future, the Soviets (notably in a speech by Molotov in July 1946) posed as the defender of a united, centralised government. However, US Secretary of State Byrnes advocated a federal political structure in a major speech at Stuttgart in September 1946 (when he also undertook to keep the US army in Germany in the long term).

Attempts to achieve a German peace treaty in 1947 through the Council of Foreign Ministers (q.v.) ended in failure. In February–June 1948 the US, Britain and France held a conference in London without the USSR and agreed to establish a West German state under certain guarantees. This was done in May 1949. The Soviets responded by founding an East German government under Walter Ulbricht.

5. Chinese Civil War, 1945–49

Conflict had actually begun in 1927 when Nationalist forces under Chiang Kai-shek first tried to destroy the Chinese Communists. After 1928 the Communists began to revive and in 1934–35 made the 'Long March' to Yenan in the north of China. In 1937 Chiang agreed to co-operate with the Communists in the war against Japan which had broken out. However, civil war was always likely to break out again once Japan was defeated. The Second World War weakened Chiang Kai-shek's power in eastern areas of China, which Japan occupied. The Communists developed guerrilla war tactics and captured areas from the retreating Japanese in 1945.

The Communists were still restricted to northern China in 1945: their armies were smaller than those of the Nationalists, and the USSR was ready to work with Chiang. American envoys, Patrick Hurley in 1945 and George Marshall in 1945–46, were unable to negotiate a lasting settlement between the Nationalists and Mao Zedong. America gave substantial aid to Chiang, including air transport, economic and military assistance and the support of 50,000 US marines (who, however, took no part in fighting). Chiang's government was corrupt, failed to tackle inflation and alienated people with high taxes. Mao was able to appeal to peasant support with the promise of land reform. Chiang's generals were appointed for loyalty rather than competence, and their conventional tactics failed against a determined guerrilla army which avoided pitched battles, concentrated on winning control of the countryside rather than the cities, and attacked only when at an advantage.

In 1945–46 Chiang's forces lost out in the struggle for control of Manchuria. In 1948 half of China was lost to Chiang and his position quickly disintegrated. Peking fell in January 1949, Mao proclaimed a People's Republic in September and Chiang retreated to the island of Taiwan. President Truman was accused of 'losing' China and the 'China Lobby' (or 'Asia Firsters') in Congress now called for greater efforts to tackle Communism in East Asia.

6. Iran crisis, March 1946

Iran was jointly occupied by Soviet and British forces in 1941, and served as a route for supplies from the Western Allies to Russia. Under wartime agreements it was due to be evacuated six months after the war, that is on 2 March 1946. The Soviets used their presence, in October 1945, to establish a separatist government in the northern province of Azerbaijan. In early 1946 the US increasingly became concerned at Soviet policy. When the 2 March deadline passed without withdrawal, the USS *Missouri* was sent to the Eastern Mediterranean. Iran was encouraged by America and Britain to appeal to the UN, and US diplomatic pressure was put on Moscow, before the Soviets agreed to withdraw their troops. They eventually left by 6 May. The crisis was seen as an early, successful example of containment (q.v.) and as an example of supposed Soviet 'expansionism' towards the Middle East. The USSR won some concessions on oil from Iran in an agreement of 4 April, but the Iranian parliament refused to ratify this. The separatist movement in Azerbaijan was ended in December 1946.

7. Black Sea Straits controversy, August 1946

Soviet interest in Turkey predated the Russian Revolution and concentrated on two issues: first, Russia had long-standing territorial claims against Turkey in the Caucasus mountains, which were raised again in

July 1945 and resisted by Turkey and Britain; second, Russia had long wanted free access from the Black Sea to the Mediterranean, through the Dardanelles, and needed a naval base there. Although subject to a fifteen-year territorial guarantee from Britain and France after 1939, Turkey felt vulnerable to Soviet pressure. In August 1946 however, when the Soviets formally proposed a joint agreement with Turkey on the defence of the Straits, the Truman administration joined with Turkey and Britain in resisting the proposal. In March 1947 Turkey, along with Greece, was provided with US aid under the Truman Doctrine (q.v.).

8. Philippines insurgency, 1946–54 and post-1968

In July 1946 the Philippines, a US colony since 1899, was given its independence, but the Americans retained a number of military bases and aided the government against the Communist 'Hukbalahap' guerrilla army (originally set up during the war, to fight the Japanese). Despite Communist success in winning over the peasantry of Luzon, a successful anti-guerrilla campaign defeated the insurgents by May 1954. A Communist guerrilla campaign revived in December 1968 against the dictatorial regime of President Ferdinand Marcos. The Communist 'New People's Army' kept up its activities after Marcos's overthrow by Corazon Aquino in 1986.

9. First Indo-China War, 1946–54

Indo-China – now divided between Vietnam, Laos and Cambodia (or Kampuchea) – had been a French colony from the 1860s. In 1940–41 the collaborationist Vichy government in France retained control of Indo-China and agreed to allow Japanese bases, but the nationalist Viet-Minh in Vietnam, resisted the Japanese. In September 1945, Viet-Minh's Communist leader, Ho Chi Minh, declared Vietnam independent. The French government of General de Gaulle was determined to restore its authority, however. Vietnam was jointly occupied after Japan's surrender by Britain (in the South) and China (in the North). The British helped to restore French authority in late 1945 and the Chinese agreed to allow French forces into the North in early 1946. By then the Viet-Minh had established a strong position in the North.

In 1946, talks between Ho Chi Minh and the French government failed to achieve a settlement. In November 1946 French forces bombarded the northern Vietnamese port of Haiphong, where there had been disturbances and the following month the Viet-Minh massacred French civilians in the city of Hanoi. A vicious colonial war now began. The French, who eventually lost 72,000 lives in the struggle, proved unable to root out the Viet-Minh, despite the formation of a local Vietnamese government in 1949 under the former Emperor, Bao Dai. Bao Dai's pro-French government was recognised by America and Britain, but the Viet-Minh were strengthened by the victory of Mao's Communists in the Chinese Civil War. Mao and Stalin recognised Ho as Vietnamese leader in 1950, leading the US to give financial aid to the French war effort in May, but the guerrilla war, under General Giap, sapped French strength. In 1953–54 the 'Navarre Plan' of the new French commander ended in disaster when a large French garrison was surrounded at Dienbienphu and forced to surrender. At the 1954 Geneva conference (q.v.) Laos and Cambodia were given their independence whilst Vietnam was divided between a Communist North and an anti-Communist South, the latter supported by the US.

10. First Arab–Israeli War, 1948–49

The Arab–Israeli conflict had its origins in the desire of the Zionist movement to re-establish a homeland for Jews in Palestine. In 1917 Britain, which became the ruling power in Palestine after the First World War, issued the 'Balfour Declaration', which promised both a Jewish homeland *and* respect for local Arab rights. The Nazi holocaust and international sympathy for Jews added to the pressures on Britain to allow greater immigration, but Arab nationalism, represented in the Arab League (1945), was also strong. In November 1947 the UN voted to partition Palestine between Jews and Arabs and, on 14 May 1948, the British quit the country. The Jewish leaders declared an Israeli state and were immediately attacked by forces from Egypt, Transjordan, Syria, Lebanon and Iraq. The Israeli Defence Forces fared best in the fighting. Attempts by the UN's Count Bernadotte to secure a new partition agreement broke down in October, when the Israelis renewed the war. Another cease-fire on 7 January 1949 effectively ended the war, except for some clashes in March. By then the Israelis controlled most of Palestine; the remaining Arab areas were annexed by Egypt (Gaza) and Jordan (the West Bank). The war led the Arabs generally to become radical and anti-Western, but created a strong Israeli state, closely allied to America.

11. Malaya emergency, 1948–60

As in the Philippines (q.v.) a large Communist movement had existed in Malaya before 1948, concentrated among the Chinese minority (40 per cent of the population). Their support was boosted by the defeat of the colonial power, Britain, at the hands of the Japanese in 1941–42. In 1945 British authority was restored but an emergency had to be declared in February 1948. The counter-insurgency campaign was particularly successful after January 1952 under Sir Gerald Templer and included such tactics as the 'strategic hamlets' later adopted by the US in Vietnam. By the mid-1950s the Communist guerrillas, cut off from the bulk of the population, were effectively defeated but the emergency remained in force until 1960.

12. Berlin blockade, 1948–49

One of the great crises of the Cold War followed the growing division of Germany (q.v.). The London agreement to form a West German state in June 1948 was opposed by the USSR. At the end of the month, the Western powers introduced a new currency into Germany. This became the basis of German economic revival and threatened to undermine economic policies in Eastern Germany. Since April, the Soviets had harassed Western land traffic into Berlin. Now the Soviets cut off access to West Berlin completely, by road, rail and canal. Since West Berlin was entirely surrounded by the Soviet zone this move threatened to starve the Allied sectors into submission. But the Western Allies maintained a right, acknowledged by the Soviets, for air access into Berlin. The US and Britain now launched the 'Berlin airlift', under which thousands of tons of supplies were flown into Berlin. The option of breaking a way open to West Berlin by force of arms (suggested by the US Governor, General Clay) was not required. The fear of a Third World War led to diplomatic contacts between Stalin and Western ambassadors in Berlin, and a neutral UN peace mission, which achieved nothing. The success of the airlift led Stalin to give way in spring 1949 and end the blockade.

13. Tito–Stalin split, 1948–49

This was the first clear sign of division within the post-war Communist bloc. Previously the regime of Josip Broz, known as Tito, had seemed a repressive police-state, entirely loyal to Stalin. But Tito had established his regime without Soviet military assistance, after a successful wartime guerrilla campaign. Tito was not one of Stalin's appointees and came to resent Soviet interference in Yugoslav affairs. He was expelled from Cominform in June 1948 after refusing to attend one of its meetings. Later in the year an economic blockade was enforced on the country by Stalin, and in 1949 Tito accepted Western economic assistance. However, Yugoslavia remained Communist. Stalin used the struggle with Tito in 1948–53 to justify a tightening of control throughout Eastern Europe. Any Communist who was suspected of 'Titoist' tendencies was liable to be executed (as with Laszlo Rajk in Hungary). Under Khruschev there was a Soviet–Yugoslav *rapprochement*, but Tito refused to join the Warsaw Pact.

14. Korean War, 1950–53

The Korean War was one of the largest and bloodiest confrontations of the Cold War, and indeed threatened to trigger a Third World War. Korea, under Japanese domination throughout the early twentieth century, was jointly occupied by US and Soviet troops in 1945 with a dividing line along the 38th parallel. Their armed forces were subsequently withdrawn. Both powers fostered new regimes in Korea: a hard-line Communist regime in the North under Kim Il Sung and a pro-American regime in the South led by Syngman Rhee. Attempts to hold all-Korean elections failed in 1948 and a series of incidents took place along the 38th parallel before, in June 1950, the powerful Northern forces launched a full-scale invasion of the South.

Stalin's exact role in events remains unclear, and Soviet forces themselves never entered the Korean War, even though US aircraft sometimes bombed Soviet territory. The Soviet Union was boycotting Security Council meetings in early 1950, as a protest at the Western refusal to allow Communist China onto the Council. This allowed the US to push through a condemnation of North Korean aggression and to fight in the name of the UN. In late June Truman also increased aid to French forces fighting Communist guerrillas in Vietnam, and sent the Seventh Fleet to defend Chiang Kai-shek in Taiwan.

US forces from Japan, under General Douglas MacArthur, led the UN military effort, and after early retreats established a 'defense perimeter' around the port of Pusan. In September, MacArthur launched the Inchon landings behind North Korean lines, which forced the latter to retreat. In the euphoria which followed, UN forces marched over the 38th parallel to begin the 'liberation' of North Korea. But in October–November the Communist Chinese began to aid the North Koreans. The Chinese feared a strong pro-American state on their border and the anti-Chinese policy pursued by America. The Chinese forces, large in number and with the benefit of surprise drove the UN forces back down into South Korea in early 1951, before a UN counter-offensive led the military front to stabilise almost where the war had begun. MacArthur and others talked of extending the war to invade China. Truman however decided to sack MacArthur and to localise the war in Korea.

Despite the military stalemate, it took another two years before the war ended. Armistice talks between the UN and the Communists proved long and difficult, with neither side willing to make concessions. The most difficult problem was that thousands of prisoners-of-war in Western hands did not wish to be sent back to China or North Korea, despite the insistence of the North Korean leadership that they be returned. The US elections in 1952 caused more delays but the new president, Eisenhower, was determined to bring a settlement. Peace prospects may also have been helped by the death of Stalin in March 1953. An armistice was finally signed in July 1953, but while this ended the fighting it did not bring a peace treaty. Korea remained divided.

15. China's invasion of Tibet, October 1950

In 1950, having secured control over most of mainland China, Mao Zedong decided to reconquer Tibet, the Himalayan country which had broken free of Chinese rule in 1911. Tibet was quickly occupied and had to give up control of its administration to Beijing. A failed nationalist rising in March 1959 led the spiritual leader, the Dalai Lama, to flee to India and Tibet was then subjected to an influx of Chinese settlers. Nationalist unrest was put down again in 1989–90.

16. Iran, 1951–54

In April 1951 the radical Iranian government of Dr Mohammed Mossadeq (1880–1967) passed a law nationalising the oil industry, which was a virtual monopoly of the British-owned Anglo-Iranian Oil Company. Britain's Labour government, facing Opposition pressure, sent a cruiser to the Persian Gulf, but decided on a peaceful solution to the problem with an appeal to the International Court of Justice. In 1953 it was the US which did most to end the dispute, when the CIA – in one of its most successful operations – launched 'Operation Ajax', under the direction of Kim Roosevelt. Demonstrators were hired, contacts established with the Iranian army and a coup was launched to restore the authority of Shah (King) Mohammed Reza Pahlevi. After the coup several Western companies took a share of the oil industry. The Shah remained a loyal US ally until the 1970s.

17. Berlin rising, June 1953

The death of Stalin in March 1953 led to expectations of change within Eastern Europe. In the USSR the new collective leadership under Georgi Malenkov adopted a 'new course' in economic policy, producing more consumer goods. But in East Germany in May 1953 the hard-line Ulbricht government decided to *increase* production demands on the workers. The result on 16 June was a workers' demonstration in East Berlin in favour of economic reform. The unrest spread to other cities and led local Soviet forces to intervene. Tanks were used against demonstrators in Berlin and leaders of the unrest were executed or imprisoned. The swift action of the Red Army put a rapid end to the 'rising' and showed that Stalin's successors would not tolerate greater independence in Eastern Europe.

18. Guatemala, June 1954

The first example of US action to overthrow a pro-Soviet regime in the Americas. Guatemalan President Jacoba Arbenz had, since 1951, carried out a number of radical reforms. In 1953, however, his expropriation of the lands of the United Fruit Company antagonised US businessmen and his political alliance with the Guatemalan Communists convinced Eisenhower that Arbenz was pro-Soviet. In late May 1954, following the arrival of Czech arms in the country, the US announced it would enforce a blockade against further shipments. On 18 June a group of Guatemalan exiles, led by Colonel Castillo Armas, invaded the country from Nicaragua and Honduras. The exiles were backed by the CIA. Arbenz's armed forces did little to defend him and on 27 June he resigned. He was soon succeeded by Armas, who followed a pro-US, anti-Communist policy. The CIA operation became the model for the ill-fated Bay of Pigs operation of 1961 (q.v.).

19. First Quemoy–Matsu crisis, 1954–55

After the fall of mainland China to Communism in 1949, the Nationalist government of Chiang Kai-shek not only retained control of Taiwan but also a number of islands close to the mainland, including Quemoy, the Matsus and the Taschen Islands. These were so close as to be within the range of Communist artillery. In September 1954, after the creation of the South-East Asian Treaty Organisation (q.v.), the Communists began to bombard the island of Quemoy. In the months that followed, the Communists maintained their pressure on the islands, and talked about 'liberating' Taiwan. The Nationalists, backed by the US, were determined not to back down and it seemed the crisis could turn into a US–Chinese war, perhaps involving nuclear arms. In early 1955 the Nationalists did abandon the Taschen Islands, but retained their hold on Quemoy and the Matsus. Peace efforts by the UN came to nothing, but at the Bandung Conference (q.v.) in April, China's Zhou Enlai adopted a moderate tone and the bombardments then eased.

20. Poland and Hungary, 1956

Khruschev's rise to predominance, his detente policy with the West and *rapprochement* with Yugoslavia again created expectations of change in the Eastern bloc. The Austrian State Treaty (q.v.) led to hopes of a Soviet withdrawal from Central Europe. In early 1956 Khruschev launched his attack on Stalinism (see de-Stalinisation). In two countries popular desires for reform came close to overwhelming the Communist system and ultimately led Khruschev to use armed force to restore Kremlin authority.

Poland

In February 1956 the death of party leader Boleslaw Bierut brought Eduard Ochab to power. He attempted some piecemeal reforms, including more open discussion. This led to calls for a free press and economic reforms. In June there were large demonstrations in the city of Poznan. The 'Poznan Rising' was quickly put down using Polish – not Soviet – troops, who killed about fifty demonstrators. Unrest revived and there were strong calls for power to be given to Wladyslaw Gomulka (q.v.), who had been imprisoned under Bierut as a 'Titoist'. On 19–20 October Khruschev himself visited Warsaw and agreed that, to control the discontent, Gomulka should become party leader. Furthermore, the Russian Marshal Rokossovsky, who had been made Polish defence minister, was dismissed and certain economic reforms were allowed. The return to normality in Poland after October probably had much to do with the bitter lesson of events in Hungary.

Hungary

In July 1956 there was a change of leadership when, after popular demonstrations in favour of reform, the conservative party leader Matyas Rakosi was replaced by Ernoe Geroe. Geroe proved an unpopular choice and demonstrations in October, similar to those in Poland, favoured a return to power by former premier Imre Nagy, who, like Gomulka, was anti-Stalinist. Unlike Poland, the return of Nagy to the premiership and the promotion of Janos Kadar to the Communist Party leadership failed to halt demands for reform. In late October workers formed factory councils, local government was taken over by 'revolutionary committees' and demonstrators demanded a free press, multi-party democracy and withdrawal from the Warsaw Pact. It was possibly to keep control of events that Nagy agreed to these three demands. Kadar, on 3 November, broke with Nagy and created an alternative government, loyal to Moscow. The Red Army then invaded Hungary. The West, crippled by the Suez Crisis, refused to give Hungary any assistance. By 11 November 3,000 people had been killed, the Soviets were in control and Nagy captured. He and others were later executed. The Church leader Cardinal Mindsentzy became a virtual prisoner for many years in the US Embassy. In most of Eastern Europe (except Poland) there was a return to hard-line Communism.

21. Sino-Soviet split, c. 1956–61

The 1949 Communist victory in China was seen in the US as marking a major advance for Soviet interests, but there were always important differences between Beijing and Moscow. Chinese Communists felt they had been ill-advised by the Soviets in the 1920s, resented Stalin's 1945 treaty with Chiang Kai-shek and were disappointed with the small scale of Soviet economic and military aid. In 1954 the Soviets surrendered the economic and transport rights in Manchuria which they had obtained in 1945, but Mao Zedong resented the behaviour of Stalin's successors when they automatically expected China to follow Soviet policy. In particular Khruschev's 'de-Stalinisation' policy offended Mao, who had not been consulted about it and who based many of his policies on Soviet methods. Mao also opposed Soviet efforts at detente with the West and favoured a strong 'anti-imperialist' policy (as seen in Chinese policy in the Quemoy–Matsu crises). Khruschev for his part resented Mao's apparent challenge to him as leader of the Communist bloc, criticised China's 'Great Leap Forward' agricultural programme (launched 1958) and refused to help in developing a Chinese atom bomb.

In 1960 China openly opposed Khruschev's policy of 'peaceful coexistence' at an international Communist conference in Moscow, and the Soviets withdrew technical advisers from China, so putting an end to many industrial projects. In 1961 Khruschev also withdrew technicians from Albania, whose Stalinist leader, Enver Hoxha, had taken an independent line. The Chinese immediately supported Albania, and in October 1961 Zhou Enlai walked out of the Soviet Party Congress after Khruschev criticised Hoxha. The Sino-Soviet split was then an open one, and Mao began to condemn the Russians as 'imperialists'. China revived old territorial disputes with Russia (1963), exploded its own atom bomb (1964), encouraged Romanian independence from Moscow and competed with Russia for influence in Third World countries, with visits by Zhou Enlai to African and Asian states in 1963–64. In 1969 there were armed border clashes between China and Russia and the 'split' was not ended until the Gorbachev era.

22. Suez crisis, 1956

In the early 1950s Britain remained the major Western power in the Middle East, but its position was challenged by Arab nationalism, especially in Egypt. In 1952 the Egyptian monarchy was overthrown by a group of army officers, led by General Neguib, then by Nasser. In mid-1956 Nasser grew closer to the Eastern bloc, and this led the US to cancel aid for the building of a dam at Aswan. In order to obtain finance Nasser then nationalised the Suez Canal, which was largely owned by Britain and France. Western countries put pressure on Nasser to reverse his decision, but he had the support of the Soviet bloc and newly emerging nations. The US, as an anti-colonial power, was unwilling to agree to armed force being used, especially in an election year. However, the

British and French established secret contacts with Egypt's great enemy, Israel. In late October the Israelis attacked Egypt, providing the British and French with the excuse to intervene to 'protect' the Suez Canal. The Anglo-French expedition, however, took time to reach Egypt, and international condemnation of it mounted. The opposition from President Eisenhower – successfully re-elected president in early November – proved particularly important and led Britain to suspend the operation.

The Suez Crisis severely damaged Britain's self-confidence and its position in the Middle East; led France to turn more towards European unity; boosted Nasser; highlighted the power of the US in the Western Alliance; encouraged Arab radicalism; and provided an opening for greater Soviet involvement in Middle Eastern affairs.

23. 'Missile gap', 1957–61

Despite its nuclear superiority and threat to use 'massive retaliation' against opponents, the US in the 1950s remained fearful of a Soviet advance in strategic arms. Exaggerated intelligence reports on Soviet bomber capabilities led to the so-called 'bomber gap' of 1955–56. The 'missile gap' of 1957–61 was far more serious, because the Soviets in 1957 did seem to outmatch US military technology, initially by launching the first multi-stage ICBM in August and then the first ever space satellite, *Sputnik*, in October. The Soviets followed this by putting a dog, Laika, into space on *Sputnik II*, while the first US satellite launch, in December, ended in failure. A report by a committee under H. Rowan Gaither criticised US defence as inadequate and recommended a massive programme to build nuclear shelters. US Democrats exploited the idea that a Soviet lead in nuclear missile arsenals would open up after 1960. But the 'missile gap' soon proved illusory. The US had an easy lead in nuclear weapons in 1957, launched a satellite (*Explorer*) in January 1958 and developed its own long-range missiles: initially the slow, liquid-fuelled Atlas and Titan, and (in the European theatre) Thor and Jupiter, but later the rapid-response, solid-fuelled, silo-based Minuteman and the submarine-based Polaris, both far superior to Soviet ICBMs. Meanwhile the Soviet lack of missiles and aircraft to strike the US was confirmed by American U-2 spy-planes (flimsy, high-altitude reconnaissance aircraft, capable of taking high-resolution pictures, deployed after 1956) and, in 1960–61, by the CIA satellite *Discoverer*. Kennedy's Defense Secretary, McNamara, conceded there was no 'missile gap'.

24. Turco-Syrian War crisis, October 1957

After the Suez crisis a rift opened between radical, pro-Soviet states in the Middle East, such as Syria and Egypt, and pro-Western regimes, such

as Turkey, Iraq and Jordan. In April 1957 King Hussein of Jordan provoked unrest at home, and upset Syria and Egypt, when he sacked his
radical prime minister, Suleyman Nabulsi. In September Syrian relations
also worsened with Turkey, a NATO member which had territorial claims
against Syria. In October the sense of crisis was heightened when
Khruschev accused Turkey of planning an attack on Syria, and Syria
took the issue to the UN. America supported the Turks. However, the
crisis subsided as quickly as it had arisen, with no real evidence that war
was ever planned.

25. Middle East crisis, July–November 1958

Following the Suez crisis, the Middle East remained a centre of instability and superpower rivalry. In mid-July 1958 the violent overthrow of the
pro-Western Iraqi monarchy – the Hashemite royal family and prime
minister, Nuri el-Said, were murdered – plunged the area into renewed
crisis. The new republican government of Brigadier Karem Kassem
seemed likely to emulate the radicalism of Egypt and Syria. Iraq, the
only Arab member of the Baghdad Pact (q.v.), took no more part in the
alliance. It seemed radicalism would spread to other Arab states. Two in
particular were vulnerable: Lebanon, where the Maronite Christian President, Camille Chamoun, asked for US assistance to restore the fragile
political balance with Muslim groups; and Jordan, where the Hashemite
King Hussein feared a similar fate to his Iraqi relatives. Within days of
the Iraq coup, US marines landed in Lebanon and British paratroops in
Jordan. Despite Soviet condemnation and calls for a Summit meeting,
the Anglo-Americans were able to stabilise the situation. In October–
November their forces were able to leave Lebanon and Jordan, where
Chamoun and Hussein survived.

26. Second Quemoy–Matsu crisis, August–October 1958

Following the first Quemoy–Matsu crisis (q.v.), Chiang Kai-shek held
onto the offshore islands, while the Communists strengthened their positions on the mainland. In early August 1958, in the wake of a meeting
between Mao Zedong and Khruschev, the Communists again began to
bombard the islands and to blockade them. As in 1954–55, however, the
US backed Chiang strongly, strengthening the Seventh Fleet and threatening to respond to any invasion of the islands. In September both the
Chinese and Americans began to relax their war of words, however. In
October the Chinese allowed supplies through to Quemoy and the Matsus,
whilst the US pressed Chiang to reduce troop levels there. The Chinese
bombardments gradually subsided.

27. Second Berlin crisis, November 1958–May 1959

The crisis began in early November 1958 when, at a reception for a Polish delegation in Moscow, Nikita Khruschev declared that US, British and French forces should leave Berlin and that Russia would transfer its responsibilities in East Berlin to East Germany. The Western powers had rejected East German efforts to open talks with West Germany in September 1958 and Khruschev was under pressure from East Germans to guarantee their security in the face of Western non-recognition and the emigration of many East Germans to the West.

On 27 November Khruschev formalised his demands to the West in a note. He proposed to turn West Berlin into a demilitarised 'free city', wanted talks on a German peace treaty and threatened to hand over access routes to Berlin to the East German government after six months – a step which would force the West to deal directly with the East German regime. A meeting of the three Western powers in December refused to negotiate under duress. Britain's Harold Macmillan threatened to breach Western unity by visiting Russia in March 1959, but meanwhile Khruschev began to moderate his demands. A Soviet note of 10 January dropped the six-month ultimatum and proposed a Summit. The Western powers rejected the Summit proposal but proposed a meeting of US, Soviet, British and French foreign ministers, which was held in Geneva in May. The conference lasted until August and allowed tensions to ease. Khruschev's original deadline passed without incident. But no progress was possible on the German question.

28. The Congo, 1960–63

The Congo (later known as Zaïre) was given its independence by Belgium on 30 June 1960, after inadequate preparations, and immediately fell into anarchy. Belgian settlers were attacked by the Congolese, which led the Belgian army to try to restore order; there was a struggle for power between President Joseph Kasavubu and the prime minister, Patrice Lumumba; and on 11 July the mineral-rich province of Katanga declared its independence under Moise Tshombe. A UN force was sent to restore order but itself became involved in fighting and was criticised by Russia. Many Americans sympathised with Tshombe, who portrayed himself as an anti-Communist freedom fighter, while the volatile Lumumba was accused of being pro-Soviet before being murdered in February 1961. Eventually in 1963 UN forces, supported by President Kennedy, ended the Katangan secession. Ironically Tshombe became prime minister of all the Congo for a time in 1964–65, but Zaïre only achieved stability under his successor, the pro-Western Joseph Mobutu.

29. Laos crisis, 1960–62

After the settlement of the First Indo-China War (q.v.), the US provided covert aid to the Laotian army to fight the Communist 'Pathet Lao', which in turn was supported by China and North Vietnam. The US opposed attempts by neutralist Prince Souvanna Phouma to form a coalition with the Communists, and in December 1960 helped establish a right-wing government under Boun Oum. A cease-fire was arranged between Boun Oum and the Pathet Lao in May 1961, and in June Kennedy and Khruschev agreed Laos should be neutralised. After more fighting a coalition was formed by Souvanna Phouma in early 1962. New fighting broke out later as a 'sideshow' to the Vietnam War. Laos fell under Communist control in 1975.

30. Bay of Pigs, April 1961

This was a CIA-backed operation to overthrow the left-wing regime of Fidel Castro, who had come to power in Cuba in 1959 and developed links with Moscow. The idea was to land a group of exiles who opposed Castro in the Bay of Pigs, without direct US involvement. But the exiles were easily overwhelmed by forces loyal to Castro and over 1,200 were captured. The operation was first planned under Eisenhower but carried out under Kennedy, who was humiliated by its failure.

31. Berlin Wall crisis, August 1961

At the Vienna Summit (June) Khruschev demanded the neutralisation of West Berlin and Western recognition of East Germany. He continued to make threats against the West after the Summit, but was met by a firm line from President Kennedy who, on 25 July, announced increases in US armed forces. In August Khruschev surprised the West by beginning to build a 'wall' of concrete and barbed wire around West Berlin. Until the end of August it seemed that US and Soviet troops might clash in the city. Khruschev had again shown his ability to take the initiative; Kennedy was powerless to stop the wall going up. The Soviet action ended the growing exodus of thousands of East Germans to the West via Berlin. Henceforward those who tried to cross the Berlin Wall were shot. In the long-term the West had to recognise Berlin's division.

32. Fourth Berlin crisis: 'Nose to nose', October 1961

In the wake of the Berlin Wall crisis, President Kennedy sent General Clay to Berlin as his special representative. Clay was determined to stand up to Soviet pressure and to deny any East German legal authority over Berlin. On 22 October 1961, after a US official refused to show his passport to East German guards at 'Checkpoint Charlie', Clay sent troops and four tanks to the checkpoint. The troops then escorted the official into East Berlin unopposed. A similar event followed on 25 October, but on the 26th Soviet tanks – not seen in Berlin since the 1953 workers' rising – appeared at the Brandenburg Gate. The following day the Soviet tanks approached Checkpoint Charlie and faced the US tanks 'nose to nose' (actually about seventy five yards apart). The Soviet tanks were withdrawn on 28 October without serious incident.

33. Soviet–Albanian split, 1961

Like neighbouring Yugoslavia, Albania became a Communist state because of indigenous forces in 1944–45, not because of liberation by the Red Army. Therefore Enver Hoxha was potentially an independent Communist leader, even if he created a Stalinist state. Albania was fearful of Yugoslav domination and so remained allied to Moscow during the Tito–Stalin split (q.v.), becoming a member of the Warsaw Pact. But Khruschev's de-Stalinisation policies and *rapprochement* with Tito upset Hoxha, who began to look to the Chinese for protection in the 1950s. In 1961 Albania accepted Chinese economic assistance and technical advice, and criticised Khruschev's policies publicly. The Soviet leader responded in October with a bitter speech attacking Hoxha, and finally, in December, the USSR broke off diplomatic relations with Albania. In 1978 Hoxha also split with China and became completely isolated in world affairs.

34. Cuban Missile crisis, October 1962

This was the gravest of Cold War crises, which seemed to carry the world to the brink of war. The discovery of Soviet nuclear missiles on Cuba by a US spy-plane came after assurances from Khruschev that he would not attempt such a move, and just before US Congressional elections. Some missiles were already in Cuba, others were on the way, but it was not clear how long it would be before they were armed. The USSR also had over 20,000 troops on Cuba and there were Ilyushin-28 aircraft, capable of carrying nuclear bombs. Khruschev's motives for installing the weapons are much debated. He may have wished merely to defend Cuba, following the Bay of Pigs operation. He may alternatively have wished to bargain for the removal of US nuclear missiles from Turkey, neighbouring the USSR. Or he may have had more wide-ranging ambitions: to humiliate Kennedy; to create circumstances in which to negotiate away the Western presence in Berlin; or to move more rapidly towards nuclear parity with America by installing missiles which could hit US targets more accurately and easily than ICBMs launched from Russia.

Kennedy was under pressure to take strong action. Some advisers wished to destroy the missile launch-sites by bombing, but this could kill many Russians and escalate into war. Others favoured a blockade of Cuba to build up pressure on Moscow, but this would not in itself remove the missiles and might lead the Soviets to blockade Berlin. Any offer to withdraw missiles from Turkey would seem to condone the Soviet action.

On 22 October Kennedy finally publicly announced that he would blockade (or 'quarantine') Cuba to prevent Soviet nuclear arms arriving. The crisis ended when Khruschev confirmed that he would withdraw his missiles in return for a US guarantee not to overthrow Castro. (For full details see Chronology.)

35. Sino-Indian War, 1962

A conflict resulting from border tensions in the Himalayas. China never accepted the 'McMahon line' border, drawn by the British between Tibet and India. Sino-Indian tensions grew in 1959 when the Chinese crushed an uprising in Tibet and occupied the Aksai-Chih area of the border. China's sudden offensive into Assam and Kashmir in early October 1962 humiliated the Indian army but was overshadowed by the Cuban crisis. In late November the Chinese announced a cease-fire and withdrawal. The war contributed to better relations between China and Pakistan: Pakistan had its own border dispute with India in Kashmir and made a border treaty with China in 1963. There were further clashes on the Sino-Indian border in September 1967.

36. Vietnam War, 1965–75

Origins

Following French defeat in the first Indo-China War (q.v.), the US began to provide direct assistance to the government of Ngo Dinh Diem in South Vietnam. Diem cancelled the all-Vietnamese elections which had been planned for July 1956 and were likely to be won by North Vietnam's Ho Chi Minh. Diem ousted the Emperor Bao Dai from office in October 1955. However, the new regime proved corrupt and unpopular. Diem gave considerable power to members of his family, his Catholicism alienated the Buddhist majority and in 1958–59 Communist guerrillas, backed by North Vietnam, began an armed struggle against him. They formed a National Liberation Front in 1960 and were known as 'Vietcong'. The US sent military advisers to the country, two of whom were killed by the Vietcong in July 1959. Under President Kennedy in 1961–63 the number of advisers increased from 900 to 11,000 and they encouraged the creation of 'strategic hamlets'. In 1963 there was widespread discontent against Diem, less from the Vietcong than from the Buddhists, some of whom burned themselves to death in protest against the government. Partly to bring reform in Vietnam, the US encouraged Diem's overthrow in October 1963, but his murder, by those who carried out the coup, led to more instability.

Outbreak

Kennedy's successor, Johnson, decided on greater involvement in Vietnam for three main reasons: (a) to fulfill containment (q.v.), and so prevent the 'domino theory' (q.v.) coming true; (b) to show that 'wars of national liberation' could be defeated; (c) to protect an ally. It seemed unthinkable that a commitment of greater US forces could end in anything other than a quick victory. The 'Army of the Republic of Vietnam' (ARVN) had a high desertion rate and was poorly led, so that the use of US combat forces seemed a necessity. In August 1964 North Vietnamese torpedo boats attacked US destroyers off the coast, giving Johnson the excuse to launch air attacks on the North and, more importantly, to secure the 'Gulf of Tonkin Resolution' from Congress, which gave him a blank cheque to deal with the situation. After his landslide re-election in November, Vietcong attacks on US personnel provided Johnson with the excuse to escalate the war. In March 1965 the first US combat troops arrived and regular bombing of the North began with 'Operation Rolling Thunder'. Over the year US forces increased from 23,000 to 180,000 and were supplemented by Australians and others. In 1966 numbers reached 380,000 and the bombing of the North continued. Buddhist discontent was put down and in September 1967 General Thieu emerged as the strongest South Vietnamese leader.

The 1968 Crisis

Despite the size of the US commitment, and the high-technology equipment (including B-52 strategic bombers) at their disposal, the war went on. North Vietnam refused to be bombed into submission, received aid from the Soviet bloc and China, and insisted on both the withdrawal of US forces and the overthrow of the South Vietnamese government. The Vietcong were supplied from the North along the 'Ho Chi Minh trail' (a complex system of routes into South Vietnam along the long border with Laos and Cambodia). US troops, many of them young conscripts with inexperienced officers, were inadequately trained for guerrilla war, demoralised by the constant dangers, and unable to distinguish between friend and foe among the Vietnamese. The South Vietnamese government remained corrupt and unpopular, with large areas of the countryside effectively under Vietcong control. In the 'Tet Offensive' of January 1968 the Vietcong suddenly took control of major towns in South Vietnam, even attacking the US embassy in Saigon. Despite heavy losses among the guerrillas, it proved a major propaganda coup, which convinced many Americans that the war was 'unwinnable'. There had been no quick victory; US commanders had failed to develop a coherent anti-guerrilla strategy and many American troops were being killed each week (eventually totalling 58,000). The war was financially costly, helping to destroy Johnson's 'Great Society' reform programme, fuelling inflation and undermining the strength of the dollar. Draft-dodging and anti-war protests had become widespread, America's NATO allies were critical of her policy, and meanwhile the USSR had been able to achieve nuclear parity. The president decided not to run for re-election (March), opened diplomatic talks with North Vietnam (May) and ended the bombing of the North (October).

US withdrawal

In January 1969 US forces in Vietnam reached their peak of 540,000 but the new president, Nixon, was committed to withdrawal. An escalation of the war by invading North Vietnam was ruled out: it would probably have led China to enter the conflict. Yet Nixon and his National Security Adviser, Kissinger, did not feel they could withdraw from Vietnam immediately because this would be to accept defeat, to betray an ally and to undermine US credibility worldwide. During 1969–73 US policy had several elements.

(a) US troop reductions to end the anti-war protests at home, lower the casualty rate and cut financial costs – the last combat troops left in August 1972.

(b) 'Vietnamisation', a policy inaugurated with the 'Guam Doctrine' (q.v.) which meant handing the fighting over to South Vietnamese forces. This was made necessary by US troop withdrawals. In order to 'buy time' for Vietnamisation to succeed, and to help the pro-US regime of Lon Nol, US and ARVN troops attacked Communist bases in Cambodia in March 1970, which helped escalate the war there. In 1971 the ARVN alone attacked the Ho Chi Minh trail in Laos (another supposedly 'neutral' country) and fared badly in clashes with the North Vietnamese Army (NVA), an experience which called Vietnamisation into question.

(c) The continued use of US naval and air forces to support the South Vietnamese, including the secret bombing of areas in

Cambodia after 1969. Most importantly in April–May 1972 the NVA 'Spring offensive' was met by the US again bombing North Vietnam on a large scale and by the mining of Haiphong harbour. This succeeded in halting the attack.

(d) US diplomatic contacts with Moscow, through detente, and the 'opening to China' (q.v.) were used to put pressure on the North Vietnamese leadership.

(e) Peace talks with North Vietnamese representatives, initially in secret, were carried out by Kissinger and finally reached a breakthrough in Autumn 1972, after the failure of the 'Spring Offensive'. President Thieu's opposition to the peace terms prevented a peace settlement before Nixon's re-election in November. In December Nixon used the 'Christmas bombing' of Hanoi and Haiphong to force the North back to the negotiating table.

1973 Settlement

In January 1973 the Paris Peace Settlement, signed by Kissinger and Le Duc Tho, led to a US withdrawal from Vietnam (completed in March) and a 'cease-fire in place', which meant that the Communists could hold on to areas they had captured. American POWs were freed and Thieu survived in power, but the 'cease-fire in place' weakened his hold on South Vietnam and neither he nor the Communists proved ready to talk to each other about an internal settlement. The 1973 treaty did not cover the civil wars in Cambodia and Laos which continued to rage between Communists and pro-American forces.

Fall of South Vietnam

In 1973–74 the US ability to support Thieu was weakened by the War Powers Act (q.v.) and the Watergate scandal (q.v.). Congress reduced its assistance to South Vietnam and forced Nixon to end air support for Lon Nol in Cambodia (August 1973). The ARVN continued to be weakened by desertions and poor leadership, despite substantial US equipment. Violence was widespread in 1974, and in early 1975 the NVA launched an offensive against South Vietnam which by April had toppled Thieu. The Lon Nol regime fell at the same time to Pol Pot's Khmer Rouge, and the Pathet Lao then seized power in Laos. After thirty years of fighting all Indo-China was Communist.

37. Dominica, April–May 1965

The Dominican Republic in the Caribbean was ruled for three decades after 1930 by the repressive dictator Rafael Trujillo, who was assassinated in May 1961. In December 1962 the radical Juan Bosch was elected President but was overthrown the following September by the military. The rightist Donald Reid y Cabral then held power, but became very unpopular, and on 25 April 1965 was in turn overthrown by supporters of Bosch. Over the next three days Dominica slipped into anarchy; a military junta was established but the US embassy feared that a Castro-style movement could seize power. On 28 April, President Johnson – claiming that Left extremists were about to take over and that American lives were in danger – authorised military action. Over 20,000 US marines were sent to the island and helped to establish the authority of an interim government under General Antonio Imbert. About 3,000 people died in the troubles. Some Latin American states agreed, on 23 May, to send forces to the island as part of an Organisation of American States 'Peace Force'. In June 1966 elections Bosch was defeated by another ex-president (from 1961–62), the right-wing Joaquim Balguer. The last US forces left the island four months later.

38. Indo-Pakistani War, September 1965

Tensions had existed between India and Pakistan since 1947 when a separate Pakistani state was formed. In 1947–48 the two countries fought a war over Kashmir, which became divided between them. In early 1965 border clashes between India and Pakistan originally concentrated on the Rann of Kutch, another disputed area. But trouble soon spread to Kashmir, and in early September India launched a full-scale invasion of West Pakistan. Despite Pakistan's membership of SEATO and CENTO, the US did not want to alienate India, the largest democracy in the world, and therefore cut arms supplies to both sides. The war saw tension between the USSR, which was close to India, and China, which had fought India in a border war in 1962. UN efforts helped bring a cease-fire after two weeks, but tensions did not ease until 1966, when talks on the border problem were held in Tashkent under Soviet auspices.

39. The Six-Day War, 5–10 June 1967

Following the two wars of 1948–49 and 1956 relations between Israel and the Arab states remained permanently strained. Border incidents and Palestinian attacks on Israel culminated in April 1967 in an Israeli bombing raid on Syria. Other Arab states, although previously divided among themselves, supported Syria. On 18 May Egypt's radical leader, Nasser, asked United Nations peace-keeping forces to leave the Sinai desert (where they had been since 1957) and on 22 May closed the Gulf of Aqaba to Israeli shipping. On 30 May the hitherto moderate King Hussein of Jordan entered a defence pact with Nasser. The United States was sympathetic to Israel and the Soviets were pro-Arab, but neither favoured intervention.

On 5 June Israel launched a pre-emptive strike on the forces massing against it. Arab air forces were destroyed on the ground and by 8 June the Israelis had driven across Sinai to the Suez Canal and had forced the Jordanians out of the West Bank of the River Jordan. Egypt and Jordan then agreed to a cease-fire. On 9–10 June the Israelis also seized the strategically vital Golan Heights from Syria, after which Syria too agreed to a cease-fire. For Israel the war was highly successful and provided it with secure borders. Arab relations with the West (except for France) were poor: an oil boycott was enforced against America from 6 June to 1 September and Egypt and Syria looked to the USSR to rebuild their forces. In November the United Nations' Resolution 242 called for peace talks on the basis of Israel's withdrawal from conquered areas and Arab respect for Israel's existence, but the Middle East remained a major area of tension with frequent border clashes between Arab and Israeli forces, especially along the Suez Canal.

40. The *Pueblo* Incident, 1968

An increasing number of border incidents between North and South Korea culminated on 21 January 1968 in fighting between a Northern terrorist group and security forces in the Southern capital, Seoul. Two days later the USS *Pueblo*, on an electronic intelligence-gathering mission, was seized by the North Korean navy in international waters and taken to the port of Wonsan. The *Pueblo* was beyond the help of other US forces and in a crisis meeting President Johnson and his advisers soon decided that any retaliatory action would endanger the lives of the eighty-three crew. The next months were therefore taken up in slow negotiations before, in December, the US issued an apology and the crew were released. The US subsequently withdrew the apology but the episode was extremely humiliating.

41. Czechoslovakia's 'Prague Spring', 1968

Until early 1968 Czechoslovakia, under Antonin Novotny, seemed a model member of the Warsaw Pact. Despite the absence of Soviet troops (who had been withdrawn after the Second World War), Czechoslovakia had seen little trouble in 1956. In the early 1960s, however, economic stagnation set in, and Communist Party members themselves began to call for reform. Novotny attempted repression in 1967 but in January 1968 the Party replaced him with a more liberal leader, Alexander Dubcek, who hoped to steer a middle course between conservative Communists and radical reformers. In March the Warsaw Pact states warned him not to go too far, but in April Dubcek promised greater parliamentary rights and a relaxation of censorship, and in May he began to plan a special party conference on reform to take place in September. Only Romania, increasingly independent of Moscow, proved ready to respect Czechoslovakian independence. Other Pact members (USSR, Poland, East Germany, Hungary, Bulgaria) formed themselves into the 'group of five'. In July Dubcek was ordered by the group of five to end Czechoslovakia's 'counter-revolutionary' trend and the country was intimidated by military manoeuvres. Finally on 21 August the group of five astonished Dubcek and the West by invading Czechoslovakia. The Kremlin was unapologetic and justified its action soon afterwards with the Brezhnev Doctrine (q.v.). After a few months Dubcek was replaced by Gustav Husak and Czechoslovakia again became a loyal member of the Warsaw Pact.

42. Sino-Soviet border clashes, 1969–89

The long Sino-Soviet border saw mounting tensions in the 1960s during China's 'Cultural Revolution'. From 1963 the Chinese claimed that the border had been drawn in 'unequal treaties'. They were also resentful of Soviet influence in Mongolia (which broke free of Chinese rule in 1911 and became, in 1924, the USSR's first satellite). Particular tensions centred on the Rivers Ussuri and Amur, on the border of north-east China, which often changed course. Heavy fighting broke out at Damansky Island on the Ussuri in March 1969 when the Chinese attacked Soviet border guards. War between the two powers seemed possible in 1969–70, and the USSR sounded out the US on its likely reaction to a nuclear strike against China.

Sino-Soviet tensions eased somewhat in the 1970s, but the split between them was deep. In 1979 there were more tensions on the Amur river, China invaded Moscow's ally Vietnam, and talks on the border dispute were broken off in 1980. The talks were revived under Gorbachev in February 1987 however and resulted in a draft settlement of all border disputes in November 1988. Gorbachev also withdrew Soviet forces from Mongolia, which became more independent of Moscow.

43. Jordan crisis, September 1970

After the 1967 Six-Day War many more Palestinian refugees than before moved into Jordan, which had ruled over the West Bank from 1948 to 1967. Radical Arabs, including leaders of the Palestinian Liberation Organisation (formed in 1964), resented the moderation in Middle East affairs of Jordan's ruler King Hussein. An assassination attempt against the king led to virtual civil war in Jordan on 1 September 1970. Tension was heightened on 6–9 September when an extremist Palestinian group hijacked three aircraft to the Jordanian capital, Amman, and blew them up. On 16 September the Jordanian army began a showdown with the Palestinians, and on 20 September Syrian forces crossed the border to support the PLO. There seemed a real danger of superpower involvement, because whereas the Syrians were armed by Moscow, the US expressed strong support for King Hussein. However neither the Soviets nor the radical government of Iraq would actively support the Syrians, whose forces withdrew from Jordan on 23 September. Hussein finally defeated the PLO in 1971 and its headquarters were moved to Lebanon, which itself soon became a troublespot.

44. Cienfuegos crisis, September 1970

In mid-September 1970 an American U-2 spy plane revealed construction work at Cienfuegos, Cuba, which suggested that a nuclear submarine base was being built by the Soviets. The US held that this broke the 1962 settlement of the Cuban Missile Crisis, and Soviet Ambassador Dobrynin was asked to stop the work. On 6 October Dobrynin gave assurances that no submarine base would be built. The US government in return formally confirmed its 1962 promise not to overthrow the Castro regime.

45. Poland: the fall of Gomulka, December 1970

The 1960s and 1970s were generally years of economic uncertainty and growing differences in the Eastern bloc. In December 1970 a new crisis came when the Polish government of Gomulka introduced price increases as a first step to economic reform. Since 1956 Gomulka had disappointed Polish hopes for a more nationalist policy externally and liberalism internally. The new prices led to riots in the Baltic coastal cities. In one incident, on 17 December in Gdynia, several demonstrators were shot. The government, fearing Soviet action, decided to replace Gomulka with a reliable administrator, Edward Gierek, and to withdraw the price increases. The crisis then eased.

46. Indo-Pakistani War, November–December 1971

Following wars over the fate of Kashmir in 1948 and 1965 (q.v.), tension between India and Pakistan grew in 1970–71 over the problems of East Pakistan (Bangladesh). West and East Pakistan, though given independence as part of the same Moslem state in 1947, were a thousand miles apart. The East had a larger population but West Pakistan was wealthier, included the capital and controlled the army. Cyclones in November 1970 killed 200,000 people in the East and discontent led to the triumph of the Bangladeshi nationalist 'Awami League' in a general election in December. Faced by this result the military President Yahya Khan post-poned the calling of parliament, arrested the Awami leader, Mujibur Rahman, and in March 1971 enforced military rule in East Pakistan. Millions of Bangladeshis fled to neighbouring India. India helped to support a Bangladeshi resistance movement, the Mukti Bahini, and on 22 November invaded East Pakistan. Whereas Pakistan was friendly to China, India had links to the USSR, which were strengthened by a Soviet–Indian Friendship Treaty (August 1971) promising that neither would help the enemies of the other. When war began the USSR air-lifted arms to India and vetoed peace resolutions at the UN. A Soviet–Chinese clash seemed possible and the US decided to send a fleet to the Bay of Bengal. For the first time under Nixon the 'hot-line' to the Kremlin was used. On 16 December however a cease-fire was achieved. The Indi-ans had easily overrun East Pakistan and secured its independence, but the US opposed any Indian invasion of West Pakistan.

47. Chile: the fall of Allende, September 1973

Salvador Allende (1908–73) became president of Chile in October 1970 with the backing of a 'Popular Front' (made up of Communists, his own Socialists, and radicals) and support from the Christian Democrats. Allende was a Marxist who had met Fidel Castro on several occasions, favoured nationalisation and land reform, and was therefore seen as a threat to US interests in Latin America. He had been opposed by the CIA, which had helped to finance alternative candidates in 1970. The US tried to undermine his regime after 1970 by propaganda and reduc-tions in economic aid. Allende in turn issued a radical nationalisation decree in 1971 and, in August 1973, threatened to reform parliament so as to allow more radical reforms. The following month however, against a background of rising social discontent, Allende was overthrown by the military, led by General Augusto Pinochet who established a dictator-ship. There was no evidence of direct US involvement in this, the first military coup in Chile since 1932, but the US was criticised for helping to 'destabilise' Allende's elected government. Allende himself died dur-ing the coup. Third World radicals criticised the USSR for failing to help Allende. Pinochet's oppressive regime survived until March 1990, when there was a return to democracy under Patricio Aylwin.

48. Arab–Israeli 'Yom Kippur' War, October 1973

Israel's rapid victory in the 1967 Six-Day War was followed by frequent clashes between Egypt and Israel, with the superpowers supporting different sides. In March 1970 the USSR increased the number of military advisers in Egypt but, following the death of President Nasser in September, the new Egyptian leader Sadat distanced himself from the USSR. Sadat's actions – making a friendship treaty with Moscow in May 1971 but then expelling Soviet advisers in July 1972 – confused the US, and his threat to make 1972 a 'year of decision' came to nothing. Israel, armed by the United States, remained far stronger than the Arabs. Sadat's policies could be explained however as an attempt to demonstrate Egyptian independence, win US respect and break the deadlock in the Middle East. Although he could not hope to win a war, it was in order to force eventual concessions from Israel that Sadat and Syria launched a surprise attack on Israeli forces on the Jewish festival of Yom Kippur in 1973.

The Egyptian–Syrian attack was well planned and, in contrast to 1967, there was no easy Israeli victory. Iraq and other Arab states sent forces to aid Egypt and Syria. Only after several days did Israel halt the Egyptian drive across the Suez Canal and the Syrian advance towards the Golan Heights. The US, keen to contain the crisis, was slow to provide arms to Israel. The Soviets tried to exploit the early Arab advances by working for a cease-fire. Once the Israelis had the advantage, however, they crossed the Suez Canal and, by 23 October, threatened to surround the Egyptian Third Army at Port Said. Henry Kissinger, recently appointed US Secretary of State, had been to Moscow on 20–22 October to discuss a cease-fire but the Israelis undermined his efforts. On 24 October Brezhnev talked of Soviet intervention in the Middle East to save Egypt, and Sadat was ready to welcome a joint US–Soviet peace-keeping force, but the US was totally opposed to a Soviet military presence in the region. The worst superpower confrontation since the Cuban Missile Crisis occurred on 24–25 October when President Nixon put US forces on a high level of nuclear alert. This action was taken without consulting America's NATO allies, many of whom were offended by it, but it was followed by a cease-fire in the war.

The October 1973 war was accompanied by an Arab oil boycott against the US and other states, and led to a large increase in oil prices by OPEC countries, which gravely harmed Western economies. It confirmed Israeli military superiority in the Middle East but succeeded in restoring some Arab military pride. Kissinger continued to demonstrate his diplomatic skill, when his 'shuttle diplomacy' of 1973–74 achieved a peaceful separation of Israeli and Egyptian–Syrian forces. However the October War was a severe blow to the policy of detente. Instead of the superpowers working together for peace, they had backed opposing sides in a dangerous Third World conflict.

49. Portugal and Spain, 1974–76

In April 1974 pro-reformist officers in the army suddenly overthrew the dictatorship of Marcel Caetano in Portugal. The dictatorship, founded by Dr Antonio de Oliveira Salazar in 1932, had failed to develop the country's economy and became involved in costly colonial wars in Africa. The coup caused concern to NATO, of which Portugal was a member, and led to two years of upheaval. Initially a presidency was established under General Antonio de Spinola. People showed their support for the new regime by coming on to the streets and exchanging red carnations, hence the term 'Carnation Revolution'. However the army and democratic politicians had little experience in power. Spinola's personal power was resented and he was forced to resign in September. A 'Revolutionary Council' was formed and the prime minister, Colonel Vasco Gonçalves, allied himself closely to the Communists, but elections in April 1975 gave most support to the Socialists (38 per cent). It was only when a group of moderate officers, led by General Ranalho Eanes, asserted their authority over the armed forces in November that order could really be restored. A constitution was published in April 1976, Eanes was elected president and the Socialist Mario Soares (after winning another election) became prime minister.

The unrest in Portugal increased the possibility of upheaval in neighbouring Spain when the dictator (since 1939), General Francisco Franco, died in November 1975. However the new ruler, King Juan Carlos, supported by Prime Minister Adolfo Suarez, was able to preside over a smooth transition to democracy. The first democratic elections since 1936 were held in June 1977. Spain joined NATO in 1983 (a decision confirmed by referendum in 1986).

50. Angola, 1974–76

The April 1974 coup in Portugal, which toppled the dictatorship, soon led to negotiations on the independence of Portuguese colonies. In Portuguese Guinea (Guinea-Bissau), where a colonial war had been underway since 1963, and Mozambique, where the FRELIMO movement had begun an independence struggle in 1964, there was a smooth transition to new governments, both Marxist-led. But in the third main colony, Angola, three groups competed for power: Agostino Neto's Marxist MPLA, backed by the Eastern bloc and controlling the capital Luanda; Holden Roberto's FNLA in the north, the original liberation movement (formed 1961), supported by Zaïre and China and aided in 1961–69 by the US; and Jonas Savimbi's UNITA, strong in the south, and eventually backed by the US and South Africa. In January 1975 the Portuguese helped establish a coalition between the three groups (the Alvor Accord) and set independence for 11 November. However by April the Accord had broken down and Angola became a focus of Superpower attention. In July the US boosted aid to the FNLA and UNITA; in September the USSR responded by supporting a massive airlift of Cuban troops to fight for the MPLA. Despite Cuban involvement the US Congress was unwilling to back further involvement. The MPLA, supported by over 15,000 Cubans, defeated the FNLA and was admitted to the UN as the recognised Angolan government in April 1976. The episode did much to undermine US faith in detente, and demonstrated growing Soviet confidence in Third World conflicts.

51. Cyprus, July–August 1974

A crisis which highlighted the divisions between two neighbouring NATO states, Greece and Turkey. The two countries had been divided over the Cyprus issue since the mid-1950s when the then-British colony saw a terrorist campaign by Colonel Grivas's EOKA movement to achieve *enosis* (union) with Greece. But whilst Cyprus was 80 per cent Greek-populated, one fifth of its people were Turkish, the island lay close to Turkey's southern coast and Turkey had ruled it before 1878. In 1959–60 a complicated agreement was reached which avoided either *enosis* or a partition of the island between Greeks and Turks. Instead the island became an independent state. But in 1964 fighting between Greek and Turkish Cypriots led a UN force to be sent to the island. There were more clashes in 1967. In July 1974 the Greek contingent in the National Guard tried to overthrow the Cypriot president, Archbishop Makarios. Within a week, Turkey, claiming to act as a guarantor of the 1960 settlement, invaded the north of the island. Talks between Turkey, Greece and Britain, in Geneva on 25–30 July, failed to resolve the issue. In mid-August the Turks extended their rule over one-third of the island, which effectively became partitioned. Greece, upset by US and British policy, withdrew its forces from NATO for a time.

52. The Mayaguez Incident, May 1975

In mid-May 1975, soon after the fall of Cambodia to the Communists, the *Mayaguez*, a US merchant ship with thirty-nine crew, was captured and taken to Cambodia. In a forceful response US aircraft attacked targets on the coast, and US marines were landed to rescue the crewmen. The action, however, proved unnecessary: by coincidence the Cambodians released the *Mayaguez*'s crew just before the attack took place.

53. South-Western Africa (Angola and Namibia), 1975–91

After the Soviet-backed MPLA took power in Angola in 1975, civil war continued between its forces, supported by Cuban troops, and Jonas Savimbi's UNITA forces in the south, backed by South Africa and (indirectly) America. Events in Angola were also closely linked to those in neighbouring Namibia, formerly German South-West Africa, which had been put under South African trusteeship in 1920. South African rule in Namibia was opposed after October 1966 by the South-West African People's Organisation (SWAPO) and in 1978 UN Resolution 435 said the country should become independent. But South Africa was concerned by the presence of Marxist governments in Angola and Mozambique, and by the advent of black majority rule in Zimbabwe (formerly Rhodesia) in 1979–80. Clashes occurred between South African forces and SWAPO throughout the early 1980s. South African forces also made incursions into Angola, whose government supported SWAPO. In Mozambique, South Africa backed the National Resistance (RENAMO) movement against the government.

In the mid-1980s the Reagan administration showed strong support for Jonas Savimbi, and in 1985 Congress withdrew the 1975 Clark Amendment, which had prevented aid to UNITA. However, at the same time, both sides in the Namibian struggle showed some desire to negotiate. South African, US, Angolan and Cuban representatives finally held a series of meetings in 1988 which resulted in a South African withdrawal from Angola (August) and two peace agreements (22 December) which provided for: (a) in Angola, the phased withdrawal of Cuban forces (estimated at 50,000) under UN supervision, ending July 1991; (b) in Namibia, a South African withdrawal under UN supervision, full independence and elections. Further complicated negotiations under US supervision resulted in a political settlement between Savimbi and the Angolan government in May 1991 but this later broke down.

54. Ogaden (Somali–Ethiopian) War, 1977–78

From the 1950s to 1974 the US had military facilities in Ethiopia, and it was the USSR which sympathised with the struggle after 1961 of Eritrea (a province on the Red Sea) for independence. The USSR also allied itself to Somalia after independence in 1960, secured a naval base at Berbera and supported Siad Barre, Somalia's president after 1969. In 1974 Barre made a friendship treaty with Moscow. The year 1974 also saw the fall of Ethiopia's pro-Western Emperor Haile Selassie, however, and the new Ethiopian military *Dergue* (junta) grew closer to the USSR, especially after Colonel Mengistu Haile Mariam became the leading figure in February 1977. In April the US cut military aid to Ethiopia. In early 1977 the US hoped for co-operation between Ethiopia and Somalia, but the situation soon became a complex one for Soviet policy because July saw a large-scale Somali invasion of Ethiopia, with the intention of seizing the Ogaden, a desert region populated by Somali tribesmen. The Organisation of African States backed Ethiopia in this dispute because of the desire of all African governments to respect each others' borders.

The Ogaden war forced Moscow to choose between its allies in the Horn of Africa. It decided to cut arms supplies to Somalia and this led Somalia to establish tentative links with the US before abrogating the Friendship Treaty with Moscow and expelling Eastern bloc advisers in November. Then, with the Ogaden War deadlocked after early Somali advances, the Soviets airlifted large amounts of arms to Ethiopia and conveyed up to 15,000 Cuban troops and 1,000 Soviet advisers there. These forces helped drive back the Somalis in Ogaden from January onwards. In America Secretary of State Vance and Defense Secretary Brown saw the Horn of Africa as geographically unimportant, and believed Soviet policy to be muddled, but National Security Adviser Brzezinski argued that the Soviets were challenging the US in an 'arc of crisis' from Africa across the Middle East to Central Asia. In January 1978 Brzezinski said the Ogaden war would complicate the SALT II talks (q.v.). In February Soviet ambassador Dobrynin promised that Ethiopia would not carry the war into Somali territory and this promise was fulfilled in mid-1978 when all the Ogaden was recaptured.

55. Vietnamese invasion of Kampuchea, 1977–89

At Christmas 1978 Vietnam, which had occupied border areas in Kampuchea since the previous December, launched a full-scale invasion of its neighbour. The Vietnamese claimed to want the overthrow of the oppressive Pol Pot regime, which had come to power in Kampuchea (formerly Cambodia) in 1975, but their action was seen as an attempt to establish Vietnamese hegemony in Indo-China. China and the Western powers therefore maintained relations with Pol Pot. The Vietnamese (with Soviet financial support) remained in Kampuchea until 1989 and established a puppet regime but could not root out Pol Pot's 'Khmer Rouge', many of whom sought refuge in Thailand. Over 25,000 Vietnamese lost their lives in the war, most in 1977–78.

56. Iran: the fall of the Shah and the hostage crisis, 1978–81

Throughout 1978 unrest grew in oil-rich Iran against the repressive, pro-American regime of Shah Rezi Khan Pahlavi. In November a general revolt broke out which included all shades of opinion from leftists to Shi'ite fundamentalists. The Shah tried to set up a military government under General Azhari, then tried to make a moderate opposition leader, Shahpour Bakhtiar, premier. Bakhtiar soon recommended that the Shah should leave Iran, which he did in January. Next month the Shi'ite Ayatollah Khomeini (q.v.) returned to the country, and in April an Islamic Republic was declared based on Islamic law. US–Iranian tension grew in October 1979 when the exiled Shah became a victim of cancer and needed treatment in New York. A mob seized control of the US Embassy in Tehran in November, taking the diplomats hostage. The women and black hostages were soon freed, but a long crisis ensued which humiliated President Carter. In April a rescue bid, planned by National Security Adviser Brzezinski, ended in failure and led Secretary of State Vance to resign. The crisis completely dominated the US presidential election campaign and the release of the hostages was delayed until January 1981, when Carter lost the presidency to Ronald Reagan.

57. Sino-Vietnamese War, February–April 1979

After the end of US involvement in Vietnam (1973), Sino-Vietnamese relations deteriorated. Vietnam developed links with the Soviet Union, culminating in a friendship treaty in November 1978. Vietnamese ill-treatment of its Chinese minority led to an exodus by the latter in 1978. Finally, China was alienated by Vietnam's invasion of Kampuchea, with which Beijing had close relations. In February the Chinese invaded Vietnam largely as a punitive measure, but they suffered heavy losses and withdrew within two months. The brief war had no marked impact on Soviet–American relations. The Sino-Vietnamese border was eventually reopened in September 1989.

58. Nicaragua, 1979–90

Since before the Second World War, Nicaragua had been ruled by the Somoza family. Unemployment among the country's landless labourers, high food prices (despite an agricultural economy) and human rights abuses eventually led to the formation of the Sandinista liberation movement, named after an inter-war revolutionary leader, Augusto Sandino. By the late 1970s middle-class groups and the Roman Catholic Church had joined the poor in opposition to Anastasio Somoza Debayle. His position was further undermined by the presidency of Jimmy Carter, who placed heavy emphasis on human rights. In September 1978 full-scale revolt broke out against Somoza. American attempts to negotiate a settlement came to nothing. In July 1979 Somoza resigned. Carter was criticised for allowing a left-wing regime to come to power in Central

America where, it was feared, it could benefit the USSR and Castro's Cuba. A determined anti-Sandinista policy began under Ronald Reagan. Trade and financial sanctions were supplemented by aid to the 'Contras', who, with CIA support, launched a guerrilla war against the Sandinistas from neighbouring Honduras. The civil war disrupted Nicaragua's political and economic life, but also destabilised the Central American region.

Fears of US involvement in the region were heightened by increasing unrest in nearby El Salvador after 1979. Victims included the liberal Archbishop Romero (shot in March 1980) and a group of American nuns. After 1980 President José Napoleon Duarte, though backed by Reagan, proved very insecure, unable to prevent a virtual civil war between left-wing guerrillas and right-wing 'death squads', the latter backed by many in the armed forces.

The determination of some Reagan advisers to help the Contras led to the Iran–Contragate scandal (q.v.), and in March 1988, in order to persuade Congress to assist the Contras, Reagan sent US forces to Honduras to deal with a supposed 'invasion threat' from Nicaragua. The Sandinista regime was under severe strain and in August 1987 other Central American states devised the Arias Plan (named after the Costa Rican president) for a cease-fire and internal settlement in Nicaragua. This was accepted by the Sandinistas and, after difficult negotiations, led to an election in 1990. To widespread surprise the Nicaraguans voted the Sandinistas and their leader Daniel Ortega out of power. The new leader was Violetta Chamorro, a former Sandinista and widow of a liberal news editor, Pedro Joaquim Chamorro, who had been assassinated in 1978. She was backed by the US and led a wide coalition, including conservatives and Communists.

59. Cuban crisis, August–September 1979

A 'crisis' which was largely self-generated by the US. In mid-1979 US Intelligence reports informed President Carter that a Soviet 'combat brigade' had been deployed on Cuba. This suggested a challenge similar to the earlier Cuban Missile and Cienfuegos crises, and was of concern to National Security Adviser Brzezinski. When the news became public it led Senator Frank Church to suspend the SALT II hearings which he was chairing. During September Carter pressed the Soviets to reduce their military presence in Cuba. It soon emerged however that a Soviet brigade had been present in Cuba since 1962, and that President Kennedy had said in 1963 that it did not break the settlement of the Missile Crisis. The Soviets feared that the 1979 'crisis' was manufactured in order to prevent the ratification of SALT II, which was already the subject of criticism in the US Senate.

60. Afghanistan: Soviet intervention, December 1979

From 1920 Afghanistan had a Friendship Treaty with Russia and Soviet aid increased after 1954, although Afghanistan also took US aid and joined the non-aligned movement in 1955, when the government was dominated by the premier, Prince Daud. He overthrew the monarchy and founded a republic in 1973 but was himself ousted and killed in April 1978. The new 'Democratic Republic' was dominated by the pro-Soviet 'Democratic People's Party of Afghanistan' (PDPA) founded in 1965, which was inexperienced in power and divided between two factions, the Khalq (mainly provincial, hard-line, and which had been totally opposed to Daud) and the Parcham (more urban in support and ready to work with other groups to secure reform). By September 1978 the Khalq faction was predominant and tried to carry out Marxist reforms, but these threatened the social fabric and Islamic religion of Afghanistan. The government also relied on Soviet military advisers (who increased from 350 to 4,000 in 1978–79) and totally alienated the US after the killing of its ambassador (during a botched attempt to free him from kidnappers) in February 1979. Tribal risings began against the government and a third of a million Afghans fled in 1978–79 to neighbouring Pakistan whose leader, General Zia ul-Haq, gave support to Afghan opposition groups.

In September 1979 the Afghan president, Nur Mohammed Taraki, visited Moscow and discussed the replacement of the Khalq's leading hard-liner, Hafizullah Amin, as a step towards restoring the government's popularity. However Taraki, on his return, was instead arrested and killed by Amin, who made himself president. It was Amin who was overthrown by Soviet intervention in Afghanistan on 25–27 December 1979, which marked the first use of Soviet combat forces outside the areas they had occupied in the Second World War.

The USSR claimed it had intervened under its treaty commitments to Afghanistan. The subsequent execution of Amin made a mockery of Soviet claims to be 'invited' to 'defend' Afghanistan. The Kremlin actually acted to maintain a neighbouring pro-Soviet regime in power, on the lines of the Brezhnev Doctrine (q.v.). They replaced Amin with Babrak Karmal, a member of the Parcham faction who tried to widen the government's appeal. The Soviets were currently concerned over US activity in the Gulf, Chinese strength in Central Asia, and the impact of Islamic fundamentalism on Moslems in the USSR. Superpower detente was already in decline, Brezhnev was ill and the military were in the ascendant in Moscow where it was probably hoped that intervention in Afghanistan would have only a short-term impact on world affairs. Instead the intervention offended Iran, China, Pakistan and the West, and was condemned by the vast majority of the UN General Assembly. President Carter said that his view of the USSR had radically altered and he took a number of anti-Soviet measures including the suspension of SALT II ratification, the boycott of the 1980 Moscow Olympics and a rearmament drive. Detente finally came to an end and the 'Second' Cold War began.

61. The Soviet war in Afghanistan, 1979–89

Outbreak

Initially, since it was winter, there was little active opposition to the 1979 Soviet intervention in Afghanistan. However, February 1980 saw considerable unrest and it was soon clear that foreign invasion had increased the unpopularity of the Marxist regime in Kabul. The Afghan army, reduced by desertions to 30,000 men, could no longer keep order and the Soviets, like the Americans in Vietnam fifteen years earlier, were forced to protect the unpopular government themselves. However Soviet involvement never matched the scale of involvement attained by the US in Vietnam. About 85,000 Red Army troops were deployed in spring 1980 and in 1988 there were 105,000 there. The peak commitment in the early 1980s seems to have been 110,000. Their opponents were the Mujahedin (soldiers of the jihad), some of whom had been fighting against Communism since before the Soviet intervention. They were divided into numerous groups, some of whom even fought each other, largely because of tribal differences. The government, which itself remained divided between Parcham and Khalq political factions, was able to exploit tribal differences to stay in power. It also used police-state methods and Marxist indoctrination, and tried to woo key groups like religious leaders and businessmen. The government held the capital, Kabul, other major cities, and some provinces.

Course

The Red Army tried to end Mujahedin activity with 'sweep offensives' at first, but conventional tactics were useless against determined, mountain-based guerrilla fighters. Thus the tactics changed to the use of air power (to pin down the guerrillas), counter-insurgency operations and the use of blatant terrorism (including aerial bombing and mine-laying) against the population. This led to high civilian casualties, flights of refugees to Pakistan and Iran, and greater unpopularity for the government. US aid to the Mujahedin increased under Ronald Reagan. It was channelled by the CIA via Pakistan and China (and even, it seems, Iran in 1986), and eventually included 'Stinger' anti-aircraft missiles in 1985–86, which proved a major blow to the Soviets.

Peace efforts by UN envoys Perez de Cuellar and (after the latter's promotion to UN Secretary-General) Diego Cordovez brought Afghanistan and Pakistan in June 1982 into 'proximity talks', so called because the two sides did not meet face-to-face until 1988. The Geneva-based talks began to make real progress however only after Mikhail Gorbachev became Soviet leader in 1985. Gorbachev also encouraged the Afghan government to hold local elections and bring non-PDPA supporters into office. In May 1986 President Babrak Karmal was replaced by Mohammed Najibullah who, though a former head of the KHAD secret police, proved amenable to Gorbachev's conciliatory policy. In 1987 Najibullah offered a cease-fire, invited Mujahedin leaders to share in government and introduced a new constitution. Then in February 1988 Gorbachev took the dramatic step of announcing the Red Army's withdrawal. On 14 April this was confirmed in the Geneva Agreement, under which Afghanistan and Pakistan promised not to interfere in each other's internal affairs and refugees were encouraged to return home voluntarily. This eased Soviet fears of Pakistani involvement in Afghanistan. The USSR and US guaranteed the Agreement but it was only a partial settlement. Since the PDPA remained in power, and would still receive Soviet backing and military supplies, most Mujahedin leaders were determined to continue their struggle.

Soviet withdrawal

The Soviet withdrawal from Afghanistan began in May 1988 and was completed in February 1989. The Red Army had lost about 15,000 dead and 37,000 wounded in the conflict, and according to Premier Ryzhkov (June 1989) the war cost the USSR the equivalent of $7.8 billion per annum. The number of Afghans killed was far higher, probably over a million, with millions more left as refugees. And, despite the wide expectations of a government collapse in 1989, the civil war continued. The Mujahedin, lacking political unity, military discipline and heavy armaments, were unable to capture major cities, as seen in the 1989 siege of Jalalabad. Their 'Afghan Interim Government' was criticised as being too closely linked to Pakistan. Their ally, General Zia, was in any case killed (in suspicious circumstances) in an August 1988 air crash. The Afghan armed forces were well armed by the USSR, while Americans were less willing to support Islamic 'freedom fighters' once the Cold War had ended. Najibullah's regime finally collapsed in early 1992, having failed to win over the Mujaheddin groups, and with Soviet support having ended when the USSR broke up.

62. Iran–Iraq (Gulf) War, 1980–88

The longest conventional war of the twentieth century broke out after years of border disputes. In 1975 the US-backed Shah of Iran used his predominance in the Gulf region to enforce a new definition of the border on Iraq. In 1979 however the situation was radically altered by the Shah's overthrow, and the rise to power in Iraq of Saddam Hussein. Iran was no longer US-backed and seemed further weakened by the turmoil of Ayatollah Khomeini's Islamic Revolution. Saddam Hussein, like other Arab leaders, saw Iran's Shia fundamentalism as a threat to his own regime. Border clashes in 1980 finally led Hussein to denounce the 1975 border agreement and invade Iran on 22 September (though Iraq claimed that Iran began the war on 4 September).

In the conflict Saddam had the support of most Arab countries. Only radical Syria and Libya showed sympathy for Iran. The UN called for a cease-fire but both America and the USSR seemed ready to allow the war to continue. The US did fear Soviet intervention in the Gulf, possibly in support of Iraq, which since 1972 had had a Friendship Treaty with Moscow. But the Kremlin was apparently preoccupied with Afghanistan, offended by Saddam's attacks on Iraqi Communists and fearful that tension with Iran would provoke discontent among the USSR's Moslem minority. The Gulf War thus became something of a sideshow in the 'New Cold War' after 1979.

Despite Saddam's hopes of easy advances into Iran the conflict soon became deadlocked. Iraq was smaller than Iran and Iraqi armed forces lacked the religious fervour of Iran's Revolutionary Guards. In 1980 the Iraqis captured Khorramshahr but not their main target, the oil port of Abadan. In March 1982 the Iranians began to advance, forcing Iraq back over the border in June. At this point Iraqi leaders were ready to make peace, but for Khomeini the war had become a religious crusade. The Iranians then invaded Iraq, concentrating their attacks on Basra, but Iraqi resistance stiffened on their own soil and Saddam proved ready to use all possible means to survive. These included: from August 1982, attacks on Iran's oil terminal at Kharg Island; from 1984, the use of chemical weapons (also used against Iraq's Kurdish minority in March 1988); from March 1984, the 'tanker war' against oil-carriers in the Gulf, to which Iran responded by sowing mines; and in spring 1985 and 1987–88, the 'war of the cities' with air and missile attacks against urban centres, to which Iran responded in kind.

In 1986 US attempts to rebuild links with Iran resulted in another humiliaton, the 'Irangate' (or 'Contragate') scandal. After May 1987, with the Soviets no longer active in the region, the US decided to get more closely involved on the Iraqi side. This decision, ironically, came after an *Iraqi* attack on a US vessel, the USS *Stark*. In July Washington agreed to put Kuwaiti tankers under protection of the US flag and the same month the UN renewed its calls for a cease-fire, also demanding the restoration of the 1980 border. Iraq agreed to the UN resolution but Khomeini did not accept what he called the 'poisoned chalice' of a cease-fire until July 1988. By then Iran was exhausted, the Iraqis had begun to advance again and US involvement had culminated in the shooting down of an Iranian airliner. Subsequent peace talks were drawn out by Saddam Hussein until 1990, when he was forced to come to terms because of the international outcry caused by his invasion of Kuwait. Up to a million people had died in the war, which left the Iraq–Iran border exactly where it was in 1980.

63. 'Polish August': the Solidarity episode, 1980–82

After the fall of Gomulka in 1970 (q.v.) the Polish government remained unpopular. Nationalist feeling was fuelled by the election of a Pole as Pope John Paul II in 1978. In July 1980 new price increases led to strikes by workers. In August shipworkers at Gdansk, led by Lech Walesa, demanded the right to organise a free trade union and the government decided to grant this right as a concession. In September the Gdansk workers founded the 'Solidarity' union which soon gained millions of members. Meanwhile Edvard Gierek, the Communist leader, was replaced by Stanislaus Kania. Official recognition of Solidarity in November was followed by a general return to work, but in 1981 relations between the union and the government remained uneasy and from December 1980 onwards many feared that the USSR would invade Poland.

Intervention was avoided largely because Poland was able to find a leader who could restore central authority. General Jaruzelski became prime minister in February 1981 and party leader in October. Finally, in December, he took Solidarity by surprise by banning the union, arresting thousands of its members and ruling through a Military Council. These actions were condemned by the West and led President Reagan to introduce sanctions against Poland. But most West European leaders were willing to treat Poland's problems as an internal affair. Jaruzelski felt strong enough at the end of 1982 to release Walesa from prison and suspend martial law.

64. Lebanon: Western intervention, 1982–84

Given its independence by France at the end of the Second World War, the Lebanon was long seen as evidence that different religious groups *could* live together peacefully in the Middle East. However, the 1958 Middle Eastern crisis (q.v.) showed the delicacy of the balance between Maronite Christians and Sunni Moslems, the two groups who dominated political life. After 1970 political instability was undermined by an influx of Palestinian refugees from Israel and Jordan, in the wake of the Six-Day War and Jordanian civil war (q.v.). Israel attacked Palestinian bases in Lebanon throughout the 1970s, fighting broke out between Moslems and Christians in Beirut in 1975–76, and the Moslems themselves were divided between Sunnis and Shias. A Syrian-led Arab peace-keeping force entered the country in October 1976, but could not enforce order. In March 1978, with the danger of an Israeli–Syrian conflict over Lebanon, a UN peace-keeping force was also sent, but instability continued.

In June 1982 the Israelis launched a full-scale invasion of Lebanon, marching to Beirut and forcing the Palestinian Liberation Organisation to quit the country in August. But the invasion proved financially costly to Israel, and alienated world opinion. US, French, Italian and British forces were sent to Beirut in September as the Israelis withdrew to southern Lebanon, but hopes of a return to order were ill-founded. In 1983 the large US and French contingents became the victims of 'suicide bomb' attacks, with 299 killed on one day in October 1983. President Reagan withdrew the peace-keeping force in February 1984. After 1987 Syrian forces increasingly dominated the country, and in 1990–91 achieved a fair degree of order.

65. Flight KAL 007, September 1983

On 1 September 1983 a South Korean Boeing 747, on an overnight flight from New York to Seoul, with 269 people on board, was shot down by a Soviet fighter over the island of Sakhalin, in Soviet airspace. This action sparked off one of the major crises of the Second Cold War. The US revealed intercepts of Soviet military messages to humiliate the Kremlin, and President Reagan claimed the Soviets had identified Flight KAL 007 as a civilian airliner before shooting it down. In fact airliners frequently violate the airspace of other countries and can easily be misidentified as military aircraft (as seen when the US shot down an Iranian airliner in mid-1988.) KAL 007, for reasons that remain obscure, was flying well off course and the Soviets may have believed it to be a spy-plane. The Soviet response to the incident was, however, clumsy and unfeeling. Their national airline, Aeroflot, was subsequently denied landing rights by many Western powers in retribution for the incident.

66. Grenada, October 1983

In 1979 the 'New Jewel' movement forcibly took power in the small Caribbean island of Grenada (a former British colony) in a revolution. The New Jewel leaders were divided among themselves but developed links with Castro's Cuba and were declared a menace to the US by President Reagan. On 14 October 1983 the prime minister of Grenada,

Maurice Bishop, was overthrown by rivals and later killed. On 20 October a 'Revolutionary Military Council' took power under General Hudson Austin. Neighbouring governments were concerned; the Governor, Sir Paul Scoon, appealed for US aid; and on 25 October the US invaded the island with about 2,000 men supported by contingents from other Caribbean islands. Reagan declared Grenada to be a 'Soviet colony' and argued that America had acted to protect its citizens on the island, but the invasion caused concern to other countries. US combat troops left Grenada in December, having installed a democratic government and demonstrated once again that the US would not tolerate the extension of Cuban influence in the Caribbean.

67. Libya, April 1986

Western states were increasingly concerned in the 1980s with terrorist activities, often carried out by groups suspected of being armed by the Eastern bloc and backed by radical Arab states such as Libya or Syria. Following the slaying of seventeen people at Rome and Vienna airports on 27 December 1985, the US State Department accused Libya's Colonel Gadaffi of aiding the Palestinian 'Abu Nidal Group' to carry out the attacks. In January 1986 the US navy carried out manoeuvres near the Libyan coast and in March sank two Libyan gunboats. Tensions reached their height in April. On the 5th two US servicemen were killed in a bomb attack in West Berlin and ten days later US aircraft bombed the Libyan cities of Tripoli and Benghazi, killing about a hundred people. The raids were criticised by the Eastern bloc and non-aligned states and led to some differences within NATO: France and Spain (unlike Britain) had denied the Americans overflying rights for the raids, and most West Europeans preferred to use non-military sanctions against Gadaffi.

68. Eastern Europe: the collapse of Communism, 1989

In the early 1980s the system of Soviet satellites in Eastern Europe was under enormous strain. Problems included a lack of legitimacy and popularity for the regimes, no real belief in Marxist-Leninism and low economic growth. Western capitalism seemed more successful and there were growing differences between members of the bloc. The 'New' Cold War of 1979–85 had added to the strains on the system by forcing East Europeans to surrender the trade links they had established with Western states in the 1970s. Gorbachev's reforms in the USSR after 1985 inevitably had an impact on the Soviet bloc. He was ready to accept greater equality among pact members and proved ready to accept the end of Communism in Eastern Europe. Without the backing of Soviet military force the various satellite regimes disintegrated in turn.

Hungary

Economic reforms in Hungary, though radical by East European standards, basically preserved an inefficient, centralised system. As early as
1983 the government tried to compensate for economic problems by
introducing political reform, with a choice of candidates in elections. By
May 1988 many Communist Party members accepted the need for greater
political change. They pushed the veteran Janos Kadar out of power at
a special conference, allowed new political parties to form and, in January 1989, became the first East European country to set free elections
for 1990. The transition to democracy was remarkably smooth and in
April 1989 Gorbachev signalled his approval by agreeing to withdraw
Soviet forces from Hungary.

Poland

After the Solidarity episode (q.v.), General Jaruzelski was able to end
martial law and reassert Communist authority. However, in November
1987 Jaruzelski proved over-confident when he put some economic reforms to a referendum and failed to obtain a clear majority. The year
1988 saw a number of strikes and the revival of Solidarity, and in early
1989 the government was forced to agree to talks with Solidarity representatives led by Lech Walesa. In April it was agreed not only to
re-legalise Solidarity and carry out economic reforms, but also to hold
multi-candidate elections. When the elections were held in June, Solidarity won enough seats to force Jaruzelski, in September, to appoint a
non-Communist premier, Tadeusz Mazowiecki.

East Germany

The hard-line regime of Erich Honecker fell victim, after May 1989, to
the liberalisation in Hungary. When Hungary opened its border with
Austria, tens of thousands of East Germans were able to flee via Hungary
to West Germany, where they were promised higher living standards. In
early October Gorbachev criticised Honecker's conservatism and soon
afterwards the latter resigned in favour of Egon Krenz. After briefly
considering repression the new government decided to introduce freedom of foreign travel, a step which led to the opening of the Berlin Wall
in November. This was the most dramatic symbol of the end of Communist repression in the East.

Bulgaria

Bulgaria had seemed securely in the grip of a conservative leader, the
veteran Todor Zhivkov, but he, like Honecker, was faced by an exodus,

of the country's Turkish minority, which threatened to harm the economy. In November Peter Mladenov, backed by Gorbachev, carried out a palace coup which toppled Zhivkov. As elsewhere the Communists changed their name (to Socialists) and held free elections in 1990.

Czechoslovakia

Like East Germany, Czechoslovakia had a strong economy relative to the rest of the Eastern bloc, and a repressive government under Gustav Husak and, after 1987, Milos Jakes. But there were opposition demonstrations in January and May 1989, and mass rallies by young people became a daily occurrence in mid-November, following the dramatic events in East Germany. The Communists tried to placate the opposition with leadership changes before surrendering their monopoly on power. The pace of change was such that in late December the best-known Czech dissident, Vaclav Havel, became president.

Romania

Here Nicolae Ceauşescu hoped to retain absolute power, because he had already established independence from Moscow. But in mid-December widespread demonstrations against him began in Timosoara, among the oppressed Hungarian minority, and on 21 December Bucharest was thrown into chaos. Ceauşescu and his wife tried to flee the capital but were captured and shot. The new 'National Salvation Front', under Ion Iliescu, included many ex-Communists.

Elsewhere in Eastern Europe, Communists clung on to power in Yugoslavia and Albania. However, *Yugoslavia* had become divided among its constituent republics since the death of Tito in 1980, and rapidly began to disintegrate, with Slovenia and Croatia declaring independence in June 1991. In *Albania* there were soon signs of opposition to the regime of Ramiz Alia, which eventually held elections in 1991 and then agreed to form a coalition government.

69. Kuwait crisis and the second 'Gulf War', 1990–91

The invasion of Kuwait by Iraq was dubbed the 'first post-Cold War' crisis. On 2 August 1990 Iraqi forces invaded the small, oil-rich Sheikhdom of Kuwait, which they had claimed for some time. The country was formally annexed by Saddam Hussein's government and the Kuwaiti population terrorised. Hussein evidently expected the world to accept his action. But neighbouring states, notably Saudi Arabia, were fearful of his actions, world opinion was outraged and the US quickly condemned the invasion. The improvement in relations between the US and USSR allowed concerted action against Saddam through the UN, which enforced economic sanctions. Although Soviet advisers remained in Iraq, the US was also able to begin a military build-up in Saudi Arabia without the fear of a superpower crisis. Britain, France and others joined the US-led force.

Only Jordan and a few other Third World states showed sympathy for Saddam, despite fears of widespread Arab unrest and Saddam's claim to be fighting for the Palestinians against Israel. The Iraqi attempt to use Western hostages as a 'human shield' intensified the international outrage against him, and in December they were released. This did not prevent an air war being launched against Iraq after 15 January 1991, a deadline for action which had been publicly set by President Bush in November. The US technological superiority was such that when a land invasion of Kuwait was launched six weeks later it proved swift and entirely one-sided: about 100,000 Iraqis were slaughtered, with very few Allied casualties. Iraq remained subject to UN economic sanctions and arms controls after the conflict.

70. Lithuania (March 1990–January 1991) and the break-up of the USSR

One vital, and largely unpredicted, feature of the Gorbachev years after 1985 was the re-emergence of regional politics in the Soviet Union which was made up of numerous national, ethnic and religious groups. Oppressed under the Tsarist and Stalinist regimes, these groups became more vocal in the era of *glasnost* (q.v.). There were fifteen constituent republics in the USSR and some (the Baltic states of Estonia, Latvia and Lithuania) had been independent between the wars. The late 1980s saw various instances of nationalist violence, notably after February 1988 in the clashes between Armenians and Azerbaijanis over who should control the region of Ngorno-Karabakh. Growing economic problems and the collapse of Communism in Western Europe (q.v.) increased expectations that the USSR might break up and a leading politician like Boris Yeltsin (q.v.) discovered that he could secure a power base at republican level: in May 1990 he became President of the largest republic, the Russian Federation. In January 1990 Gorbachev tried to forestall any immediate break-up by promising a new law on nationalities which would allow secession, but he was slow to draw this up.

Gorbachev's most pressing nationalist challenge in 1990–91 was in the Baltic states, especially Lithuania. In August 1989 one million people in the three republics joined hands in a 430-mile human chain in a pro-independence gesture. This followed: the formation of local political groups (1988); declarations of sovereignty by Estonia (November 1988), followed by Lithuania and Latvia (July 1989); and a declaration by the

Lithuanians that their 1940 annexation by the USSR had been illegal (August 1989). In December 1989 the Lithuanian Communists declared themselves separate from the Soviet party and on 11 March 1990, despite a personal appeal from Gorbachev, the Lithuanian Supreme Soviet declared itself independent under President Vytautas Landsbergis. The Red Army, still present in Lithuania, disarmed the Lithuanian National Guard and arrested those who refused to be conscripted into the army. But Gorbachev preferred an economic blockade (including an oil embargo) rather than violence to force Lithuania into line and on 29 June a compromise was reached: Lithuania suspended its declaration of independence whilst talks began on the promised Union Treaty.

By the end of the year, however, there was no Union Treaty, old Communists were being promoted in Moscow by a worried Gorbachev and the moderate foreign minister, Shevardnadze, resigned on 20 December, warning of the danger of a return to dictatorship. On 2 January 1991 Landsbergis therefore ended the suspension of Lithuanian independence and sparked a new crisis. Five days later the Red Army sent special forces into several republics to enforce conscription. The violence was worst in Lithuania, and to a lesser extent Latvia. Nineteen people were killed as the army seized key buildings and there was real fear of a general return to suppression. Though events in the USSR were overshadowed by the Gulf War (q.v.), the American government expressed its concern. Yeltsin too backed the Baltic states' desire for independence and Gorbachev quickly decided repression could not go on. By the end of January the violence had ended and on 7 March he published a draft Union Treaty which allowed a wide degree of autonomy. A referendum on the Treaty was boycotted by six republics, however, since they wanted full independence. It was when the Union Treaty was about to be signed in August that conservative Communists launched a coup against Gorbachev, hoping to restore a totalitarian system and prevent republican autonomy. Their failure paved the way for the winding-up of the USSR in December, which left all fifteen republics independent, though eleven of them agreed to form a loose Commonwealth of Independent States. Apart from the January 1991 crisis over Lithuania and, of course, the August coup, these stages in the breakup of the USSR caused remarkably limited international concern.

71. The break-up of Yugoslavia (1991–92) and the Bosnian conflict (1992–95)

Although the end of Soviet domination of Eastern Europe (1989), the break-up of the USSR (1991), and the separation of the Czech Republic and Slovakia (January 1993) were achieved with remarkably little bloodshed or international upheaval, the disintegration of Yugoslavia proved more troubled. Yugoslavia had first been set up as a union of South Slav peoples in 1918 but its internal differences were clear in the Second World War when many Croats and Slovenes backed Fascism and fought against the Serbs. The Communist leader, Tito, set up a centralised state in 1945 but the 1974 constitution allowed for a collective Presidency between the country's several republics, the strongest of which were Serbia, Croatia and Slovenia. Tito's death in 1980 removed an important unifying force and after 1987 there was growing resentment in many republics over the Serb nationalist policies of Serbia's President, Slobodan Milosevic.

In September 1989 Slovenia declared a limited form of autonomy, sparking an economic war with Serbia (December). Elections in April–May 1990 in Slovenia and Croatia confirmed that these republics wanted to turn Yugoslavia into a loose confederation but, with the Serbs unwilling to concede this, Slovenia and Croatia moved to a declaration of full independence in June 1991. The Serbs, with control of the Yugoslav army, tried to oppose this by force but by October had effectively conceded Slovenian independence. In Croatia, where there was a large Serb minority, events were more complex. Croatia (like Slovenia) was able to win international recognition for its independence in January 1992, but about one-third of the country remained in the hands of autonomous Serb minorities, notably in the region of Krajina. A UN peace-keeping force was deployed in Croatia in early 1992, but there was another outbreak of Serb–Croat violence early the following year and by then events were closely entangled with an even more complex problem in Bosnia.

Bosnia-Herzegovina was the most ethnically-mixed republic of Yugoslavia, including Moslems (an ethnic as much as a religious group in this case), Serbs and Croats. On 3 March, following a referendum, Bosnia declared itself independent under its President, Alija Izetbegovic, but clashes began almost immediately between the Moslems and Serb irregulars, the latter backed by the Yugoslav army, controlled by Serbia and its ally-republic, Montenegro (which together continued to call themselves Yugoslavia). On 27 March the Bosnian Serbs declared their own republic and there were immediate attempts by the European Community (EC), to negotiate a peace settlement based on an ethnic division of Bosnia. Izetbegovic, however, argued that this would reward Serb aggression and that, given the complicated ethnic mix, a unitary state should be preferred. A vicious inter-ethnic war began in which there were atrocities on all sides, but with the Serbs especially criticised for their policy of 'ethnic cleansing', involving expulsions and genocide. The capital, Sarajevo, was under almost continuous Serb siege. In 1992 alone about one million people were killed and 2.5 million became refugees. Over the next three years numerous cease-fires were called, then broken. The situation became even more intractable when the Croats (allies of the

Moslems at first) tried to carve out their own territory in late 1992, whilst in the north, around Bihac, a rival Moslem group claimed authority.

The response of the international community, and especially of the UN and EC, was much criticised. The UN had placed an arms embargo on the whole of the former Yugoslavia in September 1991 but the American Congress in particular argued that this effectively helped the Serbs, who were better-armed than the Moslems. The UN sent troops to Sarajevo in June 1992 but to help with humanitarian aid rather than to play a peace-making role. Sanctions were introduced against Serbia in May 1992 and had some impact on that country but did not moderate the extremism of the Bosnian Serbs, led by Radovan Karadzic. The UN Human Rights Commission condemned 'ethnic cleansing' and a number of war trials were eventually begun in The Hague, but they found it impossible to bring key culprits, like the Bosnian Serb commander, General Mladic, to justice. In May 1993 the UN declared several Moslem-held towns to be 'safe areas' (Srbrenica, Tuzla, Zepa, Gorazde and Bihac) but could not effectively defend them: Gorazde fell to the Serbs in April 1994.

In October 1992 the UN also declared a 'no-fly' zone over Bosnia, to prevent attacks by the Yugoslav air force, but only in March 1993 was NATO given authority to shoot down aircraft which violated the zone and only in February 1994 did NATO actually act. In addition to enforcing the 'no-fly' zone, NATO also tried to force the withdrawal of Serb artillery from Sarajevo. But there were serious differences within the alliance on what to do. The US was keen to see West European countries resolve the problem, but Britain and France, with peace-keeping troops on the ground, were reluctant to become involved in a full-scale conflict. Even limited action by NATO aircraft alienated opinion in Russia, which was sympathetic to Serbia, and raised the danger of a Serb riposte: NATO air strikes in May 1995 led the Serbs to seize over 300 UN peace-keepers as hostages for several weeks. This crippled the UN peace effort and was followed in July by one of the worst atrocities of the war when the Serbs overran the 'safe area' of Srbrenica.

Soon after this, however, the conflict moved towards a settlement, as the Serb position weakened and, stunned by the UN failure, America began to play a fuller role. In March 1994 the US had already brokered a settlement between the Moslems and Croats, leading to a Moslem–Croat federation in Bosnia, and later a Bosnian–Croat military alliance. In August 1994 the Bosnian government took over the rebel enclave of Bihac and in March 1995 launched a successful offensive against the Serbs. When, in July 1995, after the fall of Zepa, the Serbs decided to attack Bihac, the Croats came to the aid of the Bosnians by attacking the Serbs in Krajina. Krajina was overrun in a rapid operation in early August which found the Bosnian Serbs helpless. Serbia proper and Russia both pressed the Bosnian Serbs to negotiate peace; NATO air strikes became even more determined, with 'Operation Deliberate Force'; and President Clinton sent his Assistant Secretary of State, Richard Holbrooke, to negotiate a cease-fire. By 5 October Holbrooke was successful and November saw three weeks of talks between Izetbegovic, Milosevic and Croatia's Franjo Tudjman in America. The result was the Dayton Accords, formally signed in Paris on 14 December, which kept some central powers in Sarajevo but otherwise divided Bosnia between the Moslem–Croat federation (51 per cent of the land) and the Serb Republic. A substantial NATO-led force was sent to enforce this, replacing the UN and including a small Russian contingent which – in a remarkable commentary on the end of the Cold War – served alongside US troops.

72. Chechenia, 1994–96

The break-up of the USSR in 1991 was followed by numerous conflicts within and between its former constituent republics. Ethnic tensions, border disputes and ideological differences all provoked disputes of varying intensity and duration. Some of the worst were the Tajikistan civil war (1992–97), the war between Armenia and Azerbaijan over Ngorno-Karabakh (1992–93, effectively won by Armenia) and the secessionist war fought by the Abkhazians against the Georgian government (at its worst in 1992–93). The Commonwealth of Independent States, a loose organisation which included most of the USSR's former republics, tried to mediate in some of these conflicts and Boris Yeltsin's Russian Federation also played an active role, sometimes supporting a particular side in a dispute. Partly to please nationalist opinion, Yeltsin was keen to maintain close co-operation with former Soviet republics (especially Belarus and Ukraine) but also needed to prevent the break-up of Russia itself, which had numerous constituent republics and ethnic groups. The most serious challenge to this policy came in Chechenia.

The Chechens are an ancient people of the Caucasus region, Sufi Moslem by religion and divided into clans. They had resisted incorporation into the Tsarist Empire until 1859, and mass deportations under Stalin in 1943 had failed to break their independent spirit. They make up 60 per cent of the population of Chechenia, part of the Russian Federation: 23 per cent are Russians (keen to remain part of Russia) and 13 per cent Ingush (another Moslem people but fearful of Chechen domination and also ready to remain part of Russia). In 1991 a former Soviet air force officer, Dzokar Dudayev, became President of Chechenia, declared its independence from the then-USSR (November) and won diplomatic recognition from several states, including nearby Iran and Turkey. Yeltsin's Russia, reluctant to use force against such separatism at first, enforced an economic blockade on Chechenia, sent troops to the border and tried to undermine Dudayev's increasingly dictatorial regime by covert actions (including support for rebel forces who began a civil war in the spring of 1994). When these measures failed to remove Dudayev, Yeltsin turned, on 11 December 1994, to armed intervention. On 19 December three Russian divisions, with air support, began an assault on the Chechen capital, Grozny. The international reaction to the invasion was muted, but, to Yeltsin's deep embarrassment, the Chechens successfully resisted for several weeks. Russian casualties mounted and the weaknesses of its armed forces were quickly exposed. The Presidential palace was only taken on 15 January 1995 and Grozny was not cleared of Dudayev's followers until February. Although Chechen towns all fell into Russian hands over the following months, the Chechens turned to guerrilla warfare and had some spectacular successes in seizing Russian hostages (at Buddenovsk, June 1995, and Kizylar, January 1996). Dudayev was killed in April 1996 but his successor, Aslan Maskhadov, continued to demand a Russian withdrawal and full independence. To the dismay of Russian nationalists, the Chechens surprised the Russian army again in August by seizing control of Grozny once more. Yeltsin then sent his National Security Adviser, Alexander Lebed, to arrange a peace settlement. Russian troops were withdrawn from Chechenia, and, although a decision on the question of sovereignty was deferred until 2000–2001, Maskhadov was elected President in 1997.

SECTION THREE

Conferences and Summits

The following includes summaries of all US–Soviet Summits, plus other major Cold War conferences, and an outline of US–Russian Summits after the Cold War.

1. Tehran Summit, 28 November–1 December 1943

The Tehran Summit marked the first 'Big Three' leaders' meeting. Roosevelt had long wanted such a conference but Stalin had been reluctant to meet Churchill and Roosevelt until the Red Army had put the *Wehrmacht* on the defensive. Following the battles of Stalingrad and Kursk he felt more confident, but insisted on a meeting close to the Soviet border. With Anglo-American forces victorious in North Africa, all three Allies could plan more confidently for the war against Germany. The Soviets, critical in the past of the failure to open a 'Second Front' against Germany, were now promised an Anglo-American landing in France in 1944. Stalin pleased the US by promising that he would enter the Far Eastern war in due course. Political issues took second place to military ones at Tehran but a discussion was held on the control of Germany in future and Roosevelt put forward his ideas on a United Nations organisation under the auspices of the 'four policemen' (the Big Three, plus China).

2. Yalta Summit, 4–12 February 1945

The second 'Big Three' Summit was held when, with victory assured, post-war political issues had to be addressed. The name Yalta later became a byword for the West's betrayal of Eastern Europe, which fell under Soviet domination. But at the time, the Conference seemed a success and, contrary to popular mythology, it did *not* see any formal division of Europe into 'spheres of influence'.

The main topics discussed at Yalta, a Crimean seaside resort, were:

(a) Eastern Europe

Unable to prevent Soviet military control of the area, America and Britain could only secure a 'Declaration on Liberated Europe' (applicable to all the continent) which largely repeated the promises in the Atlantic Charter (q.v.) for the restoration of sovereignty, the destruction of Fascism and the promotion of economic well-being.

(b) Poland

This was the most divisive subject, since Poland was at the heart of Stalin's security interests in Eastern Europe. An eastern border of Poland was established which gave the USSR substantial gains, and it was agreed in principle to compensate Poland with land from Germany. On political issues, the Western Allies agreed to accept the Soviet-imposed Communist administration as the basis of a provisional government, but it was to be expanded to include representatives of the London-based government-in-exile, and elections were to be held.

(c) Germany

The idea of dismembering Germany was discussed, but left for further study. The British successfully pressed for France to be given a share in the occupation of Germany, so that France could help control the latter in future. The US agreed with Stalin that a figure of twenty billion dollars (half of which should go to Russia) should be the 'basis for discussion' of reparations from Germany; a three-power Reparations Commission was established in Moscow.

(d) United Nations

Stalin agreed to take part in the UN, but showed no great interest in it and was most concerned to preserve the predominance of the Great Powers within the planned Security Council.

(e) Far East

Roosevelt's other major aim was to secure Soviet entry into the war against Japan. Stalin agreed to do this within three months of Victory in Europe, but in return he would receive the southern half of Sakhalin Island and certain rights over ports and railways in Manchuria (North-East China). These secret concessions were later criticised.

3. Potsdam (Berlin) Summit, 17 July–2 August 1945

The last of the 'Big Three' wartime Summits was held in the former German capital two months after V-E Day. America was now represented by Truman, and Churchill was replaced after 27 July by a new prime minister, Labour's Clement Attlee. Despite Western complaints about the lack of democracy in Eastern Europe, the Polish issue was no longer divisive. The USSR confirmed its decision to enter the war against Japan, although the successful test of the atom bomb during the conference meant that Soviet help might not be needed. (Truman mentioned the 'powerful bomb' to Stalin only briefly.) Post-war issues were now uppermost and it was agreed to set up a 'Council of Foreign Ministers' to draw up peace treaties with the defeated states. The most vital issue at the conference was Germany.

Some general principles for the occupation of Germany were easily agreed, such as the so-called 'four Ds': Disarmament, Denazification, Democratisation and Decartellisation. It was agreed to give Poland all German lands down to the Rivers Oder and Neisse. The most complex issue was that of reparations. It was agreed that each occupying power should take reparations from its own zone, but that to reward the USSR for its contribution to the war, the Soviets should also obtain 25 per cent of reparations from the Western zones, some of which should be in exchange for food and raw materials. The total amount of reparations should be decided once the Allied Control Council in Germany had established a 'level of industry plan' for the country, which left the Germans with a fair standard of living.

4. Conferences of the Council of Foreign Ministers (CFM), 1945–49

The CFM was established at the Potsdam Conference in mid-1945 in order to draft peace treaties with the ex-enemy states and to discuss other post-war problems. It comprised the foreign ministers of the US, USSR, Britain, France and China. The CFM became the main forum for high-level discussions between Soviet and Western governments in the late 1940s. The following meetings took place.

London, September–October 1945

This was the first occasion on which most people realised there were serious East–West differences. The Big Three, having recently discussed Germany's future at Potsdam (q.v.), decided to discuss peace treaties with Hitler's European allies – Italy, Finland, Bulgaria, Romania and Hungary. The US and British foreign ministers, Byrnes and Bevin, objected to the lack of democracy in Bulgaria and Romania; the USSR's Molotov complained about Soviet exclusion from the occupation of Japan. The conference eventually broke down on a technicality.

Moscow, December 1945

This meeting was called by Byrnes in order to heal the rift with Moscow; France and China were excluded. The conference agreed on how to proceed with the peace treaties in future. The US and Britain accepted political realities in Romania and Bulgaria.

Paris, April–July 1946

This conference, which extended over two sessions, saw long arguments on such issues as the future of Trieste (claimed by both Italy and

Yugoslavia), but ultimately proved able to draft peace treaties with Hitler's European allies. China (being involved only in Far Eastern issues) took no part in this, or later, conferences. An exchange of views on Germany at the end of the conference showed deep divisions between the Soviets, French and Anglo-Americans.

In July–October Allied states met at a Peace Conference in Paris to discuss, and recommend amendments to, the peace treaties which the CFM had drafted. The defeated states were also represented, but had no decision-making powers.

New York, November–December 1946

Here the CFM redrafted the peace treaties with Italy and the East European states, taking into account a large number of the amendments recommended by the Paris Peace Conference. The treaties (q.v.) were signed in Paris in February 1947.

Moscow, March–April 1947

The US, USSR, Britain and France turned their attention to the German peace treaty and the associated Austrian settlement. By March 1947, however, East–West differences on the German problem (q.v.) were already very deep. The conference became a long series of arguments on such issues as reparations, Germany's western border and control of the Ruhr.

London, November–December 1947

The East–West rift had deepened thanks to the Marshall Plan and the formation of Cominform (q.v.). The positions of the Great Powers on Germany were as far apart as at Moscow. The conference ended in mid-December without setting a date for another meeting.

Paris, May–June 1949

A further meeting of the CFM was dominated by fruitless exchanges on a German peace treaty. The conference was held as a concession to the USSR for ending the Berlin Blockade.

Another attempt to hold a CFM was made in 1951 but the foreign ministers' deputies, meeting in Paris, could not even agree on an agenda.

5. Berlin Conference, 25 January–18 February 1954

The Berlin Conference was the first Soviet–Western foreign ministers' meeting since 1949. The main issue at the conference was the peace treaty with Germany, which was not made directly after the war. However, divisions on this issue were too deep to allow a settlement. The Western powers put the emphasis on the need for free elections to create a united German government; the USSR instead wanted East Germany (a country not recognised by the West) to have an equal role with West Germany in forming a unified government. The conference did not end in failure, however, since it was agreed to meet again in April to discuss two Far Eastern issues: Korea and Indo-China.

6. Geneva Conference, 26 April–21 July 1954

The second meeting of 1954 between the Soviet, American, British and French foreign ministers was held to discuss the future of Korea and Indo-China. Other parties to these disputes were allowed to attend the conference, including Communist China, which was not officially recognised by the West. A peace treaty for Korea proved impossible to negotiate. The conference proved most significant therefore for bringing a settlement of the Indo-China War. Here the colonial power, France, suffered the humiliating loss of Dienbienphu on 7 May 1954. A complex settlement was reached on 20–21 July which ended the war, allowed French troops to withdraw from Vietnam and created independent states in Laos and Cambodia. Vietnam was divided at the 17th parallel between a Communist North and the French-installed government of Bao Dai in the South; but the country was supposed to be reunited through free elections in 1956. The settlement proved only tenuous, however: the 1956 elections were never held.

7. Bandung Conference, 18–24 April 1955

The first major international gathering of 'developing' nations. It proved a major boost for anti-colonialism and non-alignment, and laid the basis for the 'Third World' movement (q.v.) although some of the states who attended were closely linked to either the Soviet bloc (China) or the West (Japan). Twenty-nine Afro-Asian countries sent representatives to the conference, held in the former Dutch colony of Indonesia. Nehru's India, a major force behind the meeting, was able to gain acceptance for an expanded version of the 'five principles' of co-operation. Racialism, colonialism, external intervention and bloc politics (including treaties like SEATO) were all criticised. The conference also discussed specific issues, condemning apartheid in South Africa, French policy in North Africa and the treatment of Palestinian Arabs.

8. Geneva Summit, 18–23 July 1955

The first East–West Summit since Potsdam, ten years before, was attended by Eisenhower (US), Khruschev and Bulganin (USSR), Eden (UK) and Faure (France), along with their foreign ministers. Cold War tensions had eased since the death of Stalin and the end of the Korean War in 1953. The conference proved friendly enough, leading to talk of 'the spirit of Geneva', but no agreement was reached on important issues which included:

(a) Germany

Although an Austrian State Treaty had been signed in May, on the basis of Austrian neutrality, a German peace treaty remained as far off as ever. The Soviets hoped to neutralise Germany but it was much more difficult to achieve this – given Germany's geographical, economic and historical importance – than it was to neutralise Austria. The Western Allies feared that neutrality could not be maintained and that such a policy would merely undermine the Western Alliance with Bonn. As to German reunification, the West wanted this to come about by free elections, while the Soviets wanted discussions to take place between West and East Germany.

(b) European security

The Soviets wanted to work towards the abolition of NATO and the Warsaw Pact, and their replacement by a new, collective system. But the Western powers saw this simply as an attempt to destroy NATO. The West was, however, prepared to consider a non-aggression agreement and (under the 'Eden Plan') a zone of limited armaments in central Europe, which could reduce tension there. Both sides agreed to study this idea.

(c) 'Open skies'

Both sides were ready to continue talks at the UN on disarmament, and President Eisenhower put forward a dramatic proposal which would reduce the danger of 'surprise' attacks and allow each superpower to verify arms agreements by allowing aerial photography over the other's air space. The Soviets, however, showed little interest in this 'open skies' proposal.

A subsequent meeting of East–West foreign ministers in Geneva in October–November confirmed the lack of progress on substantive issues.

9. Khruschev's US visit and the Camp David Summit, 15–27 September 1959

Camp David was the first solely US–Soviet Summit. In August 1959, after months of tension over the second Berlin crisis (q.v.) President Eisenhower suddenly invited the Soviet leader, Khruschev, to America. Eisenhower was hopeful of making peace with the Soviets before his presidency ended, and he believed that Khruschev's view would moderate if he was exposed to the American way of life. Khruschev's long visit, during which he toured widely, allowed him to see America at first hand, but his faith in Communism was undimmed. At Camp David, on 26–27 September (following earlier talks in Washington), he and Eisenhower agreed in principle that a full Summit should be held in 1960, Khruschev having ended his threatening policy over Berlin and there being mutual agreement that disputes should be settled peacefully. On substantive issues, such as Germany and disarmament, however, the two superpowers continued to differ.

10. Paris Summit/U-2 incident, May 1960

The Paris Summit had first been suggested at the Eisenhower–Khruschev meeting at Camp David in September 1959. Doubts about such a meeting from West Germany's Adenauer and France's de Gaulle, were overcome at a Western Summit in Paris in December 1959. It was clear that the Western powers were unlikely to make any concessions to Khruschev on the German question. The lack of enthusiasm from both sides may help to explain why the Summit was abandoned, although the actual reason was the so-called 'U-2 incident'.

On 1 May 1960 a U-2 spy-plane – a flimsy, high-altitude aircraft developed by the CIA in the mid-1950s to take high resolution photographs of the USSR – was shot down over Russia. Initially the US denied it was a spy aircraft, but the Soviets were able to exploit the situation by displaying the captured pilot, Gary Powers. On 11 May Eisenhower had to admit the truth. Three days later the leaders arrived in Paris for the Summit, but within forty-eight hours the meeting was cancelled.

11. Vienna Summit, 3–4 June 1961

The only Kennedy–Khruschev Summit was marked by bullying behaviour from the Russian leader, who was determined to maintain support for 'wars of national liberation' and demanded that the West recognise the sovereign status of East Germany. Kennedy, recently humiliated over the Bay of Pigs fiasco, was surprised by Khruschev's behaviour but refused to give way. The only substantive point the two did agree on was that there should be 'a neutral and independent Laos'.

12. Glassboro' (New Jersey) 'Mini-Summit', 23–25 June 1967

The only high-level meeting between US and Soviet leaders between 1961 and 1972 took place while the Soviet prime minister, Andrei Kosygin, was in America to speak at the United Nations about the recent Arab–Israeli Six-Day War. He met President Johnson on 23 and 25 June. Issues discussed included the Middle East and Vietnam, but the superpowers each took opposite sides on these questions: the USSR wanted Israeli withdrawal from recently conquered territory, and criticised US policy in Vietnam. The meeting had no major result.

13. Beijing (Sino-American) Summit, 22–28 February 1972

Tentative diplomatic links were established between America and China in 1969–70, after twenty years of alienation. The Romanian and Pakistani governments acted as intermediaries. The US relaxed trade barriers and in April 1971 a US table tennis team was invited to China ('ping-pong diplomacy'). In July 1971 Kissinger made a secret visit to Beijing which was followed by a surprise announcement that Nixon himself would visit China. The news shocked America's allies in East Asia, such as Japan, South Vietnam and South Korea, but the greatest blow was to Taiwan. In October 1971 the US conceded that Beijing should take the Chinese seat on the UN Security Council – which Taiwan therefore lost. The Summit took place at the start of the US election year and greatly boosted Nixon's re-election prospects. It included a meeting between Nixon and Mao Zedong, although the main Chinese negotiator was premier Zhou Enlai. The 'Shanghai Communiqué' of 28 February included a declaration against Soviet attempts at hegemony in East Asia, but also acknowledged continuing differences over Taiwan. In 1973 the US and China established 'liaison offices' in each other's capitals, but a full normalisation of relations was delayed until 1978 under Jimmy Carter (q.v.).

14. Moscow Summit, 22–26 May 1972

The first Nixon–Brezhnev Summit represented the high point of 1970s detente and was most notable for the signature of the SALT I Treaties (q.v.), which had largely been finalised beforehand. Nixon used the diplomatic coup to strengthen his prospects for re-election as president. Apart from SALT, a number of agreements were signed including one on health, a joint space venture (the 1975 Apollo–Soyuz mission), an agreement to avoid accidents at sea and the establishment of a Commercial Commission. There was also an agreement on certain 'basic principles' to govern US–Soviet detente, including restraint in crises and the avoidance of confrontation.

15. Washington Summit, 16–24 June 1973

The second Nixon–Brezhnev Summit was overshadowed by the Watergate scandal, although Congress agreed to suspend the Watergate hearings during Brezhnev's visit. The Washington Summit did not have the drama and significance of the 1972 Moscow meeting, despite the venue being moved between Washington, Camp David and San Clemente, California. Agreements were signed on agriculture, transport and cultural exchanges; principles were set out for talks on a SALT II Treaty; and a commitment was made on the prevention of nuclear war – the US and USSR would consult together if nuclear war ever threatened to involve one or both of them.

16. Moscow Summit, 27 June–3 July 1974

The third and final Nixon–Brezhnev Summit was overshadowed by the Watergate crisis. The Moscow Summit included one important nuclear arms agreement: both sides agreed to limit themselves to one anti-ballistic missile field, instead of the two agreed on in the 1972 ABM Treaty. There was also an agreement on energy research, a ban on small nuclear tests and discussion of the SALT II Treaty.

17. Vladivostok Summit, 23–24 November 1974

The principal Ford–Brezhnev Summit was arranged by Secretary of State Kissinger as a 'getting-to-know-you' meeting. Ford went to Vladivostok at the end of a major tour of East Asia. The short meeting was most import- ant for laying down a 'base agreement' on the SALT II Treaty, with both sides accepting a limit of 2,400 strategic missiles and bombers, of which 1,320 could have multiple warheads. The Summit upset US relations with China and was not followed by the expected Brezhnev visit to America in 1975.

18. Vienna Summit, 15–18 June 1979

The only Carter–Brezhnev Summit was most notable for the signature of the SALT II (q.v.) Treaty, but the long delays to this treaty, the question- ing of detente in America and Soviet fears of US–Chinese co-operation meant that the meeting took place in an uncertain atmosphere. The summit proved a low-key affair, with Brezhnev clearly in failing health and little personal rapport between the two leaders. Six months later detente was dead, killed by the Afghanistan crisis.

19. Geneva Summit, 19–20 November 1985

Held between Ronald Reagan and the new Soviet leader Mikhail Gorbachev, Geneva was the first Summit for six years. The two hoped to establish personal contacts after a long period of poor relations and did not expect to reach major arms control agreement. They got on unexpectedly well, however, agreed to meet again, and reached a number of minor agreements on civilian aircraft landing rights, cultural exchanges and the opening of new consulates.

20. Reykjavik Summit, 11–12 October 1986

This was a hastily arranged meeting proposed by Gorbachev to Reagan in mid-September and announced on 30 September. The Summit followed a number of exchanges on the reduction of nuclear missiles in Europe, but also came after a period of poor Soviet–American relations, especially with the arrest of the US journalist Nicholas Daniloff, in response to America's arrest of a KGB agent, Gennadi Zakhorov. The men were effectively 'exchanged' on 29 September. At the Summit both leaders were ready to consider dramatic nuclear weapons reductions in Europe, including Gorbachev's 'zero option', but were unable to reach agreement because Reagan would not give up his 'Strategic Defense Initiative'.

21. Washington Summit, 7–10 December 1987

Despite the failure of the 1986 Reykjavik Summit both superpowers were keen to reduce their Intermediate Nuclear Forces (INF) in Europe. Talks between US Secretary of State George Schultz and Eduard Shevardnadze (15–18 September 1987) defined the basic lines of an INF treaty, and the Washington Summit was chiefly intended to see the signature of this document, the first agreement signed by superpower leaders since 1979. The Summit was well-managed, highly successful and used to boost both leaders' reputations in their respective countries.

22. Moscow Summit, 29 May–2 June 1988

The centrepiece of the last Gorbachev–Reagan Summit was the exchange, on 1 June, of the instruments of ratification which brought the INF treaty into effect. The Summit saw an agreement by which each power would inform the other of nuclear missile launches. There was also a statement of the general lines of a strategic arms agreement. The details of such an agreement none the less remained complex.

23. Gorbachev's US visit (New York Summit), December 1988

On 7 December 1988 Gorbachev made the first speech as Soviet leader to the UN since Khruschev's visits in 1959–60. He echoed calls by many in the US for 'a new world order' and announced new cuts in Soviet armed forces. The visit allowed Gorbachev to meet both outgoing President Reagan and his successor George Bush, but since this marked a transitory phase between two presidencies a full discussion was impossible. Gorbachev was in any case forced to shorten his visit and return to the USSR, where an earthquake had devasted Armenia.

24. Beijing (Sino-Soviet) Summit, 15–18 May 1989

The Beijing Summit marked the first meeting of Soviet and Chinese leaders since 1959. The Chinese had made an improvement in relations dependent on Soviet withdrawal from Afghanistan, the end of Vietnamese domination over Kampuchea and the reduction of Soviet forces on the Sino-Soviet border. Mikhail Gorbachev answered all these concerns after 1985. His Summit with Deng Xiaoping was used to confirm reductions in Soviet military forces in Asia, to normalise relations and establish personal contacts. However, the visit was overshadowed by large-scale student demonstrations in Tiananmen Square.

The demonstrations had begun on 18 April, three days after the death of the Chinese Communist General Secretary, Hu Yaobang. The students, some of whom began hunger strikes on 14 May, regarded the reformist Soviet leader as a hero. Soon after Gorbachev's departure, however, martial law was declared, and the demonstrations were ruthlessly crushed by the army on 3–4 June.

25. Malta Summit, 2–3 December 1989

The first Bush–Gorbachev Summit came almost a year into Bush's presidency, because of the reassessment of US policy which took place in 1989. The Summit was organised partly because of pressures for the US to support Gorbachev, and by the time it was held the Soviet system in Eastern Europe was in a state of collapse. Bad weather disrupted the Summit, which was held on a Soviet ship. No substantive agreements resulted, and there was no communiqué, but the two men co-operated well and both said the Cold War was at an end.

26. Washington Summit, 30 May–4 June 1990

The second Bush–Gorbachev Summit was a friendly meeting where major strategic arms cuts were agreed in principle, although a full START

Treaty was not expected until 1991. Conventional arms cuts in Europe and chemical weapons control were also discussed. Problems were created by Soviet opposition to a reunified Germany joining NATO, by US criticism of Soviet policy in the Baltic states and by the continuing refusal of the US to provide large-scale economic aid to the USSR.

27. Helsinki Summit, 9 September 1990

Hastily called to discuss the crisis created by Saddam Hussein's invasion of Kuwait, the third Bush–Gorbachev meeting was proclaimed the first 'post-Cold War' Summit. The atmosphere was co-operative, both sides insisted on Iraqi withdrawal from Kuwait and there was full agreement on the enforcement of economic sanctions against Iraq. But while the US was ready to consider military force against Saddam Hussein, the Soviets wanted to continue talks with him. They also kept military advisers in Iraq and wanted reassurances that US forces would leave Saudi Arabia when the crisis ended.

28. Moscow Summit, 30 July–1 August 1991

The fourth Bush–Gorbachev Summit was called mainly to see the signature of the long-awaited START Treaty (q.v.), which took place on 31 July. The meeting also saw pressure from Bush for a more liberal Soviet policy in the Baltic states, for Soviet concessions to Japan on the disputed Kurile Islands and for more rapid change in the Soviet economy. The two leaders also discussed a possible Middle East peace conference, but the meeting was overshadowed by continuing regional unrest in the USSR and by the failure of the Western powers to supply adequate economic aid to Gorbachev.

29. US–Russian Summits after the Cold War

With the end of the Cold War it became normal for US and Russian leaders to meet quite frequently at international gatherings. But the key bilateral Summits after December 1991 were as follows:

1 February 1992: Camp David, First US–Russian Summit. Primarily discussed nuclear weapons.

16–17 June 1992: Washington. Agreed an outline START II Treaty and signed other co-operation agreements.

2–3 January 1993: Moscow. Bush–Yeltsin. Signed the START II Treaty (q.v.).

3–4 April 1993: First Clinton–Yeltsin Summit, primarily marked by US launch of a $1,600 million aid package to Russia.

12–14 January 1994: Moscow. Clinton calls Russia an 'equal' partner but offers no more economic aid. He and Yeltsin agree their countries will not aim nuclear missiles at each other.

27–28 September 1994: Washington. Discussed Bosnia, arms sales to Iran, the implementation of START II and greater bilateral trade (Clinton saying that the 1975 Jackson–Vanik amendment need no longer limit trade).

9–10 May 1995: Moscow. Clinton celebrates V-E Day. He and Yeltsin discuss Chechenia, NATO enlargement and sale of Russian nuclear reactors to Iran.

23 October 1995: Hyde Park, New York State. Clinton and Yeltsin discuss a Russian role in Bosnian peace-keeping, following Yeltsin's visit to UN.

20–21 March 1997: Helsinki. Clinton and Yeltsin agree on signature of a Russian–NATO Founding Act (q.v.) and on outline of a START III Treaty to cut each nuclear arsenal to about 2,000 missiles within ten years. Clinton agrees next G-7 meeting should become, with Russia, a G-8 meeting.

SECTION FOUR

Major treaties and organisations

Major Treaties and Organisations involving the Western and Eastern Blocs

1. Lend-lease aid, 1941–45

Begun in March 1941, before US entry into the Second World War, lend-lease allowed President Roosevelt to provide material to Allied states without the need for repayment. Most went to Britain but it was extended to the USSR in November. Aid was for war purposes and ended abruptly with the defeat of Japan.

2. Atlantic Charter, August 1941

A propagandistic declaration issued by Roosevelt and Churchill after they met off Newfoundland in August 1941. It promised independence for conquered nations after the war, territorial changes only by consent and freer trade. Essentially a statement of liberal-democratic principles, Churchill made clear that it would not affect Britain's imperial position. Stalin, while accepting the Charter in principle, said it must be interpreted according to circumstances.

3. Anglo-Soviet Pact, 1942–55

The first major formal treaty between the USSR and the Western Allies was signed by Soviet foreign minister Molotov and Britain's Anthony Eden in London after several months of talks. Eden had (in December) visited Moscow, but difficulties were caused by the Soviets' desire for a Western 'Second Front' against Germany and Stalin's desire to retain territorial gains he had made under the Ribbentrop–Molotov Pact. The twenty-year treaty avoided any details about a post-war settlement, but committed the two countries to pursue the war against Germany and her allies, and to resist any renewal of German aggression once victory was won. A similar treaty was signed between France and the USSR in December 1994. Both treaties were cancelled by the USSR in 1955 when Britain and France agreed to German rearmament.

4. United Nations Relief and Rehabilitation Administration (UNRRA), 1943–47

An organisation established in 1943 to begin relief work, tackle refugee problems and provide food to liberated countries. It operated down to June 1947, mainly using American funds, and provided aid primarily to Italy and Eastern Europe.

5. Percentages Agreement, October 1944

An agreement on the Balkans (south-eastern Europe) made by Churchill and Stalin when they met in Moscow in October 1944. With the Red Army marching into Eastern Europe, Churchill was anxious to protect British influence in the Balkans, particularly Greece. Churchill agreed to give the Soviets primary influence in Romania and Bulgaria, in return for British primacy in Greece; in Yugoslavia and Hungary influence was divided. The exact significance of the agreement, and how long it was intended to last, is still debated.

6. United Nations, June 1945

A new world security organisation, to succeed the old League of Nations (wound down in 1946) was first vaguely promised by Roosevelt and Churchill in the 1941 Atlantic Charter. The term 'United Nations' was first applied to the Allied countries fighting in the Second World War. Like the League of Nations, the UN was meant to break with traditional power politics (spheres of influence, great power rivalries, secret diplomacy, arms races) and to replace this with 'collective security' whereby all non-aggressive states would be represented in a single organisation, disputes would be settled through conciliation and arbitration, disarmament would be negotiated and any aggressors would be punished by economic or military sanctions.

Supporters of the UN hoped to avoid the problems that crippled the League of Nations. In particular, the US and USSR were in the new body. The UN was well-financed; it could act quickly through the permanent Security Council; it conceded a special role to the great powers as permanent members of the Security Council; and it provided for the creation of regional security bodies. But the UN, like the League of Nations, soon became a victim of the national sovereignty of its members and particularly the independence of the major powers. The British insisted it must not interfere with the colonial empires. The Soviets never showed much enthusiasm for the UN and insisted on a strong role for the major powers. Disagreement between the major powers prevented the creation of a strong military committee (to handle military sanctions) or effective regional security systems. The Soviets never joined in such economic institutions as the International Monetary Fund or World Bank.

The UN was first seriously discussed by the Big Three foreign ministers in Moscow in 1943. A plan for the organisation was drafted at Dumbarton Oaks in 1944, and the organisation was founded at the fifty-nation San Francisco conference in April–June 1945. The UN Charter entered into effect on 24 October ('United Nations Day') and the first ordinary session was held in London in early 1946. A permanent headquarters was established in New York in 1952. The UN was based on the principles of world peace and human rights, but it also recognised the right of all its members to equality and self-determination, and this principle clashed with the other aims. Thus the UN pledge to avoid armed force and the 1948 Declaration on Human Rights are often ignored. The main UN institutions are as follows.

(a) Security Council

Eleven members, increased to fifteen in 1965, including five permanent members with a veto (US, USSR, China, Britain, France) and others elected for two-year periods. Sits permanently, can hear appeals from any member, approves any UN political action and its approval is needed to amend the Charter or admit new members. Decisions require a simple majority-plus-one vote. The veto was frequently used by the USSR from the outset, and increasingly by the US since 1970, often crippling the Council's work. Until 1971 Nationalist Taiwan held the Chinese seat.

(b) General Assembly

All members, meeting annually (September–December) with one vote each. Elects members to other UN bodies, including non-permanent members of the Security Council. Debates and votes on issues, hears reports from UN bodies and has a number of sub-committees. But votes are only binding on those who support them, the Assembly only makes 'recommendations' not decisions, and debates can be unruly, tedious, even irrelevant.

(c) Secretariat

Several thousand officials, under the General Secretary, usually a respected diplomat from a minor power, who sits on the Security Council as a non-voting member and has assumed international standing as a mediator in disputes.

(d) International Court

Fifteen judges, elected by the General Assembly for nine years. Provides legal rulings on disputes, but has to be asked to do this, and cannot enforce decisions.

(e) Subsidiary bodies

A large number of institutions are linked to the UN as agencies or subsidiaries. Some are much older than the UN (International Postal Union; International Labour Organisation), some were inherited from the League (Trusteeship Council which managed colonial mandates) and others have been established since to deal with specific problems (like the Food and Agriculture Organisation, founded 1945 or the World Health Organisation, founded 1948).

The UN took several major post-war decisions (partition of Palestine in 1948; independence for Libya in 1951), passed resolutions on conflicts (notably Resolution 242 in 1967 on Arab–Israeli tension), sent peace-keeping forces to various places (Sinai in 1956–67, Cyprus, Lebanon) and sometimes became embroiled in war itself (especially in the Congo, 1960–64). Ex-enemy states were gradually readmitted (Italy in 1955, Japan in 1956, the two Germanies in 1974). More importantly, the increasing number of independent nations in 1957–64, increased the number of members and shifted the balance away from Western domination, to a situation where the Eastern bloc and Third World countries could outvote the US and its allies. The UN has proved useful for 'behind the scenes' diplomacy, helping countries to talk to each other when they have broken off diplomatic relations. For the most part, the UN between about 1946 and 1988 was crippled by Cold War tensions. It underwent a revival in the late 1980s, when it helped resolve the Iran–Iraq War, but was criticised in 1992–95 for its failure to achieve an early settlement of the Bosnian War.

7. European peace treaties, February 1947

A number of treaties with Hitler's European allies were drafted by the Council of Foreign Ministers (q.v.) of the major powers in 1945–46, and discussed at a peace conference in Paris of major Allied states in summer 1946. The defeated powers themselves, though represented at Paris, had no say in the decisions. The main territorial provisions of the peace treaties, signed in Paris, were as follows:

(a) *Italy* (i) Loss of all colonies: Libya became independent in 1951 on the recommendation of the UN; Italian Somaliland was united with British Somaliland; Eritrea was merged into Ethiopia, which became independent. (ii) Trieste (claimed by Yugoslavia) became a Free Port under Allied control, but was eventually handed back to Italy by the Western powers in 1954. (iii) Italy also lost territory to France, Austria, Greece (the Dodecanese islands) and Yugoslavia.

(b) *Finland* Lost Karelia, Petsamo (her only access to the Arctic Ocean) and other areas to the USSR.

(c) *Romania* Lost Bessarabia and North Bukovina to the USSR and South Dobrudja to Bulgaria.

(d) *Bulgaria* Gained South Dobrudja.

(e) *Hungary* Lost all its gains since 1937 under its alliance with Hitler.

Additionally *all* the defeated powers had to pay reparations and were subjected to limitations on the size of their armed forces.

8. Austrian State Treaty, May 1955

In 1943 the Allies had declared the *Anschluss* (the 1938 union between Austria and Germany) to be 'null and void'. Although Austria was placed under joint occupation by the US, USSR, Britain and France in 1945, it was – in contrast to Germany – allowed its own government. The Soviets set up a provisional government under the veteran Socialist leader Karl Renner in April 1945 which was recognised by the other occupation powers in October. Four-power talks after the war failed to settle Austria's future. In early 1955 the new Khruschev–Bulganin government in Moscow proved ready to conclude an Austrian treaty on condition the country did not join the Western Alliance. The State Treaty, signed after surprisingly short negotiations, and confirmed by the Austrian parliament in November, guaranteed Austria's independence as a neutral state, and led to the withdrawal of all foreign troops. The treaty paved the way to the Geneva Summit (q.v.).

9. Hot-line agreement, June 1963

The agreement set up a direct teletype link between the White House and the Kremlin, following the Cuban Missile Crisis of October 1962, to be used whenever a similar crisis threatened.

10. Test-Ban Treaty, August 1963

The major example of US–Soviet detente following the Cuban Missile Crisis. The effect of radiation (from an atmospheric nuclear test) on a

Japanese fishing boat, *Lucky Dragon*, in 1954 had first caused public concern about nuclear fall-out in the environment. Anti-nuclear movements grew up in the West such as Britain's Campaign for Nuclear Disarmament (CND) and Germany's 'Campaign Against Nuclear Death', and by 1958 both superpowers realised the publicity value of controls on nuclear tests. In March the Soviets announced a moratorium on tests, and in July the first round of Geneva talks began between America, the USSR and Britain on nuclear test controls. Finally, in October, both the US and USSR began a voluntary moratorium on tests. The Geneva talks were unable to reach agreement mainly because of Soviet refusal to accept rigorous US demands for 'on site' inspection of *underground* nuclear tests, but the voluntary moratorium remained unbroken until August 1961 when the Soviets began a new round of atmospheric tests. President Kennedy responded by resuming underground and (from April 1962) atmospheric tests. Both he and British premier Macmillan favoured a ban on atmospheric tests, which was easy to verify even if controls on underground tests proved impossible. In the wake of the Cuban Missile Crisis, Khruschev agreed to talks and a treaty was negotiated quite swiftly which barred the three signatories from carrying out nuclear tests in the atmosphere, underwater or in space.

11. Nuclear Non-proliferation Treaty, 1 July 1968

A treaty signed in Geneva, by most of the world's countries, after several years of talks. It forbade those countries with nuclear weapons from helping others to acquire them. For the US it prevented a spread of such weapons to volatile Third World Conflicts; for the USSR it prevented nuclear arms being obtained by West Germany. The treaty was crucially undermined by the refusal of several key states to sign it, including those such as India, Pakistan, Israel, South Africa, Brazil and Argentina who were most likely to develop nuclear weapons. However, to demonstrate their own desire to control nuclear weapons, the US and USSR announced – simultaneously with the treaty signature – that they intended to hold Strategic Arms Limitation Talks.

12. *Ostpolitik* agreements, 1970–72

During 1949–63, under the Christian Democratic Chancellor Konrad Adenauer, West Germany was closely tied to the Atlantic Alliance, adopted a strong anti-Communist policy and refused to recognise the sovereignty of East Germany. Adenauer refused to negotiate German reunification except on the basis of free elections and the right to remain part of the Western Alliance. In the early 1950s, however, certain politicians, such as the Free Democrat Karl Pfleiderer, argued that West Germany needed a new *Ostpolitik* (eastern policy) based on links to Eastern European countries, a recognition of Soviet power in central Europe and acceptance of Germany's division into two states. This view gained in force with the survival of East Germany throughout the 1950s, and especially with the building of the Berlin Wall in 1961.

In the early 1960s efforts towards greater contact with the East became identified with Willy Brandt, the Social Democrat's candidate for Chancellor. Pressures for an active *Ostpolitik* led Adenauer's successor, Ludwig Erhard, to expand trade with Eastern Europe and to negotiate an agreement with East Germany allowing West Berliners to visit East Berlin at Christmas. But it was only when Brandt became foreign minister (in a coalition with the Christian Democrats) in 1966–69 and then Chancellor in 1969–74 that *Ostpolitik* made real advances. As foreign minister, Brandt established diplomatic links with countries who recognised East Germany and adopted a more active policy in central Europe. Then, in the early 1970s, a number of treaties were made with Eastern states, gradually culminating in better relations with East Germany itself. With the Free Democrat Walter Scheel as his foreign minister, Brandt made treaties with the USSR and Poland in 1970. These included the renunciation of force in international affairs, the acceptance of the German–Polish border and the acceptance of Germany's division. In 1970 Brandt also met the East German premier Willi Stoph, though without any result. The East German government became willing to develop links to the West only after Communist leader Walter Ulbricht was replaced by Erich Honecker. There was some doubt in Western capitals about *Ostpolitik*: Americans feared a process of 'selective detente', whereby the USSR would offer different concessions to NATO states, breaking up the Alliance. But in 1971 all four occupation powers co-operated with the German governments to reach an agreement on freer access between East and West Berlin. The 'Eastern Treaties' with Moscow and Warsaw were ratified in May 1972. Brandt then negotiated the 'Basic Treaty' with East Germany which laid the basis for future dialogue on the basis of 'two Germanies in one nation'. Both countries were able to enter the UN in 1974. *Ostpolitik* was maintained by Brandt's successors and led to greater West German trade with the Eastern bloc. It may have helped to undermine Honecker's regime before its collapse in 1989.

13. SALT I talks and the 1972 Treaty

The idea of a Strategic Arms Limitation Treaty (SALT) took root in the 1960s under the pressure of several developments. These included the cost of weapons, popular calls for arms control, the success of US–Soviet detente after the Cuban Missile Crisis (notably the 1963 Test Ban Treaty), the achievement of nuclear parity by the USSR and technological progress on two fronts in particular:

(a) Anti-Ballistic Missile (ABM) systems

As protection against nuclear attack the Soviets developed the ABM 'Galosh' system around Moscow in the late 1960s. Pressure grew on the US to deploy its own ABM after the explosion of a Chinese hydrogen bomb in June 1967. American Defense Secretary McNamara disliked the idea of an ABM system because it would upset the nuclear balance, tempting anyone with an effective ABM to launch a 'first strike', and leading the other side to increase its own nuclear offensive capability so as to 'swamp' the ABM system. Talks between President Johnson and Soviet premier Kosygin at Glassboro' failed to resolve the problem, however, and in September 1967 the US announced its own ABM system, 'Sentinel' (renamed 'Safeguard' in 1969) to be built around fifteen major cities. Though supposedly an 'anti-Chinese' system, nevertheless it caused great concern to the USSR.

(b) Multiple Independent Re-entry Vehicles (MIRVs)

In the 1960s, while the US developed a nuclear 'triad' – aircraft, submarine-launched missiles (SLBMs) and inter-continental ballistic missiles (ICBMs) – the Soviets, less technologically advanced, developed land-based missiles such as the huge SS-9, which seemed large enough to wipe out the American 'Minuteman' ICBMs in a 'first strike'. This fact, together with the ABM development (see above), led to pressures for a technological leap ahead of the Soviets by building MIRVs – missiles with several warheads, each of which could be separately targeted. MIRVs could overwhelm an ABM system and were cheaper than new missile systems: indeed, after 1968, the US 'froze' its number of long-range missiles and concentrated on technological improvements like MIRV. MIRV testing was announced by the Pentagon in December 1967.

US decisions on the ABM and MIRV led the USSR to agree to SALT talks in June 1968, but plans for these talks to be opened by a US–Soviet Summit were ruined when Warsaw Pact forces invaded Czechoslovakia. The new Nixon administration in 1969 embraced the idea of 'nuclear sufficiency', but when faced with pressures to drop both the ABM (which was costly and required huge areas of land) and MIRV (which would escalate the arms race) Nixon proceeded with both systems, partly it seems as 'bargaining chips' for talks with Moscow. On SALT Nixon and his National Security Adviser, Kissinger, were determined to proceed carefully and talks did not begin until November 1969. The talks faced numerous practical problems such as the verification of an agreement and the treatment of US 'forward-based systems' (FBS) of nuclear weapons in Europe. In 1971 key decisions on SALT were actually taken in Washington, in the so-called 'backchannel' link between Kissinger and Soviet ambassador Dobrynin. Moves were carefully timed by Kissinger to coincide with other advances in detente.

The Moscow Summit of May 1972 became the venue for finalising and signing two treaties. Firstly, an ABM Treaty restricted both sides to building two ABM 'fields', of a hundred missiles each, one around their capital cities and one to protect ICBM sites. Secondly, there was an 'Interim Agreement on Offensive Missiles', with a 'freeze' on strategic weapons as follows: 1,054 ICBMs for the US and 1,618 for the USSR; 656 SLBMs for the US and 740 for the USSR; 455 strategic bombers for the US, with 140 for the Soviets. The treaty was to last for five years.

The ABM and SALT I Treaties were a major step in nuclear arms control, the most important agreements signed by Nixon and Brezhnev, and were of central importance to detente. Yet they soon drew considerable criticism. They omitted controls on new strategic systems, most importantly on MIRVs. The US had a clear lead in the total numbers of nuclear warheads. But the Soviets had a larger number of ICBMs and SLBMs, the treaty failed to control the Soviet deployment of newer 'heavy missiles' (such as the SS-19), and in 1973, to American surprise, the Soviets tested their own MIRV. Together these developments raised the danger that the USSR could overtake the number of US warheads in due course. SALT I was intended to lead to an improved agreement in SALT II.

14. Helsinki Accords (August 1975) and the Conference on Security and Co-operation in Europe (CSCE)

The idea of a European Security Conference was first launched by the USSR in 1954 and consistently pressed by the Warsaw Pact in the late 1960s, but NATO states resisted the proposal because it seemed like a tactic to 'decouple' America from Europe and destroy NATO. After the 1961 Berlin Wall crisis, however, there was no direct East–West crisis in Europe, France under de Gaulle and (later) West Germany under Brandt favoured detente, and by 1971 the US too became more actively favourable to East–West links. In December 1971 the Atlantic Council accepted the Warsaw Pact call for a Security Conference, although NATO insisted that there must also be talks on conventional force reduction (see Conventional Forces in Europe). Preparatory talks opened in November 1972, and in July 1973 a conference opened in Helsinki between thirty-three countries, including NATO, Warsaw Pact, non-aligned and neutral states (Albania being the principal absentee). The talks included two non-European countries: the US and Canada.

On 30 July–1 August 1975 President Ford, General Secretary Brezhnev and other leaders met in Helsinki to sign the 'Final Act' of the talks. This included three 'baskets'.

(a) So far as 'security issues' were concerned principles such as sovereignty and non-interference in internal affairs were stated, and European borders were declared to be 'inviolable'. This meant that borders could be changed, but not by force. The principle was seen as confirming the post-war territorial settlement, including the division of Germany and Soviet dominance in Eastern Europe.

(b) Co-operation was promised in such areas as trade, technology and cultural exchanges.

(c) The major gains for the West were that fundamental human rights were to be respected and there was to be a free exchange of ideas and people across Europe. It was hoped that this would help to undermine the Communist hold on East Europeans in the long term. The detente process was to be maintained by further meetings of a 'Conference on Security and Co-operation in Europe'.

The Helsinki Accords represented the height of European detente in the 1970s, strengthening *Ostpolitik* (q.v.) and committing both sides to maintain the peace. The 'Final Act' was weakened however by the fact that two separate military blocs continued to exist in Europe. In the East there was little respect for human rights, as seen in the suppression of the 'Charter 77' human rights group in Czechoslovakia; in the US critics argued that the West had given a veneer of respectability to the Soviet system in Eastern Europe for little gain. At the next CSCE meeting, at Belgrade in 1978, NATO and Eastern bloc states fell out over human rights and CSCE talks did not revive in importance until the late 1980s. With the end of the Cold War the body became more important, biennial Summits were held and Russia pressed for it to be given stronger powers. At the Budapest Summit of December 1994 it became a permanent organisation (OSCE) and set up its first peace-keeping operation, monitoring the situation in Nagorno–Karabakh. In 1997 the OSCE monitored elections in Chechenia.

15. Normalisation of Sino-American relations, December 1978

Despite the success of the 1972 Beijing Summit (q.v.) between Nixon and Mao, the US and Communist China remained separated by a wide ideological gulf. They continued to differ over Taiwan and were beset by other problems – Watergate and the collapse of Vietnam for America; the death of Mao and an ensuing power struggle in China. Also, Beijing was suspicious of Soviet–American detente. In 1978, however, each side had reason to co-operate with the other. China was seeking to modernise through Western links (even making a friendship treaty with its old foe, Japan, in August) and was anxious about Soviet policy, especially when Moscow allied itself to Vietnam in November. In America detente was being questioned, the Ogaden War had renewed criticism of Soviet policy in the Third World, and National Security Adviser Brzezinski, who visited Beijing in May, was eager to 'play the China card' against Moscow. Brzezinski did most to secure the normalisation of relations, which was agreed in December 1978. Normalisation was helped by the reduction of US troops in South Korea in the late 1970s and by an agreement on Taiwan, under which the US ended its defence pact and 'official' relations with Taiwan, and China undertook not to invade the island. Normalisation was followed in January–February by the first visit of a leading Chinese Communist, Deng Xiaoping, to the US. In response the Soviets backed Vietnam in its brief war with China in 1979 and strengthened their armed forces (including SS-20s) on the Chinese border.

16. SALT II talks and the 1979 Treaty

Although SALT I (1972) was always intended as an 'interim' agreement on strategic nuclear weapons, the negotiation of a second treaty proved a long one. Nixon's second administration (1972–74) was overshadowed by the Watergate scandal. The 1973 Middle East War undermined detente, Americans were concerned over new Soviet missile tests, and there were differences in Washington between Secretary of State Kissinger and Defense Secretary James Schlesinger. When Gerald Ford became president in August 1974, Kissinger tried to revive support for detente and a provisional SALT II deal was mapped out in November, at the Vladivostok Summit: there should be 'equal ceilings' of 2,400 long-range weapons (missile-launchers and bombers) for the US and USSR, of which 1,320 could have MIRV capability. (This was easier to defend in the US than the 'unequal' ceilings of SALT I.) Detailed talks in Geneva then quickened in pace but criticism of detente mounted in the US and technical problems prevented a treaty being finalised before the 1976 elections. The new administration under Carter at first seemed likely to pursue a treaty on the Vladivostok lines, as Secretary of State Vance wanted, but National Security Adviser Brzezinski and Defense Secretary Brown hoped to improve on Vladivostok, with bigger arms reductions. Relations were also upset by the 'normalisation' of relations between the US and China in December 1978, and a treaty was not finally signed by Carter and Brezhnev until 18 June 1979 (in Vienna).

Weapons developments which complicated the SALT II talks in the mid-1970s included:

(a) Soviet missile developments

In 1973 the Soviets tested a MIRV which, given their greater strategic arsenal and larger weapons (greater 'throw weight') might allow them eventually to overtake the US in total warheads. The Soviets were also developing new, large ICBMs, and submarine-launched missiles, possibly with the intention of attacking US nuclear forces in a first strike. Brezhnev insisted the USSR wanted 'nuclear parity', but American opponents of detente warned of a 'window of vulnerability' which would open up in the 1980s. Groups like the bipartisan 'Committee on the Present Danger' – formed November 1976 and including such Democratic foreign policy experts as Paul Nitze and Eugene Rostow – put pressure on Carter to improve the US defence position.

(b) 'Backfire' bomber

The NATO designation for the Tupolev-22M, which was designed to replace older medium-range bombers for use against Western Europe and China. It became an issue under Ford because the bomber *was* capable of reaching the US.

(c) US 'Cruise' missiles

Cheap, small, unmanned, jet-engined missiles became more accurate in the 1970s with the US 'Tomahawk', fitted with a 'terrain contour matching' guidance system that enabled it to avoid radar. Cruise missiles could be air-launched (ALCM), ground launched (GLCM) or sea-launched (SLCM), and were easy to conceal. The USSR was anxious to control them, as an important new element in the strategic equation in which the US was well ahead of Soviet technology.

(d) B-1 bomber

Developed to replace the aging B-52s as a strategic nuclear weapon, and intended to penetrate Soviet air defences, the B-1 bomber proved extremely costly and was abandoned by Carter in June 1977. Carter was criticised for this 'unilateral' action: he could have used the B-1 as a 'bargaining chip' in SALT II.

The SALT II Treaty confirmed the 'equal ceilings' of 2,400 long-range weapons agreed at Vladivostok, but also included three sub-ceilings: 1,320 launchers could be MIRVs *or* ALCMs; a maximum 1,200 could be MIRVs;

and only 820 MIRVs could be on ICBMs. There were also limits on the number of 'heavy' ICBMs, on deployment of new ICBMs and on the number of warheads in MIRVs. An additional protocol set limits on ALCM and GLCM deployment, and Brezhnev gave a written assurance that the 'Backfire' would not be used as an intercontinental bomber. SALT II was intended to last until 1985 and to be replaced by a SALT III Treaty, but in January 1980, following the Soviet invasion of Afghanistan, President Carter suspended its ratification. Nonetheless, the US and USSR largely continued to respect its terms.

17. Intermediate Nuclear Forces (INF) talks and the 1987 Treaty

The deployment of Soviet SS-20 missiles in the late 1970s, and the December 1979 'dual-track' decision (q.v.) by NATO on Cruise and Pershing II missiles, led to increasing public pressures for INF talks. Despite renewed Cold War tensions after 1979, such talks finally got underway between the superpowers in Geneva in November 1981. At that time President Reagan proposed the 'zero option' for the complete destruction of INF weapons but the USSR was reluctant to give up its SS-20s when NATO deployments were yet to take place. The INF talks went slowly until July 1982 when the delegation leaders in Geneva, Paul Nitze and Yuri Kvitsinsky, drew up the so-called 'Walk in the Woods Agreement', by which each superpower would restrict itself to only seventy-five intermediate-range weapons in Europe. The US Defense Department still felt that the deal gave the Soviets advantages, however, since they would have MIRVed SS-20s while the US would be restricted to slow-moving Cruise missiles. The opportunity for a deal was lost, and subsequently the USSR relied on threats and the peace movement in the West to undermine NATO's INF deployment. In November 1983, after Cruise and Pershing IIs arrived in Europe, the Soviets walked out of the INF talks.

The INF talks, like those on strategic arms, were finally revived in March 1985, (almost simultaneously with Gorbachev's arrival as Soviet leader). Progress quickened in January 1986 when Gorbachev accepted the 'zero option'. In February 1987 Gorbachev also agreed that the INF and START talks could be 'delinked' (as the US wanted) and that there should be on-site verification of disarmament. The treaty, signed by Reagan and Gorbachev in Washington on 8 December 1987, was a major *disarmament* (as opposed to arms *control*) agreement. It promised the elimination of all INF systems within three years, these being defined as missiles with a range between 500 and 5,500 kilometres. The USSR, with about 1,950 missiles, gave up more than the US, with 850. The USSR also accepted 'on site' verification. Although it was a dramatic step, the treaty only affected about 6 per cent of total nuclear arsenals.

18. German reunification, October 1990

The opening of the Berlin Wall in November 1990, and the changes in the East German government, reopened the question of German reunification. Chancellor Kohl of West Germany supported reunification and steered a careful course to achieve this. He was keen to show the Soviet Union that reunification would not pose a security threat. He also supported closer co-operation in the European Community, to demonstrate that Germany had given up its old nationalist ambitions. Remarks by Kohl, in early March 1990, called the German–Polish border into question, and provoked an international outcry. But he was quick to retreat on this point. His position was boosted by the victory of Lothar de Mazière's 'Alliance for Progress' in East Germany's first free elections since 1949.

Talks between the East and West German governments after March resulted in an agreement in May for an economic union, which took effect on 1 July, when the West German Deutschmark became an all-German currency. Meanwhile, on 4 May, the foreign ministers of East and West Germany, and the four occupation powers – the US, USSR, Britain and France – began the so-called 'two-plus-four talks' to discuss security issues and the end of occupation rights. The key issue in these talks was whether a reunited Germany could become a member of NATO – a right which the Western representatives were determined to confirm but the Soviets opposed. (This had been a point of contention in all talks on reunification since 1952.) In August the date for reunification was set for 3 October, with East Germany effectively accepting the West German constitution and political system. A two-plus-four treaty was finally signed in Moscow on 12 September. Key elements in the treaty were as follows.

(a) The new Germany was made up of West and East Germany, plus Berlin, where four-power occupation came to an end.
(b) Germany renounced all territorial claims beyond these borders, notably those against Poland.
(c) Any threat to the peace settlement became 'unconstitutional' under German law: Germany could only use force in line with its constitution and the UN Charter.
(d) Germany would restrict its armed forces by 1994 to 370,000 (a figure less than the current West German forces).
(e) West Germany's 1954 undertaking not to manufacture or use atomic, bacteriological or chemical weapons was confirmed.
(f) After 1994 German troops could be stationed on former East German soil, from which Soviet troops would withdraw: but, while Germany could remain in NATO, no other NATO

forces could enter former East German territory, nor could atomic weapons be based there.

In order to cement the agreement the West Germans had to enter talks on economic assistance with the USSR, which were finalised later. With reunification carried out amidst considerable celebration in October, the next West German elections, fixed for December, became an all-German contest in which Kohl easily triumphed.

19. Paris Accords and the Conventional Forces in Europe Treaty, 19–21 November 1990

The agreement in 1971–2 by NATO and the Warsaw Pact to hold a European Security Conference, was accompanied by Western insistence on conventional arms talks to reduce the Eastern bloc's predominance in ground forces. Such talks also helped to head off calls in the US, especially from Senator Mike Mansfield in 1971, for unilateral reductions in US forces in Europe. The 'Mutual Balanced Force Reduction' (MBFR) talks got underway in Vienna in 1973 but soon became bogged down in statistical differences about arms levels on each side. Later the MBFR talks became a victim of declining East–West relations. Only after the 1987 Intermediate Nuclear Forces Treaty did a revival of progress in the talks become possible.

In January 1989 a CSCE review meeting in Vienna agreed on a new round of 'conventional stability talks'. These were renamed in March, when discussions formally opened between NATO and the Warsaw Pact in Vienna, as the 'Conventional Forces in Europe' (CFE) talks. At the same time all CSCE members met in a 'Conference on Disarmament in Europe' to discuss confidence- and security-building measures. Later in the year the importance of these talks was boosted by the fall of Communist regimes in Eastern Europe which destroyed the old East – West divide and made it vital to build a new security system. In 1990, with the USSR troubled and the Red Army withdrawing from Czechoslovakia and Hungary (remaining only in East Germany and Poland), the West was in a stronger negotiating position in the talks. Therefore, Western leaders were unwilling to turn the CSCE into a powerful force, as Gorbachev wanted, or to wind down NATO.

The Paris Summit of thirty-four countries in November 1990, saw two major agreements:

(a) The CFE treaty between NATO and the Warsaw Pact (signed 19 November) generally followed NATO wishes and ended the Soviet armoured superiority in Europe. Precise limits on manpower were avoided in favour of restrictions on military hardware, such as tanks, artillery and aircraft. Limits were set on each alliance bloc, and there were sub-limits on the amount of arms held by single countries. Thus there would be 20,000 tanks for each alliance, with 13,300 for any individual state. The Soviets were able to escape limits in 'Europe' by shifting forces east of the Urals into Asia, something which led to accusations of 'cheating'. In effect the treaty recognised a decline in Soviet military power which had already occurred.

(b) Another Helsinki-style declaration by all CSCE states covered individual rights and guaranteed democratic freedoms, including private property, but once again had no means of implementing such high-sounding ideals. A small CSCE Secretariat was established and a 'Conflict Prevention Centre' was set up in Vienna, but their significance was initially unclear. Despite being heralded as 'the end of the Cold War' the Paris meeting proved something of a disappointment as Europeans recognised that declining East–West tensions and German reunification had not ended all the continent's problems. Eastern European states were in desperate need of economic aid.

20. Strategic Arms Reduction Talks and the 1991 START I Treaty

When the SALT II Treaty (q.v.) was signed in 1979 it was intended to follow it with SALT III talks, but the revival of Cold War tensions at the end of that year made early progress on these impossible. After Ronald Reagan became president in 1981 he renamed the strategic nuclear weapons talks START, in order to put the emphasis on *reductions* rather than mere *limitations* in numbers. START talks began between the super-powers in Geneva in June 1982, at which time the strategic arsenals of both sides were estimated as follows:

US   1,052 inter-continental, land-based missiles; 576 submarine-launched missiles; and 316 long-range bombers (with multiple warheads, about 9,000 warheads in total).

USSR   1,398 inter-continental, land-based missiles; 989 submarine-launched missiles; and 150 long-range bombers (about 8,400 warheads in total).

The START talks were complicated by new developments such as the MX missile (q.v.), by US questioning of earlier SALT deals and by Reagan's 'Strategic Defense Initiative' (March 1983). The talks were suspended in December 1983, after NATO's deployment of Cruise and Pershing missiles, and did not revive until Gorbachev became the Soviet leader in 1985. But the US then wanted to concentrate on an Intermediate Nuclear Forces Treaty (q.v.), which was signed in 1987. Under George Bush 'Star Wars' remained a problem for a time, limits on Cruise missiles had to be defined, and much time was spent in 1989–90 on the Conventional Forces in Europe Treaty (q.v.). The last technical problems were finally solved in July 1991, when Gorbachev was under pressure to agree to a treaty in order to obtain Western economic aid. START I was signed at the Moscow Summit of 31 July 1991. Its execution was made difficult by the break-up of the USSR and it did not enter into force (between the US and Russia) until 5 December 1994, after Belarus, Kazakhstan and Ukraine (where Soviet nuclear missiles had been based) acceded to the Non-proliferation Treaty, giving up their nuclear weapons. The main features of the treaty were as follows.

(a) Ceilings were placed on launchers (ICBMs, SLBMs and bombers) at 1,600 each, *and* warheads, at 6,000 each. Of these 6,000 warheads, 4,900 could be on ballistic systems, 1,540 on 'heavy' missiles and 1,100 on mobile, land-based weapons.

(b) Overall strategic arsenals were cut by about 30 per cent when certain special cases and omissions were considered. Total US missiles and bombs were reduced from 12,000 to about 9,000, the Soviets from 11,000 to about 7,000.

(c) Submarine-launched Cruise missiles were limited to 880 each under a separate agreement.

(d) The USSR agreed to reduce the warheads on 'heavy' SS-18s by 50 per cent.

(e) Limits would be carried out over eight years with verification procedures including on-site inspection.

(f) Nuclear technology would not be given to third parties (except for US sales of Trident missiles to Britain).

21. The START II Treaty (3 January 1993) and the end of Ukrainian nuclear weapons (14 January 1994)

Negotiated with remarkable speed by the US and Russia in Geneva during the second half of 1992, after being subject to an outline agreement between Bush and Yeltsin in June of that year, START II was signed just before Bush left office and was described by Yeltsin as the most significant arms control agreement ever. It represented a two-thirds cut in the nuclear arsenals of the US and Russia (START I had cut them by about one-third) and was accompanied by pressure on Ukraine to liquidate entirely its nuclear arsenal. At that time, with 1,600 warheads, Ukraine had the third largest nuclear arsenal in the world. A US–Russian–Ukrainian treaty to achieve the latter aim was finally signed a year later. This paved the way not only for the fulfilment of the START II Treaty, but also of

START I, which had been signed when Russia and Ukraine were still part of the USSR. Thereafter it was up to Russia alone to fulfil the terms entered into by the Soviet Union.

START II was, as with previous SALT and START Treaties, a complex document, but its main terms were as follows:

(a) land-based ICBMs with multiple warheads (MIRVs) and land-based 'heavy' ICBMs to be completely eliminated by 2003 (but single-warhead ICBMs would remain);

(b) the total strategic nuclear systems on each side should not exceed 4,250 (and could be lower) after *seven* years;

(c) the total number of strategic systems on each side should not exceed 3,500 (and could be as low as 3,000) after *ten* years;

(d) within the limits under (c) (that is, after ten years) up to 1,750 systems could be submarine-launched ballistic missiles;

(e) an inspection system was agreed.

22. NATO enlargement and the May 1997 Russia–NATO Founding Act

The end of the Cold War and collapse of the Soviet Union led to growing pressure from some former members of the Warsaw Pact to join NATO. This would help tie them to the West, providing them with security guarantees and military assistance, but it provoked deep suspicion in Moscow, especially when former Soviet republics like the Baltic states were interested in NATO membership. Reluctant to alienate either the Russians or the newly independent eastern Europeans, NATO was cautious to develop a policy. In January 1994 the alliance launched its Partnership for Peace (PFP) programme, offering military co-operation short of full membership (including joint training, consultation, etc). But NATO also held out the prospect of full membership in future. Over the following year numerous neutral states, ex-members of the Warsaw Pact and former Soviet republics signed PFP agreements but, in December 1994, Russia refused because NATO would not rule out enlargement. A PFP agreement with Russia was only made in 1995 following a Clinton–Yeltsin meeting.

NATO agreed to defer a decision on enlargement until after the Russian Presidential election in 1996, for fear of stirring up nationalist and Communist opposition to Yeltsin. Then, in late 1996, negotiations began on an agreement to govern future relations with Russia. The result was the 1997 Founding Act which stated:

(a) NATO and Russia do 'not consider each other adversaries', they will overcome confrontation and build co-operation;

(b) Russia agrees to NATO's enlargement eastwards;

(c) a permanent Russia–NATO command will be created to discuss security problems (but without any Russian veto on NATO actions);

(d) NATO has 'no intention' to deploy nuclear weapons or 'substantial', permanent troop numbers in new member states.

The wording of the agreement was weaker than Russia hoped and Yeltsin made clear that he was still not happy with enlargement, but, at its Madrid Summit in July 1997, NATO invited Poland, the Czech Republic and Hungary to become members, effective as of April 1999. The door was 'left open' for others to join and in January 1998 Clinton confirmed that this could include the Baltic states.

Major Treaties and Organisations involving the Western Powers

23. Treaty of Dunkirk, March 1947

An Anglo-French alliance had been proposed since 1944 as a way to renew the *entente cordiale*. The Treaty of Dunkirk was a fifty-year alliance directed against a revival of German aggression, but also promising wider co-operation. It was closely based on the Anglo-Soviet and Franco-Soviet alliances in order not to antagonise Moscow. Sometimes seen as the first step to NATO, it had only short-term significance.

24. Marshall Plan 1947–52 and organisation of European economic recovery

An economic recovery programme for Europe was proposed by US Secretary of State George Marshall in a speech at Harvard University in June 1947. The speech followed growing US concern about the economic situation in Western Europe, where local Communists could hope to exploit the sense of popular demoralisation. The US was also concerned to keep a healthy trade partner in Europe. American attempts to foster a new, thriving world economic system, through such institutions as the World Bank and IMF, had not progressed far and a situation known as the 'dollar gap' had arisen: Europeans needed to import US raw materials and capital equipment but had little to export to America, and so ran up large dollar debts.

The Marshall Plan actually amounted to little in detail other than an offer of assistance to Europe *if* the Europeans themselves co-operated together and drew up a comprehensive recovery programme. It was not clear at first whether East Europeans would be included, but in talks in Paris in June–July between the Soviet, British and French foreign ministers, the Soviets criticised the Marshall Plan as likely to undermine the independence of European countries. Subsequently the Soviets kept Eastern European states out of the Plan. At British and French invitation, sixteen West European countries met in Paris between July and September 1947 to draw up a recovery plan, which was submitted to the US. (The sixteen were: Britain, France, Belgium, Holland, Luxembourg, Italy, Eire,

Portugal, Denmark, Norway, Sweden, Iceland, Finland, Austria, Greece and Turkey. West Germany was represented by its allied military governors.) The US agreed to supply certain countries, including France and Italy, with 'interim aid', in late 1947. This helped France and Italy to cope with a series of Communist-inspired strikes, and helped the Italian Christian Democrats to victory in the April 1948 general election. The 'European Recovery Programme' lasted for four years, providing seventeen billion dollars in aid. The US established an 'Economic Co-operation Administration' under the businessman Paul Hoffman, to handle the programme, and the Europeans established an 'Organisation of European Economic Co-operation' (OEEC) which undertook the task of sharing the aid out. The Plan forced European countries to work together, to lower trade barriers and to aid each other. Growth was also stimulated after 1950 by the Korean War. By 1952 Europe was at the start of a period of sustained growth. The OEEC remained in being, and in 1961 was joined by the US and Canada to become the Organisation of Economic Co-operation and Development (OECD).

25. Organisation of American States (OAS), April 1948

Formed by a conference in Bogota, the OAS followed previous Pan-American conferences and included most states in the Western hemisphere, Canada being the principal exception. Under the 1947 Rio Pact, also called the Pact of Petropolis, OAS states were committed to provide mutual aid if one was attacked. The OAS included regular ministerial meetings and was effectively dominated by the US, which used the organisation to condemn Communism (notably at the 1954 Caracas Conference) and to ostracise Castro's Cuba in 1962 (at the Punta del Este Conference).

26. Brussels Pact, March 1948/Western European Union, October 1954

The extension of the March 1947 Anglo-French alliance to Belgium, Holland and Luxembourg was proposed in January 1948 as a first step to building West European co-operation after the breakdown of talks with the USSR. The five Western European countries also wanted to demonstrate to the US that they were ready to work for their own defence. The negotiations were quickened after the Communist coup in Czechoslovakia in February and completed in March. The treaty, signed in Brussels, included commitments to non-military co-operation (cultural, financial, political) and bound the five countries to go to war if any member was attacked. No enemy was specified, so that the treaty could become effective against both Germany (previously seen as the most likely enemy) or the USSR (now seen as a more likely threat). The Brussels Pact states established a ministerial council and their own military command structure, they jointly negotiated with America and Canada about the creation of NATO (q.v.) and laid the basis in 1949 for the Council of Europe (q.v.). NATO absorbed many of the Brussels Pact's functions in 1950–51. In October 1954, at a NATO meeting in Paris, it was agreed to turn the Brussels Pact into the 'Western European Union' with West Germany and Italy as new members. The WEU had little significance for the next thirty years. But Spain and Portugal, both members of NATO, joined the WEU in November 1988 and in the 1990s, when Greece also joined, it was seen as a possible centre for European Community (EC) military co-operation in the new security situation created by the collapse of the Warsaw Pact. Links were created between the WEU and the EC in the 1992 Maastricht Treaty, but the British in particular were keen that this should not damage the primacy of NATO in Western defence.

27. North Atlantic Treaty Organisation, April 1949

Following several requests from European countries, talks on a military alliance began between the US, Canada and the Brussels Pact (q.v.) states in Washington in July 1948. By September it was agreed to make an Atlantic Pact, partly because of fears that war could break out in Europe and partly because European states needed the psychological reassurance of a US security commitment. Work on a treaty quickened after the re-election of President Truman, and it was signed on 4 April 1949. As well as the original negotiating powers, the pact was joined by Norway, Italy, Portugal, Iceland and Denmark. The pact was later extended to Greece and Turkey (1952), West Germany (1955) and Spain (1982, confirmed by a referendum in 1986). Its terms included a commitment by all members to provide mutual assistance to any member which was attacked. But in order to protect the US Senate's right to make war, this pledge was only to be carried out in accordance with members' constitutions. This led European members to want a continued US military presence in Europe, to ensure that the Senate would declare war in the event of a Soviet attack. The Pact also provided for regular meetings of a ministerial-level Atlantic Council. Non-military co-operation (under Article 2) remained largely undeveloped.

The outbreak of the Korean War in mid-1950 led to the bolstering of NATO defences with a major rearmament effort, US reinforcements to Europe and the appointment (December 1950) of Dwight Eisenhower as the first Supreme Allied Commander Europe (SACEUR). However, US insistence that West Germany should be rearmed at this point led to bitter arguments in the alliance and to the ill-fated attempt to create a European Defence Community (q.v.). German rearmament was only finally achieved in 1955–56, by which time NATO had given up hope of matching the USSR in conventional forces. Military plans in the late 1950s relied on ground forces ('The Shield') holding a Soviet assault until US nuclear weapons ('The Sword') were brought to bear. Controversy over the control of nuclear weapons led to the still-born proposal for a Multilateral Force (q.v.) in 1961–64. Subsequently NATO developed a doctrine of 'graduated response' to a Soviet invasion.

After 1958 NATO was disrupted by the desire of France's Charles de Gaulle to be more independent of the US. He called for a US–British–French 'directorate' in NATO (1958), then pulled the French Mediterranean fleet out of NATO (1959). Finally, in 1966 de Gaulle withdrew French troops from the integrated command and forced the removal of the Supreme Headquarters Allied Powers Europe (SHAPE) from Fontainebleau to Brussels (1967). France remained a signatory of the North Atlantic Treaty, however. Her policy of remaining outside the integrated command was also adopted for a time in the 1970s by Greece (after the 1974 Turkish invasion of Cyprus), and in the 1980s by Spain.

After 1967, following the Harmel Report, NATO undertook to pursue detente with the Warsaw Pact as well as continuing its traditional security role. Following this, in 1971, the Atlantic Council took up long-standing Warsaw Pact proposals for a European Security Conference. Serious strains were caused in the early 1970s between the US and European members of NATO by Vietnam, by economic problems (especially inflation and currency instability), by the growing strength of the European Community and by calls in America (notably in 1966–73 by Senator Mike Mansfield) for a reduction of US spending in Europe. Henry Kissinger's hopes of resolving NATO's problems in 1973, by making it the 'Year of Europe' came to nothing: France suspected the US of wanting to reconstitute its domination over Europe and events were soon overtaken by the October Middle East War. NATO remained troubled by the vacillating policies of Jimmy Carter and the 'new' Cold War after 1979, but was still basically united against the Warsaw Pact menace. In 1990 NATO achieved its long-standing aim of embracing a reunited Germany within the Alliance. The London Summit Meeting of NATO leaders in July 1990 declared NATO to be 'the most successful defensive alliance in history', said that Cold War tensions had ended and planned to cut back Western armed forces. (See also NATO enlargement and the Russia–NATO Founding Act, pp. 168–9 above.)

28. Council of Europe, May 1949

The Council sprang from proposals in May 1948, from the Hague Congress of European federalist groups, for the creation of a European parliament. Despite British doubts about the effectiveness of such an institution, the French and Belgians put the idea to the Brussels Pact.

Negotiations led in May 1949 to a Statute, signed in London by most West European democracies, which created a 'Council of Europe', to meet in annual sessions. The body was made up of a Council of Ministers and an Assembly. The Assembly, formed from national delegations, had only consultative powers: it could debate and vote on problems, but not force governments to take action. Nonetheless, particularly in the early years, its votes carried moral weight. It established the European Court of Human Rights. It also helped to draw ex-enemy states, such as West Germany, back into the community of nations, and condemned oppressive regimes, such as the military government in Greece (1967–74). After 1989 membership of the Council was seen as the first step towards drawing Eastern and Western Europe back together.

29. Australia–New Zealand–US Pact, September 1951

Signed one week before the Japanese Peace Treaty (q.v.), the ANZUS Pact promised military co-operation between the three countries, consultation on security issues and united action in the event any member was attacked, although (to protect the rights of the US Senate) this would only be done in accordance with each country's constitution. The alliance was largely the result of the US need to reassure the two Pacific democracies about Japanese revival. However, like America's treaties with Japan and the Philippines (made at the same time) ANZUS also represented an attempt to build an anti-Communist system in the East Asia–Pacific region. Finally the alliance reflected the decline of British power in the Far East, with two important Commonwealth states turning to the US for protection. ANZUS functioned well until the early 1980s when it was disrupted by US–New Zealand disagreements on the deployment of nuclear weapons. In August 1986 the US suspended its obligations to New Zealand under the Pact.

30. Japanese Peace Treaty, September 1951

After the formal surrender in September 1945, Japan, while retaining its own government, was placed under American occupation, with General Douglas MacArthur as Supreme Commander. The first US attempts to organise a peace conference on Japan in 1947 came to nothing, the Soviets arguing that this was the responsibility of the Council of Foreign Ministers (q.v.), but in April 1950 President Truman gave the work of drafting a treaty to the Republican lawyer John Foster Dulles. By then the US was committed to the economic revival of Japan, a process which quickened after the Korean War broke out. Wartime hatreds between US and Japan had subsided and America's wartime ally, China, had now become Communist. Japan's prime minister, Shigeru Yoshida, was strongly pro-Western. In September 1950 the US gave a proposal for a Japanese Peace Treaty to the fifteen-member Far Eastern Commission (established in 1945 and made up of leading countries who had fought Japan). Many Far Eastern states were doubtful about Japanese revival and the USSR was critical of America's action, but in July 1951 the Americans invited interested states to a peace conference in San Francisco. (Communist China, not recognised by the US, was excluded.) The USSR, along with Czechoslovakia and Poland, attended the conference and tried to have Japan 'neutralised'; but, after failing to achieve this, refused to sign the treaty. A state of war between the USSR and Japan continued to exist until October 1956 when Khruschev and Ichiro Hatoyama agreed to open diplomatic relations.

The other countries signed a Peace Treaty with Japan in September 1951. The terms were as follows:

(a) Japan's territorial losses since 1945 were confirmed. At that time Korea had become independent, Formosa (Taiwan) had been returned to China and south Sakhalin had been lost to the USSR.

(b) The Ryukyu and Bonin islands, including Iwo Jima, were left under US administration. Iwo Jima was not restored to Japan until 1972.

(c) The principle that Japan should pay reparations remained, but in fact no reparations were demanded from her.

(d) Japan agreed to settle disputes peacefully and accept the UN Charter. (The 1946 Japanese constitution already forbade the creation of armed forces.)

Also in September 1951 the US and Japan concluded a security treaty which allowed the former to keep its military bases in Japan. In 1960 (by which time Japan had 'self-defence forces') this treaty became a more equal, mutual security pact.

31. European Defence Community, 1952–54

A long debate, which dominated the Western Alliance in the early 1950s, centred on the question of German rearmament. West German rearmament was first seriously suggested by the US in September 1950, at a meeting of Western foreign ministers in New York. It was intended to deal with the threat posed by Soviet conventional arms superiority in Europe. The Korean War had recently begun, West Germany lay in the front line of any Soviet assault, the US public wanted to see Europe do all possible for its own defence and the Soviets had formed an armed 'police-force' in East Germany. To induce West Europeans to accept German rearmament, the US put the proposal as part of a 'package deal' which also included additional US forces in Europe and the appointment of an American Supreme Commander for NATO. The idea of West German rearmament drew condemnation from the Eastern bloc: some feared the Kremlin would launch a preventive war to stop it. There were doubts about rearmament too in Germany itself, where pacifists, socialists and anti-militarists united to oppose the proposal under the slogan '*Ohne Mich*' (without me). In Western Europe, the French in particular opposed the idea, having experienced three German invasions in one lifetime (1870, 1914 and 1940).

In October the French produced the 'Pleven Plan' (named after premier René Pleven) for German rearmament only in a European army. The idea was that a federal European army, with a European minister of defence, would prevent Germany having its own independent general staff, and would thus prevent a revival of German militarism. In December 1950, after considerable debate, a NATO meeting in Brussels decided that France could proceed with the European army proposal. Talks began in Paris in February 1951 between France, West Germany, Italy, Belgium and Luxembourg, later joined by Holland – the same countries which formed the European Community (q.v.). Despite doubts about the military efficiency of a federal army, the US and Britain supported the proposal and a treaty was signed in May 1952 creating a European Defence Community (EDC). But it took several months to secure ratification in Germany, and in 1953–54 doubts about German rearmament remained strong in France. French politicians questioned the need for German rearmament at a time when the Korean War had ended. There was also opposition to the 'surrender' of French forces to a European institution.

In August 1954 the French National Assembly defeated EDC and, after four long years, threw the German rearmament issue back into the melting pot. After a critical few weeks, NATO finally solved its differences at a conference in London during September–October. Here it was agreed to rearm West Germany as a sovereign member of NATO, but on condition that Germany agreed not to possess atomic, bacteriological and chemical ('ABC') weapons. A new institution, the Western European Union, was created which preserved a 'European dimension' within NATO, and Britain undertook to maintain a certain level of forces in Europe (designed to help France to control German ambitions in future). This settlement was approved by the NATO Council in Paris in October and the agreements entered into force in May 1955.

32. Balkan Pact, August 1954

An alliance between Greece, Turkey and Yugoslavia, known as the Balkan Pact, was made at Bled on 9 August 1954. All three countries were fearful of Soviet power in the Balkans: Greece and Turkey were NATO members and Yugoslavia had broken free of Soviet domination in 1948 under Tito. The Pact built on earlier military talks (since 1952), was encouraged by NATO and promised co-operation in the military and non-military fields. But the Pact's significance was rapidly undermined when Tito became reconciled to the Soviets in 1955. Greece and Turkey then fell out over the future of Cyprus. The Pact became defunct on 24 June 1960.

33. South-East Asian Treaty Organisation (SEATO), September 1954

A treaty to protect South-East Asia had first been proposed by the US in spring 1954, during the last stages of the First Indo-China War. An alliance was signed on 8 September in Manila. Most newly independent nations in the region refused to take part, and it was therefore made up of Western states (US, Britain, France, Australia, New Zealand) and their close allies (the Philippines, Thailand and Pakistan). SEATO had a central headquarters in Bangkok, held joint military exercises and included intelligence co-operation against Communists, but it never gained widespread respect in the region. Its creation antagonised China. The treaty offered protection to certain non-members, including Laos, Cambodia and South Vietnam, but only committed members to 'consult' about Communist expansionism. Only a few SEATO members (Australia, Thailand, Philippines) joined the US with small forces in defending South Vietnam from Communism after 1965. The organisation was wound down in the 1970s.

34. Baghdad Pact (February 1955) and Central Treaty Organisation (CENTO)

The Baghdad Pact was partly the result of British efforts to maintain its position as the leading power in the Middle East. In 1945 British power in the region was based on the Suez Canal, but efforts to renew the 1936 Anglo-Egyptian treaty failed and the Egyptian government rejected a British proposal in 1951 to create a Middle East defence organisation. Britain had a loyal Arab ally in Iraq, where there were British air bases. In February 1955 Iraq's prime minister, the conservative Nuri el-Said, signed a treaty in Baghdad with Adnan Menderes of Turkey, another pro-Western Middle Eastern state. In April Britain linked itself to this arrangement by signing a new Anglo-Iraqi treaty. When Pakistan and Iran joined, the British had formed an alliance of all states in the 'northern tier' of the Middle East, forming a barrier against Soviet expansion.

From the outset the Baghdad Pact was troubled. Radical Arab states such as Egypt criticised it, and even the US refused to join. The 1956 Suez Crisis exposed British weakness in the region, and in 1958 radicals overthrew the monarchy in Iraq – the only Arab member of the Pact. In October 1958 the Pact's headquarters moved from Baghdad to Ankara, Turkey. Iraq formally left the Pact in March 1959, but there was an attempt to rejuvenate it. The US made military agreements with the remaining members, and in August 1959 the alliance was renamed the Central Treaty Organisation (CENTO), because it was in a central position between NATO and SEATO. The alliance remained a small group of pro-Western states, lacking much military effectiveness and of little relevance to Middle Eastern affairs. It was wound down in the late 1970s.

35. European Community, March 1957

Numerous factors helped to create an interest in European unity in the late 1940s: the Second World War led many to argue that the destructive division of Europe into nation-states must end; economic co-operation seemed to promise a large, expanding, single market; some Europeans hoped to create a 'third force' to match the two superpowers. The US, keen to create a stable and wealthy bastion against Communism, gave encouragement to the unity ideal after 1947 with the Marshall Plan (q.v.). Britain, still seeing itself as a Great Power with a world role, refused to merge its identity with the Continent. France, however, proved ready to take up the leadership of the European unity movement, partly as a way of controlling German nationalist ambitions. West German politicians such as Konrad Adenauer were ready to join in the unity movement as a way to tie the new Germany to other liberal democracies and so prevent a revival of militarism and Fascism.

The first step to a 'European Community', in which member states surrendered some sovereignty to common institutions, was taken in May 1950 when France launched the Schuman Plan. The Plan united the coal and steel industries of France, West Germany, Italy, Belgium, Holland and Luxembourg in a European Coal–Steel Community (ECSC) founded in Luxembourg in 1952. In 1950–54 the same states failed to create a European Defence Community (q.v.), but in 1955–57 they negotiated the creation of two new communities: the European Atomic Energy Authority (EURATOM) and the European Economic Community (EEC) were formed by the March 1957 Treaties of Rome. The ECSC, EURATOM and EEC were merged into a single Community in 1968. The EEC, the most important institution, included a strong Council of Ministers (representing member governments) and a weak parliament (not directly elected until 1979), as well as an executive Commission based in Brussels.

In the 1960s France's Charles de Gaulle, reluctant to surrender power to Community institutions, forced the 'Luxembourg Compromise' by which members could veto important decisions. In the 1970s and early 1980s the EEC, like the rest of the Western economy, was beset by low growth and inflation. However, the EEC also had its successes. In the 1960s it created a single trade area over the six member states and achieved good growth rates. In 1973 this was extended to Britain, Ireland and Denmark; later it was joined by Greece (1981), Spain and Portugal (1986), Austria, Sweden and Finland (1995). Subsequently, the 1988 Single European Act proposed to create free movement of goods, capital and labour by 1993, and strengthened the EC's central institutions. The 1992 Maastricht Treaty marked a further strengthening and extension of EC activities and paved the way for a single currency among most members in 1999. It also led the EC to become the 'European Union' in 1993. The Community arguably helped to sustain democracy and boost confidence in Western Europe. The economic success of the EEC (especially West Germany) and of Japan helped to undermine US economic dominance of the West in the 1960s, and led to various schemes for 'trilateral' co-operation between the US, Western Europe and Japan in the 1970s. One result was the series of annual Summit meetings between the 'Group of Seven' (G-7) major industrial states (US, Japan, West Germany, France, Britain, Italy, Canada) after 1975, which become the G-8 (with Russia) in 1997.

36. Multilateral (nuclear) Force, 1961–64

In 1960 NATO commander Lauris Norstad favoured the creation of a 'multilateral atomic authority' within the Alliance, and the new Kennedy administration took up the MLF idea in earnest in 1961 as part of its 'Grand Design' for new US–European relations. The MLF could (a) help in overcoming resentment at America's control over the West's largest nuclear arsenal; (b) induce Britain and France to give up the idea of independent nuclear arsenals (thus reducing nuclear proliferation), and (c) forestall West German attempts to obtain a nuclear arsenal (which would have upset the Soviet Union).

NATO members, especially West Germany, expressed interest in the MLF, although many questioned the military viability of a mixed-manned force. America would retain control over most Western nuclear missiles, and Britain and France were reluctant to surrender their independent deterrents. The proposal was abandoned by Lyndon Johnson. In December 1966, however, a Nuclear Planning Group was formed within NATO at ministerial level, which allowed for consultation (though not effective decision-making) on nuclear matters. Abandonment of the MLF helped bring the Non-proliferation Treaty with the USSR, which had consistently argued that the MLF effectively gave nuclear arms to Germany.

37. Camp David Agreement, September 1978

After the 1973 Arab–Israeli War (q.v.), Kissinger's 'shuttle diplomacy' separated the armed forces of the two sides but left deep political divisions between them: the Arabs refused to recognise Israel; Israel retained territories it had conquered in the 1967 Six-Day War (q.v.). In 1977 President Carter decided to play an active role in the Middle East, despite the high risk of failure. Attempts to introduce the Soviets into the peace process in October 1977 upset Israel which also refused to deal with the Palestinian Liberation Organisation and was determined to hold onto the West Bank and Gaza. Instead the hardline government of Menachem Begin expressed a willingness to withdraw from the Sinai peninsula in return for recognition by Egypt's Anwar El-Sadat. In response Sadat flew to Jerusalem in November for talks. Despite serious difficulties, Egyptian–Israeli talks continued in 1978, culminating in the thirteen days of talks at Camp David between Carter, Sadat and Begin in September. The result was an agreement on a peace treaty (signed in March 1979), by which Egypt recognised Israel's existence and Israel gradually withdrew from Sinai. The agreement was a surprising success in itself, but the peace process (from which the USSR was excluded) led to Egypt's isolation in the Arab world, and no wider settlement was possible until the 1990s, when Norway helped to mediate an agreement (announced in August 1993) on the creation of a Palestinian Authority in the Israeli-occupied West Bank and Gaza.

Major Treaties and Organisations involving the Soviet Bloc

38. Communist International, 1919–43

Founded in March 1919 by Lenin to supersede the Socialist Internationals (first founded in 1864), the 'Comintern' was intended as a front organisation for Communist parties which would foment revolution across the globe. Various Communist parties were established over the next few years, based on the Bolshevik model. But 'world revolution' never occurred and the Comintern soon effectively became a vehicle of Soviet foreign policy. The organisation was disbanded by Stalin in 1943 to please his Anglo-American allies, but much of its machinery continued to exist.

39. Ribbentrop–Molotov Pact, 1939–41

This was an agreement made between Germany's dictator Adolf Hitler and the Soviet leader Josef Stalin, negotiated by their foreign ministers in August 1939, just before the outbreak of the Second World War. The Pact ended the attempts of Britain and France to reach a deal with the USSR themselves, and freed Hitler to invade Poland without fear of Soviet attack. The Pact also allowed Germany to receive large amounts of raw materials from Russia until June 1941, when Hitler broke the Pact and invaded the USSR. For Stalin, the Pact offered peace and the chance to obtain territories. Under the agreement with Hitler the Soviets not only obtained half of Poland, but were free to annex land from Romania, to absorb the Baltic states (Estonia, Latvia and Lithuania) and to launch the 1939–40 'Winter War' against Finland.

40. Communist Information Bureau (Cominform), 1947–56

Created at a conference in Sklarska Poreba, Poland, in September 1947, the Cominform was widely seen in the West as a reconstituted Comintern (q.v.), designed to foment revolution. Its establishment was accompanied by a more vitriolic line in anti-Western propaganda than had previously been seen from Moscow. There were calls for Socialist unity against US 'imperialism' and a new analysis of international affairs was presented by the Soviet representative, Zhdanov, who saw the world as being divided into 'two camps', Socialist and Capitalist. Cominform also seems to have been an attempt to respond to the Marshall Plan by uniting Eastern bloc states behind the USSR (previously Poland and Czechoslovakia had shown an interest in accepting US aid) and disrupting the US aid programme, by forcing the French and Italian Communist parties to abandon the 'parliamentary road' to power and launch strike action.

Cominform was made up of Communist parties, not governments, and its membership was restricted to certain European parties, mainly in Eastern Europe: USSR, Bulgaria, Czechoslovakia, East Germany, France, Hungary, Italy, Poland, Romania and Yugoslavia. It did not therefore aim at world revolution. It created an 'Information Bureau', designed to exchange information among members, in Belgrade. The location of the Cominform in Belgrade and the exclusion of Albania from the organisation were apparently designed to please Tito of Yugoslavia, but in 1948 the organisation was used by the USSR as a vehicle to condemn Tito, who split from the Soviet bloc. Cominform remained the principal organisation for Eastern bloc political co-operation until 1955, when the Warsaw Pact was founded and Khruschev began to re-open links to Tito. The organisation was then wound down.

41. Council for Mutual Economic Aid (Comecon), 1949–91

Largely a reaction to the American Marshall Plan, Comecon was founded in January 1949 as an economic organisation for the Soviet bloc. The organisation did little in its early years: trade within the bloc was dominated by the USSR, and each country created its own Stalinist economy (with state-controlled agriculture and concentration on heavy industrial production). Under Khruschev in 1961–62 there was an attempt to develop the 'international division of labour', and in 1963 talk of a supranational economic institution for Comecon. This was largely in response to the success of the EEC. But other Comecon states were resentful of Soviet domination and opposition to Khruschev's schemes was led by Gheorghieu-Dej of Romania. The 'Complex Programme' of 1971 led to more joint projects and information exchanges between members, an investment bank was created (1970–72) and so too was an atomic energy organisation. But more effective integration was undermined by the continued reticence of Romania and the entry into the organisation of underdeveloped countries such as Mongolia (1962), Cuba (1972) and Vietnam (1978). The organisation had a top-heavy bureaucracy and never developed a common external trade policy. Comecon was wound down in 1991.

42. Sino-Soviet Alliance, February 1950

In December 1949, two months after his victory in the Chinese Civil War (q.v.), Mao Zedong travelled to Moscow to make an alliance with Stalin. The treaty took several weeks to negotiate, and was made up of several elements.

(a) Both signatories would assist each other if Japan, or countries allied with her, adopted a policy of aggression. This served as a warning against the revival of Japanese militarism at a time when the US was reconstructing the Japanese economy.

(b) The USSR agreed to end the rights, obtained after the 1945 Yalta Conference, to control Port Arthur, Dairen and the railways in Manchuria.

(c) The USSR made a small loan to China, which was evidently less than China wanted.

(d) The Soviets took a share in joint-stock companies in China and thereby gained greater influence in the Chinese economy.

(e) The treaty was to last thirty years.

Although it gave China reassurance in foreign affairs and some economic aid, the treaty did not prevent the Sino-Soviet split (q.v.).

43. Warsaw Pact, 1955–91

The 'Treaty of Friendship, Co-operation and Mutual Aid' was signed by the USSR, Bulgaria, Czechoslovakia, Poland, Romania and Albania in the Polish capital on 14 May 1955, only a week after West German entry into NATO to which it was seen as a riposte. The twenty-year treaty (renewed 1975 for ten years and 1985 for twenty) was designed to provide for mutual assistance in the event of an attack on any member and for consultation on political and military matters. The Pact superseded previous bilateral treaties of mutual assistance. It established a secretariat, a political committee and a joint command structure based in Moscow, with a Soviet Supreme Commander (initially Marshal Koniev). A Chinese representative attended the signing ceremony and pledged his country's support, and Mongolia was associated with the Pact as an observer. The treaty was extended to East Germany (1956) and was followed by treaties (1956–57) which confirmed the Soviet right to base troops in Eastern Europe.

The Warsaw Pact closely mirrored NATO in form and its signature was followed by Soviet suggestions that both alliances be disbanded. Although the treaty pledged its members to settle international disputes peacefully, its commitment to 'fraternal mutual aid' was used to justify

Soviet intervention in Hungary in 1956 and Czechoslovakia in 1968. Fear of Soviet domination led Romania to distance itself from the Pact. Not being central to the Pact's defences, Romania was able to secure the withdrawal of Soviet troops (1958). Albania left the Pact in September 1968. The Pact held regular meetings at ministerial level and had an important role in demonstrating the political unity of the Eastern bloc, especially after the dissolution of Cominform. The 1989 revolutions in Eastern Europe, alongside the INF Treaty (1987), conventional force reductions (1990), Soviet troop withdrawals from Eastern Europe and German reunification all called the value of the Pact into question, and it was formally disbanded on 1 July 1991.

SECTION FIVE

Major office-holders
(to December 1997)

Unless otherwise stated, the dates cited in the lists below are date of appointment.

1. United States

Presidents

Dates mark beginning of term in office.

Franklin D. Roosevelt (Democrat)	4 March 1933
Harry S. Truman (Democrat)	12 April 1945
Dwight D. Eisenhower (Republican)	20 January 1953
John F. Kennedy (Democrat)	20 January 1961
Lyndon B. Johnson (Democrat)	22 November 1963
Richard M. Nixon (Republican)	20 January 1969
Gerald R. Ford (Republican)	9 August 1974
Jimmy Carter (Democrat)	20 January 1977
Ronald W. Reagan (Republican)	20 January 1981
George H.W. Bush (Republican)	20 January 1989
William J. (Bill) Clinton (Democrat)	20 January 1993

Secretaries of State

Edward R. Stettinius	30 November 1944
James F. Byrnes	2 July 1945
George C. Marshall	8 January 1947
Dean G. Acheson	21 January 1949
John F. Dulles	21 January 1953
Christian A. Herter	22 April 1959
Dean Rusk	21 January 1961
William P. Rogers	22 January 1969
Henry A. Kissinger	22 September 1973
Cyrus R. Vance	23 January 1977
Edmund S. Muskie	3 May 1980
Alexander M. Haig	21 January 1981
George P. Schultz	25 June 1982
James A. Baker	20 January 1989
Lawrence S. Eagleburger	23 August 1992
Warren Christopher	20 January 1993
Madeleine Albright	20 January 1997

National Security Advisers

The first 'Special Assistant for National Security Affairs' was General Robert Cutler, appointed January 1953.

Subsequently the post was held by Dillon Anderson (1 April 1955), Cutler again (20 January 1957) and Gordon Gray (21 July 1958). But the position, commonly referred to as National Security Adviser, only became of great political importance after 1961.

McGeorge Bundy	20 January 1961
Walt W. Rostow	1 April 1966
Henry A. Kissinger	20 January 1969
Major General Brent Scowcroft	2 November 1975
Zbigniew Brzezinski	20 January 1977
Richard V. Allen	20 January 1981
William Clark	4 January 1982
Robert C. McFarlane	17 October 1983
Admiral John M. Poindexter	4 December 1985
Frank Carlucci	2 December 1986
Lieutenant-General Colin Powell	5 November 1987
Major-General Brent Scowcroft	20 January 1989
N. Anthony Lake	20 January 1993
Samuel R. Burger	5 December 1996

Secretaries of Defense

James V. Forrestal (first appointee to the post)	26 July 1947
Louis A. Johnson	28 March 1949
George C. Marshall	21 September 1950
Robert A. Lovett	17 September 1951
Charles E. Wilson	28 January 1953
Neil E. McElroy	9 October 1957
Thomas G. Gates	2 December 1959
Robert S. McNamara	21 January 1961
Clark M. Clifford	3 January 1968
Melvin P. Laird	22 January 1969
Elliott L. Richardson	2 February 1973
James R. Schlesinger	2 July 1973
Donald H. Rumsfeld	20 November 1975
Harold Brown	23 January 1977
Caspar W. Weinberger	20 January 1981
Frank Carlucci	5 November 1987
Richard Cheney	10 March 1989
Les Aspin	20 January 1993
William J. Perry	20 January 1994
William S. Cohen	20 January 1997

Directors of the Central Intelligence Agency

Rear-Admiral Roscoe H. Hillenkoetter	29 August 1947
Lieutenant-General Walter Bedell Smith	1 October 1950
Allen W. Dulles	7 January 1953
John A. McCone	27 September 1961
Vice-Admiral William F. Rabone	11 April 1965
Richard Helms	19 June 1966
James R. Schlesinger	21 December 1972
William E. Colby	10 May 1973
George H.W. Bush	2 November 1975
Admiral Stansfield Turner	7 February 1977
William J. Casey	20 January 1981
William H. Webster	3 February 1987
Robert M. Gates	20 January 1991
R. James Woolsey	20 January 1993
John Deutch	10 March 1995
George J. Tenet	19 March 1997

Chairmen of the Joint Chiefs of Staff

The post was created as a statutory appointment on 10 August 1949. Admiral William D. Leahy had fulfilled a similar function as 'Chief of Staff to the Commander-in-Chief' since 1942. Leahy became ill and had been replaced on a 'temporary' basis in February 1949 by General Dwight D. Eisenhower.

General Omar N. Bradley	August 1949
Admiral Arthur W. Radford	August 1953
General Nathan F. Twining	August 1957
General Lyman L. Lemnitzer	October 1960
General Maxwell D. Taylor	October 1962
General Earle G. Wheeler	July 1964
Admiral Thomas H. Moore	July 1970
General George S. Brown	July 1974
General David Jones	July 1978
General John W. Vessey	July 1982
Admiral William J. Crowe	July 1985
General Colin L. Powell	July 1989
General John M. Shalikashvili	October 1993
General Henry Shelton	October 1997

Chairmen of the Senate Foreign Relations Committee

All dates of election are January, unless otherwise stated.

Tom Connally	July 1941
Arthur H. Vandenberg	1947
Tom Connally	1949
Alexander Wiley	1953
Walter F. George	1955
Theodore F. Green	1957
J.W. Fulbright	1959
John Sparkman	1975
Frank Church	1979
Charles Percy	1981
Richard Lugar	1985
Claiborne Pell	1987
Jesse Helms	1995

Ambassadors to the USSR (to December 1991)

Dates are the date post assumed.

W. Averell Harriman	23 October 1943
W. Bedell Smith	3 April 1946
Alan G. Kirk	4 July 1949
George F. Kennan	14 May 1952
Charles E. Bohlen	20 April 1953
Llewellyn E. Thompson	16 July 1957
Foy D. Kohler	5 July 1962
Llewellyn E. Thompson	16 July 1967
Jacob D. Beam	18 April 1969
Walter J. Stoessel	4 March 1974
Malcolm Toon	18 January 1977
Thomas J. Watson	29 October 1979
Arthur A. Hartman	26 October 1981
Jack F. Matlock	2 April 1987
Robert Strauss	20 August 1991

2. Soviet Union (for Russia see p. 193 below)

For most of the history of the Soviet Union there was no rigorous constitutional definition of the powers of the president, prime minister or Communist Party Leader. Vladimir Ilyich Ulyanov, known as *Lenin*, held the post of 'Chairman of the Council of People's Commissars', but was effectively dominant because of his intellectual leadership of the Bolsheviks.

Josef Stalin established his predominance after Lenin's death (1924), in the position of Secretary-General (leader) of the Communist Party of the Soviet Union (CPSU), a post he held from 1922 to 1934, but, from 1934 until his death on 5 March 1953, Stalin's main position was Chairman of the Council of Ministers (i.e. prime minister). The Chairmanship of the Presidium of the Supreme Soviet (i.e. Soviet President) was powerless.

Georgi Malenkov became both Chairman of the Council of Ministers and leading Secretary of the CPSU on Stalin's death. (The title Secretary-General had lapsed after 1934.) But other Communist leaders insisted that Malenkov share his powers, and within a week *Nikita Khruschev* became leader of the CPSU, adopting the title 'First Secretary' in September 1953. It was in this position that Khruschev triumphed over Malenkov, whose removal from the premiership was announced in February 1955. From then on, until Gorbachev, the dominant figure in Soviet politics was the CPSU leader. From February 1955 until March 1958 *Nikolai Bulganin* served as Chairman of the Council of Ministers. After March 1958 Khruschev took over Bulganin's position and thus became both First Secretary of the party and head of government.

On 14 October 1964 Khruschev was forced to retire and replaced as party leader by *Leonid Brezhnev* and as prime minister by *Andrei Kosygin*. From April 1966 the party leader was again known as the General Secretary. On 16 June 1977 Brezhnev also took over the office of Soviet president, which had become of greater significance under a new Constitution. The Constitution on the other hand reduced the powers of Premier Kosygin, who resigned and was succeeded by *Nikolai Tikhonov*.

Brezhnev died on 10 November 1982 and was succeeded the next day by *Yuri Andropov* as Secretary-General of the Communist Party. Andropov died on 9 February 1984 and was succeeded four days later by *Konstantin Chernenko*. Both Andropov and Chernenko also took the position of Soviet president.

Mikhail Gorbachev became Secretary-General of the Communist Party on 11 March 1985, the day after Chernenko's death, but it was *Andrei Gromyko* who became the new president on 2 July. *Nikolai Ryzhkov* succeeded Tikhonov as prime minister on 27 September 1985. Gorbachev finally replaced Gromyko as president in September 1988, and so combined the two leading posts in the Soviet political system. In March 1990 Gorbachev extended his powers to become Executive president, and on 14 January 1991 *Valentine Pavlov* succeeded Ryzhkov as premier. Pavlov was sacked after the August 1991 coup which ended the old Communist power structure. In December the USSR ceased to exist.

Foreign ministers

Vyacheslav M. Molotov	3 May 1939
Andrei Y. Vyshinsky	4 March 1949
Vyacheslav M. Molotov	6 March 1953
Dimitri T. Shepilov	1 June 1956
Andrei A. Gromyko	15 February 1957
Eduard Shevardnadze	2 July 1985
Alexander Bessmertnykh	15 January 1991
Boris Pankin	28 August 1991
Eduard Shevardnadze	19 November 1991

Defence ministers

Joseph V. Stalin	25 February 1946
(first single minister for the armed forces)	
Nikolai A. Bulganin	3 March 1947
Alexander M. Vasilevsky	4 March 1949
Nikolai A. Bulganin	6 March 1953
Georgi K. Zhukov	9 February 1955
Rodian Y. Malinovsky	26 October 1957
Andrei A. Grechko	12 April 1967
Dimitri F. Ustinov	29 April 1976
Sergei Sokolov	22 December 1984
Dimitri T. Yazov	30 May 1987
Yevgeni Shaposhnikov	23 August 1991

Heads of the KGB

Ivan A. Serov	March 1954
Alexander N. Shelepin	December 1958
Vladimir Y. Semicastny	November 1961
Yuri V. Andropov	April 1967
Vitali Fedorchuk	May 1982
Viktor M. Chebrikov	December 1982
Vladimir Kryutchkov	December 1988
Vadim Bakhatin	August 1991

Chiefs of General Staff

Georgi Zhukov	February 1941
Boris M. Shoposhnikov	July 1941
Alexander M. Vasilevsky	May 1942
Sergei M. Shtemenko	November 1948
Vassili D. Sokolovsky	December 1952

Matvei V. Zakharov	May 1960
Sergei S. Biryuzov	March 1963
Matvei V. Zakharov	September 1964
Viktor G. Kulikov	September 1971
Nikolai V. Ogarkov	January 1977
Sergei F. Akhromeyev	September 1984
Mikhail A. Moiseyev	December 1988
Vladimir Lobov	August 1991

Supreme Commanders of the Warsaw Pact forces

All appointees to the post were Soviet.

Marshal Ivan Koniev (first appointee)	14 May 1955
Marshal Andrei A. Grechko	24 July 1960
Marshal Ivan I. Yakubovsky	7 July 1967
General Viktor G. Kulikov	9 January 1977
General Peter G. Lushev	2 February 1989

Ambassadors to the US

Maxim M. Litvinov	November 1941
Andrei Gromyko	August 1943
Nikolai Novikov	April 1946
Alexander Panyushkin	October 1947
Georgi N. Zarubin	June 1952
Mikhail Menshikov	December 1957
Anatoly F. Dobrynin	January 1962
Alexander Bessmertnykh	May 1986
Viktor Komplektov	January 1991

3. Russia (from December 1991)

President

Boris Yeltsin	December 1991

Prime ministers

Boris Yeltsin	December 1991
Yegor Gaidar	15 June 1992
Viktor Chernomyrdin	15 December 1992

Foreign ministers

Andrei Kozyrev	December 1991
Yevgeni Primakov	9 January 1996

Defence ministers

Boris Yeltsin	16 March 1992*
General Pavel Grachev	8 May 1992
Colonel-General Igor Rodionov	17 July 1996

* Date when post was created.

4. China

Chinese leaders

Following the creation of the Chinese People's Republic in October 1949, power was vested pre-eminently in the hands of *Mao Zedong*, whose position was formalised under a new constitution in 1954 as Chairman of the Central Committee. As in the Soviet Union, the party was predominant over the government, whose prime minister during 1949–76 was *Zhou Enlai*. In January 1976 Zhou died and was succeeded by *Hua Guofeng*, who also became the party Chairman when Mao died in September. But from 1978 the most powerful figure in the leadership was *Deng Xiaoping*, who held a number of positions. Deng secured Hua's replacement by *Zhao Ziyang* as premier in September 1980, and by *Hu Yaobang* as Chairman in June 1981.

On 16 January 1987, following popular disturbances, Hu himself gave way to Zhao Ziyang as Chairman but Zhao gave up the premiership to *Li Peng* in November 1987. The Tiananmen Square demonstrations of April–June 1989, which followed the death of Hu Yaobang, led to the replacement of Zhao Ziyang as Chairman by the hard-line *Jiang Zemin* who also become President in March 1993. However, Deng Xiaoping remained the decisive force in the leadership until his decline in the mid-1990s. He gave up his last party post (Chairman of the Central Advisory Committee) in November 1987, and his last government post (Chairman of the Central Military Commission) in March 1990, and died in 1997.

Foreign ministers

Zhou Enlai	20 October 1949
Chen Yi	11 February 1958
Ji Bengfei	20 January 1972
Qiao Guanhua	14 November 1974
Huang Hua	2 December 1976
Wu Xueqian	19 November 1982
Qian Qichen	12 April 1988

5. Great Britain

Prime ministers

Winston S. Churchill (Conservative)	10 May 1940
Clement R. Attlee (Labour)	26 July 1945
Winston S. Churchill (Conservative)	26 October 1951
Sir Anthony Eden (Conservative)	6 April 1955
Harold Macmillan (Conservative)	10 January 1957
Alexander Douglas-Home (Conservative)	19 October 1963
Harold Wilson (Labour)	16 October 1964
Edward Heath (Conservative)	19 June 1970
Harold Wilson (Labour)	4 March 1974
James Callaghan (Labour)	5 April 1976
Margaret Thatcher (Conservative)	4 May 1979
John Major (Conservative)	28 November 1990
Tony Blair (Labour)	2 May 1997

Foreign Secretaries

Anthony Eden	23 December 1940
Ernest Bevin	28 July 1945
Herbert S. Morrison	12 March 1951
Anthony Eden (knighted 1954)	27 October 1951
Harold Macmillan	12 April 1955
Selwyn Lloyd	22 December 1955
Sir Alex Douglas-Home, 14th Earl of Home (renounced title October 1964)	27 July 1960
Richard A. Butler	20 October 1963
Patrick Gordon Walker	16 October 1964
Michael Stewart	22 January 1965
George Brown	11 August 1966
Michael Stewart	16 March 1968
Sir Alex Douglas-Home	20 June 1970
James Callaghan	5 March 1974
Anthony Crosland	8 April 1976
Dr David Owen	21 February 1977
Peter Carrington, 6th Lord Carrington	5 May 1979
Francis L. Pym	2 April 1982
Sir Geoffrey Howe	11 June 1983
John Major	24 July 1989
Douglas Hurd	26 October 1989
Malcolm Rifkind	2 May 1995
Robin Cook	2 May 1997

6. France

Presidents of the Fifth Republic

Dates are date of election.

Charles de Gaulle	8 January 1959
Georges Pompidou	15 June 1969
Valery Giscard d'Estaing	19 May 1974
François Mitterrand	10 May 1981
Jacques Chirac	17 May 1995

Prime ministers

Charles de Gaulle	9 September 1944
Félix Gouin	26 January 1946
Georges Bidault	23 June 1946
Léon Blum	16 December 1946
Paul Ramadier	22 January 1947
Robert Schuman	24 November 1947
André Marie	26 July 1948
Henri Queuille	11 September 1948
Georges Bidault	28 October 1949
Henri Queuille	2 July 1950
René Pleven	12 July 1950
Henri Queuille	10 March 1951
René Pleven	10 August 1951
Edgar Faure	20 January 1952
Antoine Pinay	8 March 1952
René Mayer	8 January 1953
Joseph Laniel	27 June 1953
Pierre Mendès-France	19 June 1954
Edgar Faure	23 February 1955
Guy Mollet	1 February 1956
Maurice Bourgès-Maunoury	12 June 1957
Félix Gaillard	5 November 1957
Pierre Pflimlin	14 May 1958
Charles de Gaulle	1 June 1958
Michel Debré	8 January 1959
Georges Pompidou	28 November 1962
Maurice Couve de Murville	11 July 1968
Jacques Chaban-Delmas	20 June 1969
Pierre Messmer	5 July 1972
Jacques Chirac	27 May 1974
Raymond Barre	27 August 1976

Pierre Mauroy	22 May 1981
Laurent Fabius	19 July 1984
Jacques Chirac	18 March 1986
Michel Rocard	10 May 1988
Edith Cresson	16 May 1991
Pierre Bérégovoy	2 April 1992
Edouard Balladur	29 March 1993
Alain Juppé	17 May 1995
Lionel Jospin	2 June 1997

Foreign ministers

Georges Bidault	10 September 1944
Léon Blum	16 December 1946
Georges Bidault	22 January 1947
Robert Schuman	26 July 1948
Georges Bidault	8 January 1953
Pierre Mendès-France	19 June 1954
Edgar Faure	20 January 1955
Antoine Pinay	23 February 1955
Christian Pineau	31 January 1956
René Pleven	14 May 1958
Maurice Couve de Murville	2 June 1958
Michel Debré	31 May 1968
Maurice Schumann	22 June 1969
Michel Jobert	5 April 1973
Jean Sauvagnargues	28 May 1974
Louis de Guiringaud	27 August 1976
Jean François-Poncet	29 November 1978
Claude Cheysson	22 May 1981
Roland Dumas	7 December 1984
Jean Raimond	20 March 1986
Roland Dumas	12 May 1988
Alain Juppé	30 March 1993
Hervé de Charette	18 May 1995
Hubert Védrine	3 June 1997

7. West Germany and (from 1990) Germany

Chancellors

Konrad Adenauer (Christian Democrat)	20 September 1949
Ludwig Erhard (Christian Democrat)	17 October 1963
Kurt Kiesinger (Christian Democrat leading 'Grand Coalition')	1 December 1966

Willy Brandt (Social Democrat)	21 October 1969
Helmut Schmidt (Social Democrat)	16 May 1974
Helmut Kohl (Christian Democrat)	1 October 1982

Note: The Free Democrats usually shared power in coalitions with the major parties.

Foreign ministers

Heinrich von Brentano*	6 June 1955
Gerhard Schröder	14 November 1961
Willy Brandt	1 December 1966
Walter Scheel	21 October 1969
Hans-Dietrich Genscher	16 May 1974
Klaus Kinkel	17 May 1992

* First foreign minister after sovereignty restored.

8. United Nations

Secretaries-General of the UN

Dates mark beginning of term in office. Countries of origin are also cited.

Trygve Lie (Norway)	23 February 1946
Dag Hammarskjöld (Sweden)	10 April 1953
(killed in the Congo, 17 September 1961)	
U Thant (Burma)	3 November 1961
Kurt Waldheim (Austria)	1 January 1972
Javier Perez de Cuellar (Peru)	1 January 1982
Boutros Boutros Ghali (Egypt)	1 January 1992
Kofi Annan (Ghana)	1 January 1997

9. NATO

Supreme Commanders of NATO (Supreme Allied Commander Europe, or SACEUR)

All appointees to the post were American generals.

Dwight D. Eisenhower	19 December 1950
(first appointee)	
Matthew B. Ridgeway	28 April 1952
Alfred M. Gruenther	1 July 1953
Lauris Norstad	13 April 1956
Lyman L. Lemnitzer	1 January 1963

Andrew Goodpaster	1 July 1969
Alexander M. Haig	15 December 1974
Bernard W. Rogers	1 July 1979
John Galvin	1 July 1987
John Shalikashvili	1 July 1992
George Joulwan	4 October 1993
Wesley Clark	1 July 1997

Secretaries-General of NATO

Lord Ismay (Britain)	March 1952
Paul-Henri Spaak (Belgium)	May 1957
Dirk Stikker (Holland)	April 1961
Manlio Brosio (Italy)	May 1964
Joseph Luns (Holland)	May 1971
Lord Carrington (Britain)	June 1984
Manfred Woerner (Germany)	June 1988
Willy Claes (Belgium)	October 1994
Javier Solana (Spain)	December 1995

SECTION SIX

Biographies

Brief biographies are provided for the Cold War period of all US Presidents and Secretaries of State, plus the more important National Security Advisers, Defense Secretaries and CIA Directors. Similarly there are biographies of all Soviet General Secretaries and foreign ministers, plus the more important defence ministers, premiers and KGB chiefs. Other biographies include major Western and Eastern bloc leaders, Third World leaders, UN Secretaries-General and certain key figures of the post-Cold War years.

Adenauer, Konrad (1876–1967): The son of a Cologne city official, Adenauer rose in the city administration to become Mayor of Cologne in 1917, and was a leading member of the Catholic Centre Party in the 1920s. An opponent of the Nazis, he was removed from his post in 1933 and spent the next twelve years in prison or in hiding. He was made Mayor of Cologne again by the Americans in 1945, but was quickly removed by the British and became involved in attempts to form a new Christian Democratic Party in Germany. He oversaw the creation of the West German constitution in 1948–49 and, despite his age, went on to win four elections as West Germany's first Chancellor in 1949–63. He was deeply committed to a Western Alliance, believing the only alternative to be Soviet domination. He was accused of helping to divide Germany, but succeeded in tying Bonn closely to NATO and to the European Economic Community.

Andropov, Yuri V. (1914–84): Born in the Caucasus and educated as an engineer, Andropov became an organiser for the Young Communists. In the late 1940s he helped consolidate Soviet control of the Finnish border areas and in 1954 became Ambassador to Hungary, where he had a leading role in dealing with the 1956 uprising. His role in Hungary helped him gain election to the Communist Party's Central Committee in 1962, and appointment as KGB Chairman in 1967, a post he held until 1982. From 1973 he was also a full member of the Politburo. In May 1982 he became a Secretary on the Central Committee and in November outmanoeuvred Konstantin Chernenko to succeed Leonid Brezhnev as Secretary-General of the Communist Party. Certain changes were made which suggested a desire for reform and he had a major role in strengthening Mikhail Gorbachev's position in Moscow, but was unable to achieve much before becoming seriously ill in the summer of 1983. He died the following February.

Baker, III, James A. (b. 1930): An American lawyer and Republican politician, Baker gained brief government experience under Gerald Ford and ran George Bush's presidential campaign in 1980. In 1981–85, with Bush as vice-president, Baker had the difficult job of White House Chief of Staff, and in 1989, when Bush was elected president, became Secretary of State. He had a high profile in promoting Bush's 'new world order' after 1990 and developed a good working relationship with the Soviets, which resulted in the CFE and START Treaties. In August 1992 he moved to become Chief of Staff in the White House in an attempt to invigorate Bush's failing re-election campaign.

Beria, Lavrenti P. (1899–1953):   A Bolshevik secret policeman, trusted by his fellow Georgian Stalin, Beria succeeded Yazhov as head of the NKVD in 1938. Beria expanded the secret police empire and had a leading role in organising the Soviet war effort. He remained in overall ministerial control of the secret police after the war, but organisational changes threatened his power. On Stalin's death in March 1953, Beria was again able to merge all secret police powers under his own control, but his colleagues in the leadership grew fearful of him and within months he was overthrown. Like many of his victims before him, he was executed as a 'foreign agent'.

Bessmertnykh, Alexander A. (b. 1933):   A Soviet diplomat, educated in the State Institute for International Relations, Bessmertnykh worked in the Washington Embassy in 1970–83, then headed the US Department of the Soviet foreign ministry. In 1986 he succeeded the veteran Anatoly Dobrynin as Ambassador to Washington. When foreign minister Shevardnadze suddenly resigned in December 1990, Bessmertnykh was chosen to succeed him, partly because of his knowledge of Washington. Bessmertnykh preserved good relations with the US, and completed the START Treaty, but his failure to oppose the August 1991 coup against Gorbachev led to his replacement.

Bevin, Ernest (1881–1951):   British trade union leader who became Minister of Labour in 1940–45 and Foreign Secretary in 1945–51. Though increasingly unwell, he was a powerful figure who did much to develop co-operation between the British Commonwealth, Western Europe and America against the Soviet Union. He had a leading role in the formation of NATO.

Boutros Ghali, Boutros (b. 1922):   Born into an Egyptian political family, Boutros Ghali had a long career as a Professor of International Law and International Relations in Cairo after 1949 before serving as Minister of State for Foreign Affairs in 1977–91, in which post he had a leading role in the Egypt–Israeli peace process. In January 1992 he became the first Arab, and the first African, Secretary-General of the UN but, despite being highly respected in many circles, he was blamed, especially in the US, for the failings of the organisation in the 1990s (in Bosnia for example) and failed to win a second term.

Brandt, Willy (1913–92):   A German Social Democrat, and opponent of the Nazis, Brandt went to Norway during the war and became for a time a Norwegian citizen. Returning to West Germany he won a parliamentary seat in 1949 and in 1957 became Mayor of West Berlin. His liberal views and resistance to Soviet pressure during the 1961 Berlin Wall crisis won great respect. He helped reform the Social Democratic Party to make its policies more popular, partly by pledging support for NATO and the European Community. In 1966 he became foreign minister in a 'Grand Coalition' with the Christian Democrats and in 1969 was elected Chancellor, in coalition with the Free Democrats. His *Ostpolitik* (q.v.) established more open relations with the Soviets and East Germans, helped win him the 1971 Nobel Peace Prize, and secured another Social Democratic election victory in 1972, but in 1974 one of his aides was exposed as a spy, and Brandt hastily decided to resign. He remained a powerful advocate of such causes as aid to the developing world and, as Chairman of the SPD in the 1980s, continued to support dialogue with the Eastern bloc.

Brezhnev, Leonid I. (1906–82):   A Soviet Communist politician, Brezhnev rose in the Communist Party under Khruschev to become Soviet President – then a powerless position – in 1960. In October 1964 he helped lead the overthrow of Khruschev and became General Secretary of the Communist Party, the most important position in the hierarchy. Brezhnev reversed many of Khruschev's internal reforms, stiffened controls on society and reinforced party authority. He ended Khruschev's 'brinkmanship' in foreign affairs and built up the Soviet nuclear arsenal to a position of superpower parity. In 1971 Brezhnev threw his weight behind a policy of detente with the US, from which he obtained controls on US nuclear weapons (through SALT) and the legitimisation of Soviet domination over Eastern Europe (at Helsinki). His conservative policies at home helped to bring economic stagnation and a decline in Communist idealism. His increasing ill-health probably contributed to the disastrous decision to invade Afghanistan.

Brzezinski, Zbigniew K. (b. 1928):   Like Henry Kissinger, Brzezinski was a naturalised American who became an academic specialising in international relations, joined various prestigious foreign policy groups and was appointed National Security Adviser (in 1977). He had met President Jimmy Carter earlier, on the 'Trilateral Commission', which sought to improve relations between America, Japan and Western Europe. His Polish birth made Brzezinski highly critical of Soviet policy. His clash over detente policy with Secretary of State Vance did much to divide the Carter presidency, and his attempt to take a tough line with Iran in the 1980 hostage crisis ended in failure.

Bulganin, Nikolai (1895–1975):   A Soviet statesman, who became Minister of Defence in 1947–49 and 1953–55, Bulganin helped Nikita Khruschev to oust Georgi Malenkov from power in February 1955. Bulganin served as premier until 1958, representing the USSR at various international meetings such as the 1955 Geneva Summit, but was replaced by Khruschev who had always overshadowed him.

Bundy, McGeorge (1919–96):   A Yale-educated American academic, who became a Harvard Professor in the 1950s, Bundy was a critic of Eisenhower's foreign policy. In 1961 Bundy was appointed by President Kennedy to be Special Assistant for National Security Affairs, in which position he played a much more active role than previous appointees. He was part of the team which successfully handled the Cuban Missile Crisis, but disagreements with Johnson over Vietnam led to his resignation in 1966, and his return to academic life. His brother William (b. 1917) was a member of the CIA in the 1950s, a top Defense Department official in 1961–64 and Assistant Secretary of State in 1964–69.

Bush, George H.W. (b. 1924):   The son of a Wall Street banker, Bush served as a pilot in the Second World War, studied at Yale and made a fortune in the Texas oil industry before entering the House of Representatives as a Republican in 1966. Under Nixon he served as Ambassador to the UN (1971–72), unofficial 'ambassador' to China (1974–75) and then, in the very difficult post-Watergate period, as CIA Director (1976–77). In 1981 he became Reagan's vice-president, and was trusted with various foreign policy duties. He thus had wide experience of international affairs when he succeeded Reagan in 1989. Bush was initially criticised for failing to respond to Soviet initiatives for detente early in the presidency. However, his tough action against the dictatorships in Panama and Iraq in 1989–91 helped secure his record popularity at a time when the Soviet Empire was in turmoil, and he strongly supported German reunification. Despite such foreign policy successes, domestic economic problems cost him the presidency in the 1992 election.

Byrnes, James F. (1879–1972):   A South Carolina Democrat, Byrnes entered the US Senate in 1931 and became responsible for war mobilisation during 1943–45. He attended the Yalta Conference, and in July 1945, after Harry Truman became president, was made Secretary of State. He was criticised in early 1946 for taking a soft line with the Russians and subsequently adopted a more forthright policy towards them. At Stuttgart, in September, he announced that US troops would remain in Germany until peace was assured. Having lost favour with Truman, he resigned in January 1947.

Carter, Jimmy (b. 1924): Born into a Georgia farming family, Carter graduated from the US Naval Academy in 1946 and pursued a career in the submarine service, before returning to peanut farming in 1953. He was elected Governor of Georgia in 1970, but was still relatively unknown in 1976 when he emerged as the Democratic front-runner in the presidential election. He then proceeded to beat the Republican candidate, Gerald Ford. Carter tried to maintain detente with the Soviet Union, but was committed to human rights and hoped to improve relations with America's allies, Western Europe and Japan. His advisers were frequently divided. He was discredited by the Soviet invasion of Afghanistan, which ended detente, and by the humiliating 'hostage crisis' with Iran (1979–81). He lost the 1980 election to Ronald Reagan, but remained politically active, being used as a diplomatic envoy by Bill Clinton on several occasions.

Casey, William (1922–87): New York-born businessman and Republican, Casey served in the Office of Strategic Services during the Second World War, and later made a fortune on Wall Street. He managed Ronald Reagan's successful presidential campaign in 1980, and was subsequently appointed director of the CIA. Intensely loyal to the president, he was the first CIA director to become a member of the Cabinet and, after the problems of the 1970s, did much to revive the CIA's fortunes. In December 1986 he collapsed at work, was found to be suffering from a brain tumour, and was forced to resign. After his death he was accused of involvement in the Iran–Contragate scandal.

Castro, Fidel (b. 1926): Castro, the Cuban revolutionary, was the son of a Spanish-born landowner. Aided by his brother Raul and the Argentinian Ernesto ('Che') Guevara, he led the 26 July Movement which overthrew the pro-American dictator Batista in 1959. Castro steered Cuba towards alliance with the USSR and soon declared himself to be a Marxist–Leninist. He quickly alienated the US but survived an attempt by the CIA to topple him at the Bay of Pigs. Facing continued US attempts (known as 'Operation Mongoose') to undermine his regime, Castro was disappointed when Khruschev backed down in the 1962 Cuban Missile Crisis. After 1962 Castro was able to create a Communist regime in Cuba, to assist other radical groups in Latin America and to send military forces to help Marxist governments in Angola and Ethiopia in the 1970s. His regime was called into question by the collapse of the Soviet Union and he was subjected to continuing US economic sanctions.

Ceauşescu, Nicolae (1918–89): Born into a peasant family, Ceauşescu joined the Romanian Communist Party in 1936 and spent several years in prison. When the Communists emerged as the dominant force in post-war politics he rose rapidly in the leadership. In 1965 he was the obvious successor to party leader Gheorghieu-Dej, who had maintained a repressive regime internally and industrialised the country, but pursued an independent foreign policy. Ceauşescu built on Dej's policies, acting independently of Moscow and playing a major role in establishing Sino-American contacts in the early 1970s. He was rewarded with trade agreements by America and Western Europe. His domestic rule was extremely harsh, political power was concentrated in his own hands, and he promoted his wife (Elena) and other family members to leading government positions. His secret police, the *Securitate*, could not save him from being overthrown and executed in December 1989.

Chebrikov, Viktor M. (b. 1923):   Chebrikov became a Communist Party bureaucrat in 1951 and rose to become a deputy chairman of the KGB in 1968–82. In 1982 he supported Yuri Andropov (former KGB head) in succession to Brezhnev and was rewarded in December with the Chairmanship of the KGB. In March 1985 Gorbachev's succession as leader owed much to Chebrikov's support. Chebrikov's brand of reform however was akin to that of the leading Communist ideologist Igor Ligachev: both wanted a more efficient Soviet government without any loss of Communist political control. Chebrikov became identified as a conservative opponent of Gorbachev and was moved in 1988 to be the Politburo member for legal affairs. A year later he was thrown off the Politburo.

Chernenko, Konstantin (1911–85):   Born in Siberia, Chernenko joined the Soviet Communist Party in 1931 and survived Stalin's purges before becoming, after 1945, a loyal lieutenant of Leonid Brezhnev. Brezhnev's rise to the leadership carried Chernenko in its wake, and he became a full Politburo member in 1978. On Brezhnev's death, in 1982, Chernenko was outmanoeuvred in the succession struggle by Yuri Andropov; however, on Andropov's death, in 1984, conservative elements managed to make Chernenko the new Secretary-General. His health was already poor, his interest in reform was minimal and he had little experience of foreign policy. He showed some interest in arms reductions talks before his death.

Chiang Kai-shek (1887–1975):   As deputy to the Chinese Nationalist leader, Sun Yat-sen, Chiang Kai-shek was given the task of training an army to fight the warlords who ruled China in the 1920s. After Sun's death, Chiang broke, in 1927, the alliance which had been made with the Chinese Communists. The alliance had alienated the landlords and businessmen. Chiang's army won control of most of eastern China but his government became corrupt. He was unable to destroy the Communists, and made an uneasy alliance with them to fight the Japanese

(1937–45). Defeated by the Communists in the civil war of 1946–49 he fled to Taiwan where the US protected him.

Christopher, Warren (b. 1925): Trained as a lawyer and with naval service in the Second World War, Christopher first worked for the State Department, as a special consultant on economic problems, under Kennedy. As Deputy Secretary of State under Carter he worked on the Panama Canal treaties (to restore the canal to Panamanian sovereignty) and on the Iran hostages crisis. As Secretary of State throughout Clinton's first term, Christopher was much criticised for a time, but eventually won some progress on Arab–Israeli relations and oversaw the Dayton Accords on Bosnia.

Churchill, Winston (1874–1965): In his early career, before entering politics, Churchill served as a cavalry officer, then as a press correspondent during the Boer War. He served in Liberal and Conservative Cabinets after 1905, and his posts included First Lord of the Admiralty in the First World War and Chancellor of the Exchequer in 1924–29. He was excluded from office in the 1930s, but took up the cause of anti-Nazism and returned to the Admiralty when war broke out in 1939. He was a natural choice to replace Chamberlain as prime minister in 1940. Although an anti-Communist he embraced the Soviets as Allies in 1941. A great war leader he nevertheless lost the 1945 General Election. As opposition leader in 1946 he criticised the 'iron curtain' in Eastern Europe and wanted a 'special relationship' with America. As prime minister in 1951–55 his fear of war and desire to play a major international role made him an early proponent of detente with the USSR.

Clinton, William ('Bill') J. (b. 1946): Educated at the Universities of Yale and (as a Rhodes Scholar) Oxford, Clinton was trained as a lawyer and became Attorney-General of his home state, Arkansas, in 1977. Elected State Governor when aged only 33, he served in this post in 1979–81 and 1983–93, using it as a springboard for his successful presidential campaign in 1992. Though elected mainly for his promises about the domestic economy, and despite fears of a US retreat from world affairs, he proved active on the international scene, backing peace efforts in the Arab–Israeli conflict, Bosnia and Northern Ireland. Despite criticism of his private life he was re-elected for a second term, when he succeeded in balancing the federal budget for the first time in a generation.

Deng Xiaoping (1904–97): A leading Chinese Communist from the 1920s onward, and a highly able administrator, closely allied to Zhou Enlai, Deng Xiaoping became number three in the Communist hierarchy in 1975. In April 1976, after Zhou's death, the radical 'Gang of

Four' were able to oust Deng, but they were themselves arrested in October – one month after Mao Zedong's death. Deng was rehabilitated in July 1977 and won the power struggle with Mao's successor as Chairman, Hua Guofeng. In 1978 Deng was in the dominant position, and in 1979 he visited the US, using the visit to criticise Soviet policy. By 1980 Deng was fully secure in power. While maintaining firm one-party rule, he pursued policies of decentralisation, modernisation and the production of consumer goods to end the old bureaucratic system and achieve growth. He also favoured an 'open door' with the outside world, to expand trade, win investment and obtain advanced technology. In 1987 he resigned from his last official post, but remained influential. In June 1989, still the major force, though seldom seen in public, he agreed that demonstrations in Tiananmen Square for democratic reform should be crushed. This harmed his standing in the West. In the mid-1990s he went into physical decline and died shortly before the return of Hong Kong to China, which he had done much to achieve.

Dubcek, Alexander (1921–92):   The Slovak Communist politician who replaced Antonin Novotny as party leader in early 1968 and backed the liberalisation of Czechoslovak government, Dubcek was surprised by the Soviet-led invasion of August that year and unable to resist it. In contrast to Hungary's Imre Nagy (q.v.) Dubcek suffered a mild fate after his defeat: he was demoted, becoming Ambassador to Turkey in 1969, and expelled from the Communist Party in 1970. He re-emerged as a major figure in 1989, during the anti-Communist demonstrations which toppled the government, and became president of the Czechoslovakian parliament.

Dulles, Allen W. (1893–1969):   Brother of John Foster Dulles (q.v.), Dulles made his name as America's wartime 'spymaster' in Switzerland, from where he controlled agents in Nazi-occupied Europe. In 1950 the head of the CIA, Bedell Smith, made Dulles his Deputy Director. Then, in 1953, Dulles was promoted to the Directorship by President Eisenhower. Dulles's long term of office saw the expansion of CIA activities, a more sophisticated organisation and such successes as the overthrow of the Mossadeq regime in Iran (1953) and the Arbenz government in Guatemala (1954). The failure of the Bay of Pigs operation (1961), however, led to his being replaced.

Dulles, John Foster (1888–1959):   American international lawyer and Republican supporter John Foster Dulles gained his first-hand experience of foreign policy at Versailles in 1919. Strongly religious and obsessively anti-Communist, he was a keen supporter of the UN, and helped to develop a bipartisan American foreign policy under President Truman. He concluded the 1951 Peace Treaty with Japan. Both his grandfather and uncle had been Secretaries of State, and he too gained this long-coveted position in 1953 under Eisenhower. Dulles was known for his tough rhetoric, but was only able to pursue a strong anti-Communist policy because this was to the president's liking.

Eden, Anthony (1897–1977):   A British Conservative politician, and specialist in foreign affairs, Eden first became Foreign Secretary in 1935. His resignation in 1938 established his reputation as an 'anti-appeaser', and in 1940–45 he was recalled to be Churchill's foreign minister, in which position he attended the major wartime summit conferences. Back as foreign secretary in 1951–55, he was suspicious of Soviet moves for detente after Stalin's death. He succeeded Churchill as prime minister in 1955, won a general election and did much to bring about the Geneva Summit with Khruschev. But Eden's premiership was soon overshadowed by the Suez Crisis, after which he resigned.

Eisenhower, Dwight D. (1890–1969):   A US general, Eisenhower worked on operations planning in Washington in 1941–42 and was made commander of the Anglo-American invasion of North-west Africa (1942), although he had never held a field command. He proved adept at handling alliance politics and was made Supreme Commander of the Normandy landings in 1944. His successes made him a natural choice as the first Supreme Commander of NATO (1950) and as Republican presidential candidate in 1952. As president in 1953–61 he is now recognised to have played a major role in foreign policy-making. Strongly anti-Communist, he nonetheless took a genuine interest in detente and nuclear arms control.

Ford, Gerald R. (b. 1913):   A Chicago-born, US Republican, Ford trained as a lawyer and entered the House of Representatives in 1949. In 1973 he succeeded Spiro Agnew as vice-president, when the latter was forced to resign over tax evasion charges. In 1974 President Nixon was also forced to resign and Ford became the first non-elected US president. A far from dynamic figure, he largely carried on Nixon's foreign policy, including detente, but was criticised for signing the 1975 Helsinki Accords. Ford lost the 1976 election to Jimmy Carter, partly because of growing problems with detente.

de Gaulle, Charles (1890–1970):   A general during the Second World War, de Gaulle, after witnessing the fall of France, went to Britain to found the Free French movement. He led France's first post-war government in 1944–46, but clashed with the political parties and resigned. In 1947 he founded the 'Rally of the French People', but only returned to power in 1958 when the government proved unable to resolve Algerian independence. He founded the Fifth Republic (with himself as a strong president), withdrew from Algeria and pursued a forthright international policy based on a belief in French greatness and independence. He recognised Communist China, visited Moscow and withdrew from NATO's integrated command. Stunned by student discontent in 1968, he resigned after an adverse vote in a referendum in 1969.

Giscard d'Estaing, Valery (b. 1926):   A French civil servant and politician, Giscard d'Estaing led the Independent Republicans (a centre-Right group) in the 1962 elections, in coalition with the victorious Gaullists. He became Finance Minister until 1966, a position which he regained under President Pompidou after 1969, when he took the difficult decision to devalue the franc. His experience, liberal views and youthful image helped him to become president in 1974. He maintained the independent foreign policy begun by de Gaulle, improved the nuclear *Force de Frappe*, worked closely with West Germany's Helmut Schmidt in the European Community and tried to maintain detente even in 1980, after the Soviet invasion of Afghanistan. At home his reputation suffered from economic problems, a failure to carry out radical reforms, and a 'monarchical' style of government. He was defeated in the 1981 presidential election.

Gomulka, Wladyslaw (1905–82):   A Polish Communist, Gomulka remained in Poland during the Second World War and became party leader afterwards. He lost out in a power struggle with the Stalinist Boleslaw Bierut, was denounced as a 'Titoist' and imprisoned, but was released and rehabilitated after 1953. He was able to pose as a nationalist leader in 1956 and was recalled to lead the Communist Party in the troubles of that year. He was able to end the collectivisation of land and introduce other economic reforms. But his loyalty to the Warsaw Pact, maintenance of a one-party state and personal power gradually lost him his original popularity. His failure to improve the economy led to disturbances in 1970 which brought his fall from office.

Gorbachev, Mikhail S. (b. 1931):   Born in a village in southern Russia, Gorbachev joined the Communist Party in 1952, studied law and agriculture, and rose in the Stavropol party organisation until he was elected to the Supreme Soviet in 1970. He joined the Communist Central Committee the following year and became a Secretary of that body in 1978. In 1979 he was made a non-voting member of the Politburo and became a full member in 1980. He was soon seen, along with the Conservative Grigori Romanov, as one of the younger men most likely to succeed Brezhnev's generation. The support of Yuri Andropov and other reformers helped Gorbachev to emerge as General Secretary in March 1985.

A relatively young and energetic leader, Gorbachev sought to reform the USSR at home (through the policies of *glasnost* and *perestroika*), while reducing commitments abroad (especially with the withdrawal from Afghanistan) and renewing detente with the West. However, his policies served to unleash nationalist discontent at home and soon threatened Moscow's hold on Eastern Europe, where pro-Soviet Communist regimes disintegrated in 1989. He failed to carry through radical economic reforms, but also alienated conservative elements who tried to oust him in August 1991 in a failed coup. After the coup he suspended the Communist Party and agreed to give independence to the Baltic states, but was forced to resign as president in December, when the Soviet Union broke up into its constituent republics. Much admired abroad, the depth of his unpopularity at home was cruelly exposed by a paltry vote in the 1996 Russian Presidential elections.

Grechko, Andrei Y. (1903–76):   A Soviet General, who joined the Red Army in 1918, Grechko was high in the command structure during the Second World War. He commanded occupation forces in East Germany in 1953–57 and was Supreme Commander of the Warsaw Pact after 1960. In April 1967 he succeeded the long-serving Malinovsky as defence minister, and himself continued in office for nine years. Promoted to the Politburo in 1973 by Brezhnev, to whom he was a loyal ally, Grechko was able to secure considerable resources for the armed forces and developed a more active military policy in the Third World. His period in office marked the height of Soviet military power.

Gromyko, Andrei A. (1909–89):   Gromyko rose rapidly in the Soviet diplomatic service while still a young man: he served as Ambassador to both Washington and London. His grasp of issues was impressive, but he was best known for his ability to 'stonewall' in discussions with the West. In 1957, after six years as a deputy foreign minister, he began the longest tenure of a Soviet foreign minister, although he did not become a full Politburo member until 1973. He was closely involved in the detente policies of the 1970s, but after 1979 was one of the hard-line Cold War Warriors in the Soviet leadership. For this reason Mikhail Gorbachev replaced him as foreign minister in July 1985. Gromyko was put in the largely honorific post of president, but lost even this in 1988.

Haig, Alexander (b. 1924):   Born in Philadelphia, Haig graduated from West Point, studied international relations at Georgetown University and saw service in Korea and Vietnam before becoming military adviser to Henry Kissinger in 1969. In 1970 Haig became deputy National Security Adviser and played a major role in developing detente with China and settling the Vietnam War. For a time in 1973 he was Vice-Chief of Staff of the Army but was hastily moved to become White House Chief of Staff, to deal with the Watergate Scandal. When President Nixon was forced to resign, Haig became Supreme Allied Commander in Europe. He retired in 1979, but in 1981 became Ronald Reagan's first Secretary of State. Haig did not fit in well with the Reagan White House, and he offered to resign several times before finally departing in June 1982.

Hammarskjöld, Dag (1906–61): A Swedish politician, Hammarskjöld became Secretary-General of the UN in March 1953. Like Trygve Lie he was seen as a compromise candidate, acceptable to East and West, but in fact he proved strong-minded and active, determined to make the UN a dynamic force for peace. In November 1956 he oversaw the establishment of the first UN peace-keeping force to help resolve the Suez Crisis. In 1960, amidst some criticism, he sent another peace-keeping force into the former Belgian Congo (later Zaïre) to help resolve its post-independence anarchy. He was killed in an air-crash in Ndola, in the Congo, on 17 September 1961.

Helms, Richard M. (b. 1913): An experienced foreign intelligence officer since the war years, Helms rose to become CIA Deputy Director of Plans in 1961, after the Bay of Pigs failure. He became Deputy Director of the CIA in 1965 under Vice-Admiral William F. Raborn. Raborn, who had made his name as head of the Polaris submarine programme, failed to fit in well at the CIA and was replaced by Helms in 1966. Despite Helms's experience, loyalty to the president, and popularity within the CIA, his directorship proved a difficult one. The early years were marked by the worsening Vietnam War; and under Nixon, Helms found himself overshadowed by Henry Kissinger. After 1973 Helms became Ambassador to Iran for three years, but, in the years of criticism of the CIA which followed, he was accused of having misled Congress about US attempts to overthrow President Allende of Chile during his directorship.

Herter, Christian A. (1895–1980): Born in France, of American parents, Herter attended Harvard University, and joined the US foreign service in 1916. He later worked as a newspaper editor and in 1942 was elected to Congress as a Republican. After four years as Governor of Massachusetts, he became Under-Secretary of State to John Foster Dulles in 1957 and, despite being crippled, succeeded the latter as Secretary in 1959 when Dulles died. His short period as Secretary of State was dominated by the Berlin Crisis and the failure of the 1960 Paris Summit.

Ho Chi Minh (1890–1969) (born Nguyen Tat Thanh): A Vietnamese nationalist leader who opposed French rule, Ho Chi Minh lived part of the inter-war years in the USSR. In 1941 he returned and led the

Viet-Minh movement against Japanese occupation. Though a Commun-
ist, he hoped for US support when he proclaimed Vietnamese independ-
ence in September 1945. In 1946–54, aided by the outstanding General
Giap, he led a guerrilla war which resulted in the establishment of a
Communist state in North Vietnam. He later began a campaign in South
Vietnam to reunite the whole country, which resulted in US intervention.
By the time of his death he could foresee eventual Communist victory.

Honecker, Erich (1912–94): Born in Western Germany, Honecker
joined the Communist Party in 1929, and spent most of the Nazi era in
prison. In 1946–55 he was head of the Communist youth movement and
rose in the East German leadership until, in 1971, he succeeded Walter
Ulbricht as party leader. Honecker developed links with West Germany,
and in the early 1980s showed some independence of Moscow, but his
regime was repressive and collapsed in 1989 under popular pressures.
Honecker was imprisoned, but in 1991 was allowed to go to the USSR.

Hoover, J. Edgar (1895–1972): The head of the American Federal
Bureau of Investigation (FBI) for almost half a century, from 1924 until
his death, Hoover was a formidable figure. He was a determined anti-
Communist, using the FBI after 1945 to monitor all possible forms of
left-wing activity in the US, including Civil Rights activists and trade
unionists. He has been blamed for allowing the McCarthyite 'witch-hunts'
of the 1950s to occur, but became too powerful (and too widely feared)
to remove.

Jaruzelski, Wojtech (b. 1923): Born into a middle-class family, Jaruzelski
fought with the Red Army against the Germans in the war and became
the youngest general in the Polish army in 1956. In 1968 his appointment as Defence Minister allowed him to develop as a political leader,
and in February 1981 he was made Poland's prime minister in the face
of the mounting crisis caused by price rises, strikes and the formation of
Solidarity. Trusted by Moscow and able to combine the support of the
army and Communist Party, he made himself party leader in October
before repressing the Solidarity movement at the end of the year. He
showed skill in easing the repression over the following years, but could
not solve Poland's deep economic difficulties. In 1989–90, as president,
he managed the transition to democracy, before being succeeded by his
old opponent Lech Walesa.

Jiang Zemin (b. 1926): Jiang joined the Chinese Communist Party in
1946 and rose in the party machine whilst also working as an industrial
manager, as Commercial Counsellor in the USSR (1950–56) and later as
an industry minister. In 1985 he became mayor of Shanghai for three

years and in 1987 joined the Politburo, having been on the Central Committee since 1981. His tough approach to the Tiananmen Square demonstrations in 1989 helped him become Chairman of the Central Committee and he tightened his grip on power in 1993 by becoming president. Cautious and loyal to the veteran leader Deng Xiaoping (q.v.), he maintained policies of economic reform and openness to the outside world after Deng's death.

Johnson, Lyndon B. (1908–73):   A Democratic politician from Texas, Johnson had formidable experience of Congress, being elected to the House of Representatives in 1937 and the Senate in 1948, where he was Democratic leader during 1953–61. As vice-president in 1961–63 he chaired the National Security Council. He succeeded Kennedy when the latter was assassinated and won the presidency in his own right in 1964, by a massive majority. He showed an interest in developing detente, but he was drawn into the costly Vietnam War, which destroyed his reputation and his hopes of social reform in America. In 1968 he decided not to run for the presidency again.

Kadar, Janos (1912–90):   Hungarian Communist, and an early member of its youth movement, Kadar was imprisoned for a time in the 1930s and was unusual among party leaders in that he remained in Hungary, working underground, during the Second World War. He was a member of the party's Politburo after the war, but was imprisoned in 1951–54 in the period of Stalinist repression, because of his 'nationalist' leanings. Ironically this nationalist image made him useful to Moscow in 1956 when he became the political leader of Hungary after the crushing of Imre Nagy's government. After a period of repression, Kadar developed some market elements in the economy, but he always maintained Communist rule and was toppled from power by radical reformers in 1988–89.

Kennedy, John F. (1917–63):   From an Irish Roman Catholic family in Massachusetts, Kennedy was a naval war hero and Harvard graduate who became Democratic presidential candidate in the 1960 election. He defeated his opponent Richard Nixon by a narrow margin. His rousing inaugural address set the tone for a strong foreign policy, but he inherited some difficult problems (Congo and Laos) and faced humiliation over the Bay of Pigs operation before demonstrating resolute leadership in the Cuban Missile Crisis. A young, dynamic figure, his assassination in Dallas in November 1963 was a major blow to US self-confidence.

Khomeini, Ayatollah (1902–89):   Born Sayyed Ruhollah in the town of Khomein, from which he took his clerical name, he studied in the Holy City of Qom and became a leading Iranian religious leader (Ayatollah).

An opponent of the US-backed Shah, Khomeini was exiled in 1964 and spent the years 1965–78 in Iraq, before being expelled and going to Paris. By then he was the acknowledged leader of the Iranian opposition and finally returned to his country in February 1979, after unrest had driven the Shah out. In April an 'Islamic Republic' was declared, based on Khomeini's political ideas. As the unrivalled leader of a theocratic government he denounced both the US and the USSR as satanic, but became particularly hated in the West, partly because of the imprisonment of US Embassy staff in 1979–81. Shortly before his death he had to acknowledge that victory was impossible in the long war with Iraq.

Khruschev, Nikita S. (1894–1971):   Khruschev joined the Communist Party soon after the 1917 Revolution, and rose to become a full Politburo member in 1939. After work in Ukraine in 1944–47 he took charge of agricultural policy, over which he clashed with Georgi Malenkov. In 1953, on Stalin's death, Malenkov became prime minister and Khruschev head of the party bureaucracy. It was Khruschev who triumphed in the power struggle which followed. By 1955 he was strong enough to develop major new initiatives in foreign policy: the formation of the Warsaw Pact, a Summit with Western leaders at Geneva, the reopening of relations with Tito's Yugoslavia, and the development of links with 'Third World' states. In 1956 Khruschev launched a major attack on Stalin's 'personality cult'. He successfully resisted an attempt by other leading ministers to overthrow him in 1957 (the 'Anti-Party Plot'), and then became both party leader and prime minister. But Khruschev's 'de-Stalinisation' programme upset other Communist leaders, created uncertainty in the USSR, and led to the 1956 Hungarian Rising. His attempts to talk with the West were interspersed with threatening actions, leading to the Second Berlin Crisis (1958–59) and the Cuban Missile Crisis (1962). His humiliation over the last incident and the failure of his agricultural projects helped to undermine his position; in 1964 he was ousted by his ministers.

Kim Il Sung (1912–94):   Korean Communist Kim Il Sung was born Kim Song-ju into a peasant family who opposed the Japanese occupation. He was favoured by the Soviets after 1945, becoming North Korean leader. He allied closely with the USSR and launched the invasion of South Korea in June 1950, sparking the Korean War. After the war Kim united the Korean Communists, who had previously been divided into several factions, and increasingly took an independent course from both China and the USSR. The regime he established was isolationist and authoritarian, and presided over economic stagnation. Rarely seen in public, the 'Great Leader' survived to become the longest-serving dictator in modern history and was succeeded by his son, Kim Jong Il.

Kissinger, Henry A. (b. 1923):   German-born, of Jewish background, Kissinger fled with his family from Germany to New York in 1938 to escape Nazi persecution. He trained as an accountant before seeing war service and deciding to study foreign policy at Harvard. He became a well-known writer on foreign policy, and gained a reputation as an academic, especially on account of his *Nuclear Weapons and Foreign Policy* (1957). He was given considerable powers as Nixon's National Security Adviser after 1969. Kissinger's role in developing detente with Russia, the 'opening' to China and peace in Vietnam led to his being treated as a 'superman' figure by 1973 when he became Secretary of State. But the collapse of South Vietnam, and moral doubts about his *realpolitik*, undermined respect for him.

Kohl, Helmut (b. 1930):   German Christian Democratic politician, who joined the party on its foundation in 1946, gained experience in local politics and rose to become party chairman in 1973. As party leader in the Bundestag after 1976 he seemed uninspiring, but in 1982 he won a vote of no confidence in Helmut Schmidt's leadership. Like Britain's Margaret Thatcher, Kohl pursued a policy of spending controls and tax reform internally, and backed both NATO and nuclear defence in international affairs. Unlike her, he was a keen advocate of European integration, to provide Germany with a non-nationalist ambition in world affairs. Kohl accepted Cruise and Pershing missiles into Germany and defeated the SPD in the 1983 and 1987 elections. Still criticised as lacklustre, he survived a series of difficulties in the late 1980s and carefully exploited the events of 1989–90 to become the first Chancellor of a reunited Germany. Although his ability to deal with the new country's economic problems was soon in doubt, with rising unemployment and the high costs of modernising the East, he was re-elected in 1994 and had a leading role in pressing for a single European currency.

Kosygin, Alexei (1904–80):   Soviet Communist leader Kosygin became an economics minister under Khruschev in the 1950s and head of the economic planning commission (GOSPLAN) in 1960. With Brezhnev, Kosygin led the overthrow of Khruschev in October 1964, becoming prime minister. Kosygin attempted some tentative reforms of the planning system in the 1960s. He also handled relations with non-Communist states and met President Johnson at Glassboro' in 1967, but was gradually excluded from power by Brezhnev and replaced as premier shortly before his death.

Kozyrev, Andrei (b. 1951):   Kozyrev joined the Soviet foreign ministry in 1974 and served in various posts before becoming the foreign minister of the Russian Soviet Federated Socialist Republic in October 1990. In

1990–91 the RSFSR President, Boris Yeltsin, pressed for greater powers to be given to the constituent republics of the USSR and, especially after August 1991 (when Mikhail Gorbachev's position was crippled in a failed coup attempt), Kozyrev was able to construct a distinctly Russian foreign policy. When the USSR disintegrated, he continued in his post, eventually becoming Yeltsin's longest-serving minister. But Kozyrev was increasingly criticised by Communists and nationalists for being too pro-Western and failing to assert himself in the Bosnian conflict. His removal was already likely in December 1995 when, on being elected a member of parliament, he had to choose between taking his seat or remaining in government. He resigned in early January.

Kryuchkov, Vladmir (b. 1928): A Soviet secret policeman, Kryuchkov joined the Communist Party in the war, took part in state prosecutions under Stalin and became allied to Andropov, with whom he worked in putting down the Hungarian rising in 1956. From 1974 to 1988 Kryuchkov was head of the KGB's foreign intelligence. In 1988 he succeeded Chebrikov – another Andropov ally – as head of the secret police. Kryuchkov soon emulated Chebrikov by criticising Gorbachev and accusing the West of fomenting discontent in the USSR. He became a leading figure in the 1991 coup to oust Gorbachev and was arrested after its failure.

Lie, Trygve (1896–1968): Norwegian politician and war-time foreign minister Trygve Lie was appointed first Secretary-General of the UN in February 1946. He was chosen as a compromise candidate, acceptable to both East and West, but was little known. He presided over the UN at a difficult time, when the Cold War was developing and the UN headquarters had to be set up. At first he was seen in the West as the 'Soviet candidate' for Secretary-General, but in the Korean War after 1950 the Soviets condemned him as pro-Western, and in November 1952 he announced he would resign.

Macmillan, Harold (1894–1986): A British Conservative politician, Harold Macmillan made his reputation as housing minister in the early 1950s. After brief periods as defence minister and foreign secretary, Macmillan became Chancellor of the Exchequer and had a major role in the 1956 Suez Crisis. Despite this, he emerged as prime minister in succession to Anthony Eden in January 1957 and won the 1959 general election. Macmillan rebuilt the alliance with America after Suez, visited Russia in early 1959 in the midst of the Second Berlin Crisis and maintained Britain's nuclear deterrent. But he also presided over economic difficulties, a growing sense of malaise in British society and the loss of much of the Colonial Empire. A series of spy scandals and a failed attempt to enter the European Economic Community undermined his position, and ill-health forced him to resign in 1963.

Malenkov, Georgi (1902–88):   A Soviet Communist, Malenkov became one of Stalin's leading ministers before the Second World War and afterwards rivalled Andrei Zhdanov in the quest for power. Following the latter's death, Malenkov became Stalin's favourite, succeeding him as party leader and prime minister in March 1953. But other ministers forced Malenkov to surrender the party leadership to Khruschev. In 1953–54 Malenkov tried to relax tensions with the West and develop a 'new course' inside the USSR based on greater production of consumer goods. But he lost out in the power struggle with Khruschev, was replaced as premier in early 1955 and ousted from the leadership in 1957 after joining in the unsuccessful 'Anti-Party Plot' to overthrow Khruschev.

Mao Zedong (1893–1976):   Mao became committed to the radical reform of China as a youth and in the 1920s turned to Marxism. He saw the need to mobilise the mass of the peasants behind the revolutionary cause and became the leader of the Communists during the 'Long March' of 1934–35. In 1949 Mao triumphed over the Nationalists in the civil war and after 1954 adopted the title of 'Chairman of the Central Committee', with a personality cult. Many of his policies were based on the Soviet model, adapted to suit Chinese conditions, including the redistribution of land, close links between the Communist Party and the administration, and the Five-Year Plans (beginning with that of 1953–57).

After Stalin's death Mao increasingly fell out with the Soviets, breaking with them completely in 1961. Committed to freeing the Chinese from the poverty and weakness of the past, he tried to transform the country in various ways. In 1957 his 'hundred flowers' speech tried to encourage constructive criticism of society, but instead led to the questioning of Communism itself from intellectuals, which in turn led him to attack them in the so-called 'Anti-Rightist' campaign. In 1958–60 Mao turned to the 'Great Leap Forward', seeking the mobilisation of peasants behind new production programmes, but his unrealistic demands led to malnutrition and famine. Millions died. Mao's final bid to reinvigorate the revolution was the 'Cultural Revolution' (q.v.), which also resulted in instability and oppression. Mao's last years were marked by a struggle to succeed him, and also by the 'opening' to America.

Marshall, George C. (1880–1959):   A US general, Marshall was, as Army Chief of Staff in 1939–45, responsible for controlling America's war strategy. In December 1945 he was sent to China by President Truman, but, despite enormous efforts, could not mediate a settlement between Communists and Nationalists. For two years after January 1947 he was

Secretary of State, in which position he launched the Marshall Aid Programme and laid the basis for NATO. In 1950–51 he also served as Secretary of Defense, but this did not prevent baseless criticisms of him by the rabid anti-Communist Joe McCarthy.

McCone, John A. (1902–91):   A shipbuilding engineer, millionaire businessman and in 1958–60 Chairman of the Atomic Energy Commission, McCone was chosen by John F. Kennedy to head the CIA after the humiliating Bay of Pigs operation. McCone's managerial abilities, his interest in intelligence-gathering technology and his performance during the Cuban Missile Crisis helped the Agency to recover from its difficulties. As a Republican, McCone was able to maintain bipartisan respect for the CIA. He did not work so well with President Johnson and resigned in April 1965.

McNamara, Robert S. (b. 1916):   A US businessman who rose to become president of the Ford Motor Company, McNamara was made Secretary of Defense under Kennedy in 1961. He continued to serve under Johnson until 1968. He had a major role in the 1961 Berlin crisis, Cuban Missile Crisis and Vietnam War. His energy and efficiency were devoted to the introduction of new planning and budget systems, to the development of nuclear strategy (see Mutually Assured Destruction) and to the foundation of such new bodies as the Defense Intelligence Agency. He later worked as President of the World Bank.

Mitterrand, François (1916–96):   A leftist French politician and a wartime resistance fighter, Mitterrand first gained ministerial experience under the Fourth Republic, and became a major critic of de Gaulle's powers during the 1960s. He tried to create a centre-Left opposition group in the 1960s, but only in 1971, when he became leader of the new Socialist Party, did these efforts begin to bear fruit. After narrowly losing the 1974 presidential election to Giscard d'Estaing, Mitterrand became president in 1981. His attempt at radical Socialist economic policies in 1981–83 ended in failure and a general election in 1986 forced him to accept a period of 'cohabitation', with the Gaullist Chirac as premier. But Mitterrand's political acumen and strong image enabled him to win re-election in 1988. He worked more closely with the US than previous Fifth Republican politicians, ultimately joining in the military campaign against Saddam Hussein's Iraq in 1991, but until then he also kept his distance from NATO and maintained links to Eastern Europe before the fall of Communism. A strong advocate of European integration, he backed the 1991 Maastricht Treaty but suffered from the narrow result of a referendum upon it, as well as from revelations about his links to the wartime Vichy regime. He survived to the end of his second term but succumbed to cancer soon afterwards.

Molotov, Vyacheslav M. (1890–1986): A leading Bolshevik, originally surnamed Skriabin, Molotov adopted his pseudonym (Molotov = hammer) in 1912. He was editor of *Pravda* in 1917, joined the Politburo in 1921 and became a close ally of Stalin, with the position of Chairman of the People's Commissars (1930–40). In 1939 he also became foreign minister, making the Ribbentrop–Molotov Pact before co-operating with the Western powers during the war. A skilled tactician, he argued forcefully with Western foreign ministers in the post-war Council of Foreign Ministers. Demoted to deputy foreign minister in 1949, he became a victim of Stalin's suspicions: his Jewish wife was subjected to internal exile. Stalin's death brought Molotov back to the foreign ministry in 1953–56, but he opposed Khruschev's reforms and tried to overthrow the latter in the 1957 'Anti-Party Plot'. The plot's failure led to Molotov's demotion to Ambassador to Mongolia. In 1964 he was expelled from the party and was allowed to return only in 1984.

Muskie, Edmund S. (1914–96): American lawyer and Democratic politician, Muskie served as Governor of Maine in 1955–59 and was a senator from 1959 to 1980, in which position he held several key Congressional posts, including membership of the Senate Foreign Relations Committee. His public standing made him an ideal successor to Cyrus Vance, when the latter suddenly resigned as Secretary of State in 1980. Muskie's short Secretaryship was overshadowed by the Iran hostage crisis, and his reputation could not prevent Carter's defeat in the November presidential election.

Nagy, Imre (1896–1958): A Hungarian Communist leader who had converted to Communism after being taken prisoner by Russians in the First World War, Nagy worked underground in Hungary in the 1920s before seeking exile in the Soviet Union.

He returned to Hungary at the end of the Second World War, but was a critic of the Stalinist political–economic system. As prime minister in 1953–55, following Stalin's death, Nagy tried to introduce more liberal policies and economic reforms. He lost a power struggle with the Communist Party leader, Matyas Rakosi, in 1955, but was recalled to power in October 1956 by popular demand. His renewed calls for reform, including a neutralist foreign policy, brought his overthrow the following month by the Red Army. He was taken to Romania and later executed, but remained an inspiration to nationalists when Soviet Communism collapsed in 1989.

Nasser, Gamal Abdel (1918–70): An Egyptian soldier and nationalist, Nasser was one of the leaders of the 'Free Officers' who overthrew the monarchy in 1952. In 1954 Nasser replaced General Neguib as leader of

Egypt, the most powerful Arab state, and in 1956 he became the hero of the Arabs because of the failure of the Anglo-French expedition against him (see Suez Crisis). Nasser tried to modernise Egypt through the redistribution of land and building the Aswan dam. In international affairs he joined the non-aligned movement, but also accepted substantial aid from the Eastern bloc. Nasser's involvement in the Yemen civil war after 1962 weakened Egypt in the face of war with Israel in 1967, when his forces were routed. In 1970 he died suddenly of a heart attack.

Nehru, Jawaharlal (1889–1964):   Born into an aristocratic family, educated in Britain and trained as a lawyer, Nehru became a leader of the Indian nationalist movement during the inter-war years. He was imprisoned by the British, but became first prime minister of an independent India in 1947. He made India a Republic and was ardently opposed to colonialism, but joined the British Commonwealth. He was a socialist who welcomed Khruschev to India in 1955, but was determined not to join the Soviet bloc. His policy was one of 'non-alignment' and he sought to create an Afro-Asian viewpoint in world affairs at the Bandung Conference (1955). His last years were marred by deteriorating relations with China, which culminated in the humiliating border war of 1962.

Ngo Dinh Diem (1901–63):   A South Vietnamese leader, Ngo Dinh Diem came from a Roman Catholic mandarin family in central Vietnam. He became a civil servant and opposed both French rule and the Communists. His anti-colonialism and anti-Communism made him attractive to the US as a new prime minister of South Vietnam in June 1954. He successfully defeated political rivals, ousted the ex-Emperor, Bao Dai, from power (1955) and refused to call nation-wide elections (planned for 1956). However, he could not construct a solid anti-Communist alliance. His regime alienated Buddhists, became corrupt and oppressive, and helped the Communists gain popularity. US sympathy for him ended and he was murdered by his own generals in November 1963.

Nguyen Van Thieu (b. 1924):   A South Vietnamese leader, Nguyen Van Thieu was for a time a member of the Viet-Minh nationalist movement, before joining the Vietnamese army set up by the French. He came to the fore as one of the South Vietnamese army officers favoured by the premier, General Nguyen Khanh, in 1963–65. In June 1965 Thieu became South Vietnam's head of state, but real power was in the hands of premier Nguyen Cao Ky until September 1967. As the leading figure in South Vietnam thereafter, Thieu defeated all political rivals, won rigged elections in 1971 and opposed a settlement with the Communists. But he was distrusted by the US, who negotiated 'peace' with North Vietnam in January 1973. In 1975 Thieu's indecision helped the Communists secure his regime's overthrow, after which he lived in exile.

Nixon, Richard M. (1913–94):   A US Republican from California, Nixon trained as a lawyer and was elected to the House of Representatives in 1946, in which position he made his name as a firm anti-Communist (being closely involved in the Chambers–Hiss spy case). He was elected to the Senate in 1950 and, helped by the rising tide of McCarthyism, became Eisenhower's vice-president in 1953–61. As vice-president he was almost killed by a mob whilst visiting Caracas (1958), and had a public argument with Khruschev (the 'kitchen debate', 1959). He lost the 1960 presidential election to Kennedy, and the 1962 race for the Governorship of California, but he returned to win the presidential elections of 1968 and 1972, the latter by an overwhelming majority. His anti-Communism ironically probably helped him keep America's trust as he developed a detente with Russia and China. But he was criticised for taking too long to extricate America from the Vietnam War, and was forced to resign in 1974 by the Watergate (q.v.) scandal.

Perez de Cuellar, Javier (b. 1920):   A Peruvian diplomat, Perez de Cuellar was ambassador to the UN in 1971–75 and UN representative in Cyprus during 1975–77. He then became Under-Secretary-General to the UN, before being elected Secretary-General in 1981. Experienced and hardworking, he nevertheless failed to prevent the 1982 Falklands war between Britain and Argentina, or to bring peace to the Lebanon, but he did reassert the UN role in the later 1980s, over for example the end of the Iran–Iraq War.

Pompidou, Georges (1911–74):   A French politician, Pompidou was catapulted to predominance by de Gaulle in 1962, when he was promoted from being the latter's executive secretary to being prime minister. Pompidou survived an early attempt to vote him from office and grew enormously in stature in 1968 when he stood firm against student demonstrators and striking workers, at a time when de Gaulle seemed to waver. Pompidou became the Gaullist candidate for president in 1969, after de Gaulle's resignation, and as president pursued a self-confident, independent foreign policy. He maintained a policy of detente with the Eastern bloc. It was probably in order to control German ambitions that Pompidou allowed Britain into the European Community. He died suddenly of cancer in 1974.

Powell, Colin L. (b. 1937):   Born into a family of Jamaican immigrants, Powell joined the US army in 1958, served in Vietnam and rose to become the commander of the second brigade of the 101st Airborne Division by 1976 before taking on a more political role as adviser to the Defense Department in 1979–81 and 1983–86. He was Reagan's National Security Adviser in 1987–88 before becoming the youngest ever Chairman of the Joint Chiefs of Staff in 1989, a post he held for four years. In this role he had overall charge of the US campaign against Iraq in the Gulf War. He refused to run in the 1996 election campaign despite evidence that he could have become the first Black American president.

Primakov, Yevgeni (b. 1929):   Educated in Oriental Studies, Primakov worked as a journalist in radio (1953–62) and on the Soviet newspaper, *Pravda* (1962–70) before joining the International Relations Institute, of which he became director in 1985–89. He was a candidate member of the Politburo in 1989–91 and elected a People's Deputy in 1989. Seen as an architect of Gorbachev's 'new diplomacy', Primakov was determined to protect Soviet interests and in 1990–91, as special envoy in the Middle East, worked for a diplomatic solution to the Gulf crisis. In September 1991 he became founder-director of the new external intelligence service, taking over part of the KGB's former role. He continued to hold this post in Yeltsin's Russia before succeeding Andrei Kozyrev (q.v.) as foreign minister, an appointment greeted with suspicion in the West. Insisting on Russia's importance as a great power, he criticised NATO's eastward enlargement and in 1997–98 (as in 1990–91) tried to dissuade America from military action against Saddam Hussein.

Reagan, Ronald W. (b. 1911):   Born in Illinois to an Irish–English family, Reagan became a sports journalist before making his film debut in 1937. A well-known 'B-movie' star, he became President of the Screen Actors Guild in 1947, at which time he supported the Democrats. Strongly anti-Communist, he switched to the Republicans in 1962, supported the right-wing Barry Goldwater for the presidency in 1964 and was elected Governor of California in 1967. He made bids for the Republican candidacy for the presidency in 1968, 1972 and 1976, before finally winning the 1980 presidential race. He was known in his first term for strong condemnations of Moscow's 'evil Empire' and for a willingness to use military force (as in Grenada). The 'Reagan Doctrine' (less well-defined than earlier presidential doctrines) promised US support for anti-Communist 'freedom fighters' in Afghanistan, Nicaragua and elsewhere. In his second term (1985–89), however, he was discredited somewhat by the Irangate scandal, and proved ready to pursue dramatic steps towards detente with Gorbachev.

Rogers, William P. (b. 1913):   A lawyer and Republican politician, Rogers served in Eisenhower's Cabinet as Attorney-General in 1957–61 and, as a loyal and reliable friend of Richard Nixon, became Secretary of State in 1969. His experience of foreign affairs was, however, limited, and he suffered from Nixon's determination to keep meaningful foreign policy decisions in the hands of the White House. Rogers led attempts to bring peace between Israel and the Arabs, but was otherwise overshadowed by National Security Adviser Kissinger, who replaced him in 1973.

Roosevelt, Franklin D. (1882–1945): An American Democratic politician, Roosevelt in his early career was Assistant Secretary of the Navy (1913–20) and an unsuccessful vice-presidential candidate (1920). He suffered an attack of polio in 1921 and was forced to use a wheel-chair: nevertheless, he re-entered politics in 1928, becoming Governor of New York and, in 1933, president. He carried out the 'New Deal' reforms of the 1930s to tackle economic depression, and was re-elected president on an unprecedented three occasions (1936, 1940, 1944). He followed an isolationist policy in the 1930s, but supported Britain's war effort after 1940. Forced into the war by Japan's attack on Pearl Harbor, he became the personification of hopes for a liberal peace. He supported the creation of the UN and had hopes of working with Russia after the war, but died a few weeks before the conflict ended.

Rusk, Dean D. (1909–94): Partly educated in Britain and Germany, Rusk was a College lecturer in the 1930s before war service took him to the operations division of the War Department. After the war he worked for the Defense Department and the State Department, and in 1952–61 was president of the Rockefeller Foundation. His experience and high standing in the US foreign policy establishment made him a natural choice as Kennedy's Secretary of State in 1961, from which position he handled the Test-Ban Treaty negotiations and directed US policy towards the Congo crisis. Rusk's loyalty led him to continue to serve as Secretary of State throughout the Johnson presidency, when he became the principal public defender of US policy in Vietnam and alienated many of his former liberal allies. In 1969 he returned to academic life.

El **Sadat**, Anwar (1918–81): Egyptian political leader Sadat came from a peasant family. He joined the Egyptian army and opposed British domination of his country. In 1952 he was a leader of the 'Free Officers' movement which overthrew King Farouk. Sadat was a close friend of Nasser after 1954, succeeding him as president in 1970. Sadat distanced himself from the Soviet Union and masterminded the October 1973 (Yom Kippur) War against Israel. He was determined to win back control of the Sinai peninsula from Israel, but his willingness to visit Jerusalem and his peace treaty with Israel (1979) alienated other Arab states and inspired a group of his own soldiers to assassinate him.

Saddam Hussein (b. 1937): Saddam joined the secular and socialist Ba'ath Party in 1957 and was involved in an attempt to overthrow the

Iraqi government only two years later. Forced into exile in Egypt, he returned to Iraq in 1963 and, though imprisoned in 1964–65 for continued plotting, rose in the party hierarchy. He had a leading role in a successful coup in 1968, joining the Revolutionary Command Council of which he became chair in 1979. Made a general in 1976, he also took over the presidency in 1979. Responsible for the decision to attack Iran in 1980, his failure to achieve anything despite eight years of war did not prevent him from invading Kuwait in 1990, which resulted in a successful American-led counter-invasion. Ruthless in exterminating his opponents, he nonetheless clung to power and continued to irk the US by developing weapons of mass destruction and periodically threatening Kuwait.

Schlesinger, James R. (b. 1929):   Educated at Harvard, Schlesinger worked as an academic economist in the 1950s, and in the 1960s was a senior member of the influential Rand Corporation. He entered government service under Nixon in 1969 and in 1971–73 served as Chairman of the Atomic Energy Commission. In 1973 Schlesinger had an eventful four months as CIA Director, trying to take control of the whole intelligence community, and to root out 'dead wood' among its employees. But in July, amid the changes brought by the Watergate scandal, he was moved to become Secretary of Defense. In this position he often clashed with Henry Kissinger and was eventually replaced by President Ford in the 1975 'Halloween Massacre'. He also served as Secretary of Energy under President Carter during 1977–79 and remained an influential voice in foreign affairs.

Scowcroft, Brent (b. 1925):   A US air force officer, Scowcroft taught political science at West Point and the Air Force Academy before gaining various National Security posts in the 1960s. He became Deputy National Security Adviser in 1973–75 and was then chosen by President Ford to succeed Kissinger as National Security Adviser. He held several official posts after 1977 in the field of foreign and defence policy and was reappointed National Security Adviser under Bush, remaining throughout the presidency. Scowcroft carried out the major review of US foreign policy in early 1989 which resulted in a series of presidential speeches. He formed part of the experienced group around the president which successfully handled the 1990–91 Kuwait crisis. Unlike Kissinger he tended to co-ordinate policy rather than take a major decision-making role.

Semichastny, Vladimir Y. (b. 1924):   Russian Communist Semichastny was a close ally of Alexander Shelepin (q.v.), whom he succeeded as head of the Youth Movement in 1958 and of the KGB in 1961. He helped to overthrow Khruschev, and was promoted on to the Central

Committee, but was demoted by Brezhnev in 1967 to become deputy premier of the Ukraine.

Serov, Ivan A. (1905–65):   A Russian Communist, Serov joined the secret police and, after 1941, was deputy head of the NKVD. He took part in the forced deportation of minorities during the Second World War and mass murder afterwards, while helping to Communise Eastern Europe. In 1953 Serov arrested the security chief, Beria, who was later executed. Serov's boss was then Sergei Kruglov, who helped form the KGB in 1953–54 before also being dismissed (and later executed). Serov then became first head of the KGB, a post he held for four years, helping to defeat the Hungarian rising, and the 'Anti-Party Plot' against Khruschev in 1957. But in 1958 Khruschev moved Serov to be head of military intelligence. In 1963 he was excluded from leading office, being too much identified with the terrors of Stalinism; soon after he committed suicide.

Shelepin, Alexander N. (1918–94):   Russian Communist Shelepin rose to become head of the Youth Movement and in 1958, of the KGB, a post he held for three years. He tried to alter the repressive image of the KGB to help his own political ambitions. He organised the overthrow of Khruschev in 1964, and was promoted to the Politburo. But Brezhnev tried to control him, making him head of the trades unions in 1967 and removing him from the Politburo in 1975.

Shepilov, Dimitri T. (b. 1905):   Soviet politician Shepilov worked with Khruschev in the Ukraine during the World War. He became editor of *Pravda* in 1952, and gained foreign policy experience in 1954 as chairman of the foreign affairs commission of the Supreme Soviet. In February 1956 Shepilov became a candidate (non-voting) member of the Politburo and four months later replaced the veteran Molotov as foreign minister, just a day before a major visit by Tito. But in 1957 he was replaced as foreign minister by Gromyko and then took part in the ill-fated 'Anti-Party Plot' to overthrow Khruschev. The plot's failure destroyed Shepilov's career.

Shevardnadze, Eduard A. (b. 1928):   Born in Georgia, Shevardnadze studied history before becoming a youth movement member and, after 1961, a Communist Party bureaucrat. His efforts at rooting out corruption in Georgia, where he became Communist Party leader, brought him to Moscow's attention. He impressed Gorbachev, whom he met on several occasions. International opinion was shocked in July 1985 when Shevardnadze was appointed foreign minister, in succession to the veteran Gromyko. Shevardnadze nevertheless proved a capable foreign minister, carrying out Gorbachev's policies aimed at relaxing tension. He became greatly respected in the West, and his resignation in 1990 was a bitter blow to Soviet reformers. He quit the Communist Party before the August 1991 coup against Gorbachev. During November–December Shevardnadze returned as foreign minister for a short time, but then focused on Georgian politics, becoming head of state.

Shultz, George P. (b. 1920): A Republican politician and business professor, Shultz served in various capacities, including Secretary of the Treasury, in the Nixon administration (1972–74). In 1982 he succeeded Al Haig as Secretary of State and remained in the post for the rest of the Reagan era. Shultz's cautious manner and quiet approach to diplomacy earned him the nickname 'the Buddha'. He was trusted by Reagan, but often differed with Defense Secretary Weinberger. Although Shultz supported the use of force in Lebanon and Libya, he adopted a positive line in dealings with the Soviets and worked well with Eduard Shevardnadze to build detente after 1985.

Smith, Walter Bedell (1895–1961): An American soldier, Smith rose to become chief of staff to Dwight Eisenhower in 1942–46, when the latter was Allied Supreme Commander. In 1946–49 Smith served as Ambassador to Moscow and in 1950–53 helped to establish the CIA, as its second director. He continued to serve his old chief, Eisenhower, as Under-Secretary of State in 1953–54, and played a major role in the 1954 Geneva Conference on Indo-China.

Stalin, Josef (1879–1953): Born Josef Djugashvili, to a peasant family in Georgia, Stalin began anti-Tsarist subversive activity in 1899, was elected to the Bolshevik's Central Committee in 1912 and became Commissar for Nationalities under Lenin after the October 1917 Revolution. Following Lenin's death in 1924, Stalin gradually eliminated all potential rivals, including Leon Trotsky, and became dictator of the USSR by 1928. He carried through the rapid industrialisation of the country at the cost of creating a police-state in which his opponents were liquidated in 'purges'. He tried to co-operate with other powers against the Nazis, but then entered into a Pact with Hitler in 1939. Attacked by Hitler in 1941, Stalin eventually (after 1943) saw the Germans forced to retreat. The war left him in control of Eastern Europe which he turned into puppet Communist regimes, as relations with his wartime allies declined. Increasingly megalomaniacal, his 'personality cult' reached its height at the 1952 Party Congress. He seemed to be planning a new 'purge' when he died of a stroke in 1953.

Sukarno, Achmed (1901–70): Sukarno led the Indonesian Nationalists in the period after 1927 against colonial rule in the Dutch East Indies.

Imprisoned by the Dutch, he worked with the Japanese for a time during the Second World War, and proclaimed Indonesia's independence in 1945. Sukarno was President of Indonesia after it successfully won independence in 1949, and he became a leading figure in Third World politics. He used the army to put down local opposition, established a dictatorship (1959), forced the Dutch out of West New Guinea (1962) and threatened war against Malaysia (1964). In 1965 General Suharto, supported by the US, replaced Sukarno and destroyed the Indonesian Communists ruthlessly.

Syngman Rhee (1875–1965): A Korean politician, Rhee was related to the royal family who opposed the Japanese domination of the country after 1895. He spent much of his early life in the US. A determined anti-Communist and ruthless politician he was favoured by the US occupation authorities in Korea after 1945, becoming first President of South Korea in July 1948. He led the country through the Korean War, but his authoritarian manner and corrupt government alienated many, and he was overthrown in 1960 after widespread demonstrations.

Thatcher, Margaret (b. 1925): A British Conservative politician, first elected to parliament in 1959, Thatcher served as Education Minister in 1970–74. In 1975 the Conservatives chose her to replace Edward Heath, who had lost three elections. Thatcher won the next election in 1979 and proved a determined prime minister, pursuing privatisation and controls on government spending. Initially little-known abroad she soon had a major impact, criticising Soviet politics in the 'Second Cold War', working closely with US President Reagan and directing the short, successful war with Argentina over the Falkland Islands (1982). Although re-elected in 1983 and 1987 her combative style alienated many, and she was forced to resign in November 1990 by growing dissent in her own party.

Tito (Josip Broz) (1892–1980): Communist leader of Yugoslavia from 1937, Tito conducted a successful partisan campaign after 1941 against the German occupation. In 1944–45 he was able to establish complete control in Yugoslavia. He seemed entirely loyal to Moscow, but became resentful of Soviet interference in Yugoslav affairs. In 1948 Stalin expelled Tito from Cominform, and in 1949 the latter accepted Western financial aid. Relations with Russia improved again in 1955, but Tito thereafter identified in foreign affairs with the non-aligned movement. Although he sought to decentralise authority within Yugoslavia he always remained a Communist, taking a tough line against dissidents such as his former deputy, Milovan Djilas.

Truman, Harry S. (1884–1972): A US Democratic politician from Missouri, Truman was elected to the Senate in 1934. He made his name in uncovering the mismanagement of government defence spending in the 1930s, and was Roosevelt's vice-presidential candidate in 1944. On Roosevelt's sudden death, in April 1945, Truman became president, a position to which he was elected in his own right, by a narrow majority, in 1948. He lacked knowledge of international affairs at first, but in 1947 enunciated the anti-Communist Truman Doctrine (q.v.) and took a tough stand against Russia over the Berlin Blockade (1948–49). He also decided to enter the Korean War in 1950, though he was blamed by many for the loss of China (1949) and deadlock in Korea.

U Thant, Sithu (1909–74): A Burmese politician and ambassador to the UN, U Thant became Secretary-General of the UN in 1961 after Hammarskjöld's death. A Buddhist, with great self-discipline, U Thant seemed unruffled by the many crises he had to face – Cuba in 1962, Vietnam and the India–Pakistan War of 1965. He sent a peace-keeping force to Cyprus in 1964, but was much criticised by Western nations in 1967 for withdrawing UN troops from Sinai. The action was followed by an Arab–Israeli war. His health declining, he decided not to stand for a further term in 1971.

Ulbricht, Walter (1893–1973): A German Communist leader, Ulbricht fled to Russia in 1933 on Hitler's entry into power. In April 1946 Ulbricht became General Secretary of the East German Socialist Unity Party (SED), formed by Communists and Socialists, and he dominated the new East German government after 1949. He remained in power despite the 'de-Stalinisation' of the Eastern bloc after 1953, and became head of state (as well as party leader) in 1960. His lukewarm approach to links with West Germany in the late 1960s aroused Moscow's displeasure and he was replaced as party leader in May 1971 by Erich Honecker. Ulbricht remained head of state, however, until his death.

Ustinov, Dmitri F. (1908–84): A Soviet politician, Ustinov joined the Communist Party in his youth, trained as an engineer and became Commissar for Armaments when only thirty-two, a post he held throughout the war and until Stalin's death. He continued to head the defence industry in the 1960s and developed the Soviet space programme. He succeeded Grechko as defence minister in April 1976, inheriting a formidable military machine. He also became a Politburo member and was appointed Marshal, despite having no active service record. He sought to maintain the importance of the military in Soviet life, though this was undermined by the campaign in Afghanistan after 1979. In 1984 he died and was succeeded by the much weaker Sergei Sokolov.

Vance, Cyrus (b. 1917): Educated at Yale Law School, Vance pursued a career as a New York lawyer, but developed a keen interest in international affairs. He entered the Defense Department under President Kennedy and, in 1964–67, was Under-Secretary of Defense. His experience, common sense and high standing helped him become Secretary of State in 1977. Vance, whose greatest triumph was the Camp David Agreement between Egypt and Israel, shared President Carter's desire to improve relations with Third World states, but recognised the importance of the Soviet Union and worked hard to secure a SALT II Treaty. However, he increasingly lost influence over policy-making to the National Security Adviser, Brzezinski. He was upset by the demise of detente in 1979 and opposed the attempt to rescue US hostages in Iran in April 1980. He decided to resign on the last issue, but remained an influential voice, taking part in attempts to solve the Bosnian civil war in the 1990s.

Vyshinsky, Andrei Y. (1883–1955): A Russian Communist, originally a Menshevik, Vyshinsky trained as a lawyer and was professor at Moscow University in the 1920s before becoming Stalin's chief prosecutor in the show trials of the 1930s. In 1940–49 he acted as deputy foreign minister to Molotov and replaced the latter in 1949. Despised in the West, his period in office marked the depths of Cold War enmity. With Stalin's death in 1953 Vyshinsky was replaced once more by Molotov and excluded from power.

Waldheim, Kurt (b. 1918): Austrian politician Waldheim became Ambassador to the UN and foreign minister, before being elected Secretary-General of the UN in 1971, as a compromise candidate. He was hard-working and determined, but personally ambitious, and could not recover the standing which the Secretary-General's office had held under Dag Hammarskjöld. The UN proved useful in separating the opposing sides after the 1973 Middle East War, but in general the 1970s saw a growing rift within the organisation between Third World states and the Western powers. In 1981 China's opposition led Waldheim to withdraw from an attempt at re-election as Secretary-General. Later it was revealed that, as a wartime officer in the German army, he had been involved in the occupation of the Balkans, but had subsequently tried to disguise his role in this. The revelations harmed the UN, but did not prevent Waldheim becoming Austrian president, 1986–92.

Weinberger, Caspar W. (b. 1917): Weinberger acted as finance director for Ronald Reagan in 1968–69, when the latter was Governor of California. He worked in Washington in various posts under Nixon and

Ford and later as a company director. In 1981 he was appointed Reagan's Defense Secretary and soon became a major force behind the presidency's foreign policy. Always close to Reagan, Weinberger joined in the president's anti-Soviet rhetoric and, along with Deputy Secretary Richard Perle, supervised a US military build-up. Outspoken and tough, Weinberger questioned the value of SALT, strongly supported Britain in the 1982 Falklands Crisis and clashed with the Secretaries of State Haig and Schultz. When Weinberger retired in 1987 he was succeeded by his close ally, Frank Carlucci.

Yazov, Dmitri (b. 1924):   A professional soldier of peasant background, Yazov fought in the Second World War and served in Eastern Europe and elsewhere, rising to become head of the Red Army's Far Eastern Command. He was still quite low in the military hierarchy when chosen, in 1987, to succeed Sergei Sokolov as defence minister, after the military were humiliated by the young West German, Matthias Rust, who flew an aircraft undetected into Red Square. Yazov carried out the withdrawal from Afghanistan, but grew in confidence as a critic of Gorbachev and the latter's military spending cuts. In 1991 he joined the botched coup against Gorbachev and was sacked.

Yeltsin, Boris N. (b. 1931):   Yeltsin was educated in Sverdlovsk, at the same Polytechnic as the later Soviet premier, Nikolai Ryzhkov, before becoming a building engineer, and a Communist Party bureaucrat. In 1976 he became the first Secretary of the Party in Sverdlovsk and in 1985 was made, with Ryzhkov's support, the Central Committee's Secretary for Construction. In December 1985 he succeeded the conservative Viktor Grishin in the highly influential post of Communist Party Leader in Moscow. Yeltsin was then seen, along with such figures as Shevardnadze, as one of the reformist younger men, from regional party backgrounds, favoured by Gorbachev. He became a supporter of political reform in the USSR and clashed with conservative Politburo members. In October 1987 an argument led to Yeltsin's expulsion from the Politburo, but he proved adept at public relations, easily won a seat in the new Congress of People's Deputies in March 1989 and later became President of the Russian Federation, from which position he became a real rival to Gorbachev. His popularity was strengthened by his August 1991 stand against the attempted overthrow of Gorbachev. As Russian president, after the break-up of the USSR, he steered a volatile course, courting the West in order to win financial aid but criticising the enlargement of NATO. Despite drunkenness, health problems and attacks from ex-Communists over Russia's poverty-stricken economy, he was re-elected president in 1996.

Zhou Enlai (1898–1976): Well-educated, from a middle-class background, Zhou was an early member of the Chinese Communist Party, and became China's prime minister from September 1949 to January 1976. Zhou was also foreign minister in 1949–58, from which position he took a bellicose line in the Korean War, had a leading role in the 1954 Geneva Conference on Indo-China and supported the non-aligned movement at Bandung in 1955. He survived as Mao Zedong's trusted lieutenant during the 'Great Leap Forward' (1958–60) and 'Cultural Revolution' (after 1965), and played a leading role in the *rapprochement* with America during 1971–72. But after 1972 Zhou fell from favour. Four years later he died of cancer.

Zhukov, Georgi (1896–1974):   Russian soldier Zhukov joined the Communists after the Revolution and became famous for the defence of Stalingrad in 1942–43. He accepted Germany's surrender in May 1945. Stalin was jealous of Zhukov's reputation and put him in minor commands after the war. He returned to prominence in 1955, when he became Minister of Defence, but Khruschev too became jealous of the Marshal's position and, accusing him of 'Bonapartism', replaced him in 1957.

Note on Reagan's National Security Advisers (1981–89)

In the twenty years before Ronald Reagan came to office, the president's 'Assistant for National Security Affairs' had played a major role in foreign policy-making. Under Reagan the position was less significant, partly through Reagan's personal choice, partly because of the unfortunate experience of the Brzezinski–Vance 'duel' under Carter, and partly because none of Reagan's National Security Advisers (NSAs) survived long in office.

The first NSA, Richard V. Allen, had been deputy NSA under Nixon and chief foreign policy adviser to Reagan in the 1980 election campaign, but was forced to 'suspend' his appointment in November 1981, following allegations of financial misconduct. Although nothing was proved against him, Allen resigned on 4 January 1982. His successor, William Clark, had been Reagan's Chief of Staff as Governor of California in 1966–69 and, after 1973, a judge in the Californian Supreme Court. Though lacking in foreign policy experience, he was made Deputy Secretary of State in 1981–82 and hoped to take a higher profile than Allen as NSA. In October, 1983, however, Clark was made Secretary of the Interior, following the forced resignation of James Watt.

Reagan's third NSA, Robert C. ('Bud') McFarlane, lasted longest. A former Marine Corps officer, he had served in the National Security Council in 1973–77, in the State Department in 1981–82 and as deputy

NSA under Clark. McFarlane hoped to restore the standing of the NSA but was reported to get on badly with the White House Chief of Staff, Donald Regan, and resigned in December 1985. In 1988 he pleaded guilty to misdemeanours in the 'Contragate' scandal. His successor was his former deputy NSA, Admiral John Poindexter, who was little known in public and also became embroiled in the Contragate scandal, resigning in November 1986, along with his assistant Colonel Oliver North.

The last two of Reagan's NSAs were both close allies of Defense Secretary Caspar Weinberger. Frank Carlucci soon succeeded Weinberger as Defense Secretary in November 1987. General Colin Powell (q.v.) then served as NSA for Reagan's last year.

SECTION SEVEN

Glossary

Alliance for Progress   Launched by President Kennedy in a speech to Latin American diplomats on 13 March 1961, the Alliance was intended to prevent the spread of Castro-type regimes by providing housing, education, health and other basic needs in Latin America through a co-operative effort. It built on policies begun by Eisenhower and aimed at long-term improvements. But many regimes in the region were reluctant to undertake social reforms, economic problems were daunting and the programme soon proved too costly, being wound down under Johnson and Nixon.

Atomic bomb   An atom was first split by British researchers in 1932 releasing considerable energy, and by 1939 it was clear that this process could be applied to warfare. Britain and America developed separate projects to build an atomic bomb. These efforts were co-ordinated under the August 1943 Quebec Agreement. A bomb was finally developed in the Los Alamos research centre in New Mexico, under a programme known as the Manhattan Project, directed by US General Leslie Groves. The bomb was tested on 16 July 1945. On 6 August a bomb named 'Little boy' was exploded on Hiroshima, destroying two-thirds of its buildings and killing over 70,000. On 9 August a second bomb, 'Fat Man', dropped slightly off target on Nagasaki, but still destroyed nearly half its buildings and killed 35,000. Japan soon surrendered.

Attempts to control the atomic bomb via the UN failed in 1946 (see Baruch Plan) and under the McMahon Act of August 1946 the US set up their own 'Atomic Energy Commission' (civilian-controlled but with a military input) and refused to share atomic secrets with other powers. This came as a blow to the British, who secretly developed their own bomb, exploded in 1952. The exposure of the British atomic scientists Alan Nunn May (1946) and Klaus Fuchs (1950) as Soviet spies undermined Anglo-US co-operation in this field. Despite America's atomic monopoly in 1945–49, and the confidence this gave to the West, the number of US atomic bombs was not large and there was no reliable long-range bomber to deliver them until the 1950s. The weapons were therefore little threat to the Soviets in the diplomatic struggles which marked the birth of the Cold War. The Soviets exploded their own bomb on 29 August 1949, earlier than Western experts expected.

'Atoms for Peace'   A proposal made by Eisenhower, put in a speech before the UN General Assembly in December 1954, for an International Atomic Energy Agency (IAEA) to develop peaceful uses of atomic energy, using fissionable material supplied by the Superpowers. The speech showed Eisenhower's interest in detente. The IAEA was created in 1957 but did little to reduce East–West tension.

Baruch Plan (1946)   In January 1946 the UN agreed to establish an Atomic Energy Commission and the US set up its own committee under Dean Acheson and David E. Lilienthal, to look at ways to share its nuclear monopoly. The Acheson–Lilienthal Report, reflecting the views of the liberal-minded atomic scientist Robert Oppenheimer, argued that the US monopoly would not last and that atomic projects should be controlled by an international body. The businessman Bernard Baruch, who became America's representative on the Atomic Energy Commission, revised the Report. Under the Baruch Plan published on 14 June, the US would share its atomic stockpile and knowledge with an international authority, but no other nation would be allowed to develop atomic weapons. Any that did would be subjected to UN sanctions. The USSR criticised the plan as effectively maintaining America's monopoly on atomic developments. The Soviets preferred an agreement banning the use of the atomic bomb. The Baruch Plan was soon abandoned.

Bipolarity/multipolarity   A peculiar feature of the post-1945 world order was its domination by two Superpowers. US–Soviet domination came about because of the defeat of France (1940), Italy (1943), Germany and Japan (1945), and the decline of British power. Arguably it was inevitable that the US and USSR would become rivals of some sort given this 'bipolar' situation, although ideological rivalries, the post-war power vacuum in Europe and the Far East, and the development of nuclear weapons made the rivalry more intense. Although the US was always the more powerful in economic terms, and initially in atomic weaponry, the Soviets had vast economic assets, a large population and substantial armed forces. Both sides developed alliances and client states, and world affairs became what has been termed a 'zero-sum' game – that is, any gain for the USSR in the international arena was seen as a loss for the US, and vice versa. In the 1960s the world moved towards a more 'multipolar' situation: the US was weakened by Vietnam; China emerged as a potential 'third power' (leading to ideas of 'triangular diplomacy' in the 1970s); Japan and the European Community, especially West Germany, emerged as powerful economic forces; non-alignment grew in popularity among 'Third World' (q.v.) states; and certain countries in the Eastern and Western blocs became more independent of the Superpowers, notably Romania under Ceauşescu and France under de Gaulle.

Brezhnev Doctrine   A Western term (not used in the USSR itself) for ideas enunciated by Soviet leader Leonid Brezhnev in a speech to the Polish Communist Party in November 1968. Following the intervention in Czechoslovakia by Warsaw Pact forces in August, Brezhnev defined the principle of 'limited sovereignty', saying: 'Whenever internal and

external forces hostile to Socialism try to reverse the development of a
Socialist country towards the restoration of capitalism . . . this becomes
. . . the concern of all Socialist countries.' The Doctrine was abandoned
by Mikhail Gorbachev when he withdrew from Afghanistan (1988) and
allowed a non-Communist premier to take office in Poland (1989).

Carter Doctrine   Enunciated by President Jimmy Carter in the 23 January 1980 'State of the Union' address. A year earlier the Shah of Iran
had gone into exile and Iran, hitherto a vital US ally in the Middle East,
fell under a fundamentalist Islamic leadership. Fears that the Soviet Union
would exploit the situation were heightened by the Red Army's incursion
into Afghanistan in December 1979. Carter's doctrine stated that: 'An
attempt by any outside force to gain control of the Persian Gulf region
will be regarded as an assault on the vital interests of the US. It will be
repelled by the use of any means necessary, including military force.'

Central Intelligence Agency (CIA) and US Intelligence   The US has had
an intelligence service since 1776 but the inadequacies of the system
which operated before 1941 were exposed by the Japanese attack on
Pearl Harbor. In 1942 President Roosevelt formed the Office of Strategic Services under William J. ('Wild Bill') Donovan to handle intelligence operations, but this experienced problems of co-ordination and
led Truman to form first the Central Intelligence Group (1946) and
then the CIA. Under the July 1947 National Security Act the CIA was
designed to collect, analyse and co-ordinate intelligence, and to 'per-
form . . . other functions' under the general direction of the National
Security Council. The CIA director was also to act as 'Director of Central
Intelligence', co-ordinating the work of all US intelligence services. The
power of 'the Agency' (also known as 'the Company') was built up in
the 1950s by Directors Walter Bedell Smith and Allen Dulles. A headquarters was built at Langley, Virginia and the CIA had a number of
successes, including the overthrow of radical governments in Iran (1953)
and Guatemala (1954) and the development of information gathering
from the U-2 spy-plane (1955) and space satellites (1961–62). The ill-
fated Bay of Pigs operation (1961) proved a setback but the Agency was
active in Vietnam.

By the 1970s the CIA, under its 'other functions', was carrying out
such 'covert' activity as propaganda, financial support for foreign political groups, and even economic warfare, as well as paramilitary actions.
It also carried out counter-intelligence work – making US systems safe
against Soviet intelligence. But in the Watergate era questions were raised
about the lack of democratic controls over intelligence work. In December 1974 *New York Times* articles by Seymour Hersh accused the CIA
of helping to overthrow the elected Allende government in Chile and

spying on US citizens. A Commission under Vice-President Nelson Rockefeller, followed by Congressional committees under Frank Church (Senate) and Otis Peake (House), confirmed US citizens had been spied upon and led to such measures as the 1978 Electronic Surveillance Act and 1980 Intelligence Oversight Act. In the early 1980s the Agency's fortunes revived under Director William Casey, who was close to President Reagan, but after 1986 the 'Irangate' scandal (q.v.) again called intelligence operations into question and it was embarrassed in the 1990s by certain spy scandals (notably with the arrest of Aldrich Ames).

Apart from its lack of democratic accountability, the CIA has (like other intelligence services) been accused of collecting intelligence material indiscriminately, failing to be objective in its analysis and putting too much faith in 'covert action'. Nor has the CIA avoided clashes with other US intelligence services which include:

(1) *Federal Bureau of Investigation* (FBI), established 1906, which carries out work *within* the US and was particularly active under J. Edgar Hoover against 'subversives'.

(2) *Drug Enforcement Agency*, which became particularly important in the international campaign against drug abuse in the 1980s and which, like the FBI, is under the Department of Justice.

(3) *National Security Agency*, a highly secret institution, established 1952 and based at Ford Meade, which handles the interception of communications and code-breaking, and seeks to keep US communications secret.

(4) *Defense Intelligence Agency*, established by Defense Secretary McNamara in 1961 to co-ordinate the work of army, navy and air force intelligence (which themselves remain separate agencies). The DIA, like the NSA, is under the control of the Defense Secretary, whose position *vis-à-vis* the CIA is strengthened by his being a Cabinet member. (Of the CIA directors in the Cold War, only Casey was in the Cabinet.)

Cold War A term first used in the late 1930s to describe Franco-German tensions, there are competing claims as to who first applied it to East–West relations after 1945 but it was popularised by the American journalist Walter Lippman, who entitled a collection of articles on international affairs *The Cold War* in late 1947. Cold War may be defined as a state of tension between powers in which many of the features of modern warfare are present – ideological division, propaganda, espionage, subversion, large arsenals of weapons, the formation of alliances, controls on society – but with no actual war between the powers themselves. Thus the Superpowers *did* become involved in 'hot wars', like the US in Korea, but not against each other.

Common European home   A concept first put forward by Gorbachev in Prague in April 1987, when he talked of a Europe 'from the Atlantic to the Urals' which was a 'cultural and historic entity rich in spiritual significance . . . even if its states belong to different social systems and military–political blocs'. This European aspect of Gorbachev's 'new thinking' echoed the earlier ideas of Charles de Gaulle. On visits to Britain, West Germany and France in April–July, however, Gorbachev disappointed his audience by failing to develop the 'common home' into anything concrete.

Containment   The policy pursued by the US to deal with the Soviet menace which was believed to exist between about 1947 and 1987. The term is identified with George Kennan, a US diplomat. In February 1946, when doubts about Soviet intentions were growing in Washington, Kennan sent the so-called 'long telegram' from Moscow. He argued that historic Russian insecurity had become married to Marxist ideology in the USSR, so that the country was committed to conflict with the US and Western way of life. This view gained widespread circulation in Washington thanks to the support of Navy Secretary James Forrestal. In July 1947 Kennan's views gained public exposure when, under the pseudonym 'Mr X', he published an article on 'The Sources of Soviet Conduct' in the influential journal *Foreign Affairs*, and said that Soviet expansionism must be 'contained by the adroit and vigilant application of counterforce at a series of constantly shifting geographical and political points'.

US resistance to Soviet expansionism was summed up in the March 1947 Truman doctrine and seen in crises over Iran (1946), Berlin (1948) and Korea (1950). Early critics of 'containment' included the journalist Walter Lippmann who argued that historical factors were more important than ideology in shaping Soviet policy, that global containment would prove costly and that the US would have to support any anti-Communist regime, however distasteful. In 1952 Republicans criticised containment as a defensive doctrine which allowed the Communists to choose the battleground, and talked of 'roll-back' and 'liberation' as more aggressive alternatives. But in effect Eisenhower refused to help liberate those, like Hungary in 1956, who tried to throw off Communism. The real crisis for containment did not come until 1968–69 in Vietnam, when it was clear that the US could not successfully fight Communism everywhere. By then, too, Communism could no longer be seen as a 'monolithic bloc' controlled by Moscow. But US presidents in the 1970s and 1980s still saw the USSR as their main adversary. Containment was officially abandoned in Bush's speech of 12 May 1989 to the Texas A&M University.

Cultural Revolution   Mao Zedong's attempt to rejuvenate the Communist revolution began in 1965 and was accompanied by a more radical

Chinese foreign policy. Internally in 1966–68 Mao dismissed his opponents within the Communist Party (including the veteran President Liu Shaoqi), and held mass rallies of young 'Red Guards'. He encouraged the Red Guards to attack all traditional ideas, and launched terror campaigns against intellectuals and party officials. Externally China supported Communists in Third World countries like Vietnam, and alienated both Western and Soviet bloc states, with attacks by Red Guards on the British and Soviet Embassies in Beijing. In June 1967 Red Guards even took over the Chinese foreign ministry, destroyed its archives and forced the foreign minister Chen Yi to issue a public 'self-criticism'. Eventually the upheaval caused by such behaviour led Mao to disband the Red Guards in 1968, and effectively to call off the Cultural Revolution itself in 1969. Mao then relied on the People's Liberation Army, under General Lin Biao, to restore order. This they did ruthlessly before Mao fell out with Lin Biao. The General died in mysterious circumstances in an air crash in 1971, while apparently fleeing to the USSR. The 'Cultural Revolution', finally abandoned in 1976, led to 'ten wasted years' in China and to the country's international isolation, which was not broken until the *rapprochement* with America in 1972.

De-Stalinisation   By the time of his death Stalin had established a political, economic and social system in the Soviet Union which (a) fused Marxism with a despotic government dominated by one man, (b) enforced Communist ideals by the use of indoctrination and a police-state, and (c) created an industrialised state with a large proletariat by the use of a centralised planning system, the ruthless exploitation of the agricultural sector and the forced direction of labour. A similar system had been forced on the Soviet satellite states in Eastern Europe.

In 1953–55 the 'collective leadership' which succeeded Stalin tried to reform the system by ending the 'personality cult', reforming the secret police into the KGB and developing a 'new course' in the economy, including more production of consumer goods. This caused some tension in the leadership which became dominated by Khruschev. In February 1956 he made a major speech to a Party Congress which attacked the personality cult and arbitrary police methods, and welcomed greater diversity in the Soviet bloc. He did *not* criticise the one-party state, the centralised economic system, the collectivisation of agriculture or the existence of the secret police. But the speech created expectations of reform in the Eastern bloc, and helped to bring about the upheavals in 1956 in Poland and Hungary (q.v.).

Detente   A French term (*détente*), meaning 'relaxation', which has been used to describe periods of 'thaw' in the Cold War such as those after the death of Stalin and the Cuban Missile Crisis. More particularly the term is used to describe the relaxation of tensions between 1971, when the first Nixon–Brezhnev Summit was planned, and 1979, when the Soviets invaded Afghanistan. US interest in detente had grown under Johnson in the late 1960s, leading to the Glassboro' 'Mini-Summit'. Problems in Vietnam, the desire to stabilise the nuclear balance, popular pressures and the fact that the USSR had achieved nuclear parity by 1968 all contributed to the US desire for detente. European leaders tended to show even greater enthusiasm: de Gaulle, as part of France's more independent policies in the 1960s, recognised Communist China (1964) and visited Moscow (1966); after 1969 West Germany's Brandt was keen to open links to Eastern Europe under his *Ostpolitik*. The Soviets apparently saw detente as a way to reduce military costs, obtain Western trade and technology and have their equality as a Superpower recognised.

By tying concessions to Soviet good behaviour (see 'linkage') and by developing the 'opening to China', Nixon and Henry Kissinger hoped to 'manage' relations with the Soviets in such a way that America remained powerful and secure, despite Vietnam. A number of crises in 1969–71 (Cienfuegos, Jordan, the Indo-Pakistan War) delayed detente but progress on a SALT I Treaty and Nixon's desire for re-election helped bring about the successful 1972 Moscow summit, followed by other Nixon–Brezhnev Summits in 1973–74 and the maintenance of detente under Ford and Carter. However, the euphoria over detente soon dimmed. Ideological differences between the superpowers remained deep. Some Americans criticised the 1972 SALT Treaty and 1975 Helsinki Accords as giving advantages to the USSR. There were congressional attempts to link trade concessions to greater Jewish emigration (the Jackson–Varik amendment) which in turn upset the Soviets. A SALT II Treaty proved difficult to negotiate and Moscow was fearful of Sino-American links. Furthermore the US and USSR remained rivals in Third World conflicts (1973 Arab–Israeli War; Angola in 1974–75; 1977–78 Ogaden War) which helped undermine detente even before its final demise over Afghanistan.

Dissidents (Soviet) The condemnation of Communist regimes as oppressive police states which abused human rights was always an important element in Western Cold War propaganda. However, despite wide-ranging opposition to the Soviet, East European and Chinese regimes (from religious groups and nationalist minorities for example), Western attentions often focused on particular dissidents. The case of gifted individuals, usually intellectuals, was used to highlight the illiberalism of the Communist system, even though such people were a minority of the population. Concern over dissidents grew particularly after 1965–66 when two Soviet writers, Yuli Daniel and Andrei Sinyavsky, were arrested and sentenced to labour camps. This came after a period of relaxation in controls under Khruschev who had allowed the publication of Alexander Solzhenitsyn's *One Day in the Life of Ivan Denisovich.*

Under Brezhnev oppression continued, carried out by Yuri Andropov as head of the KGB. Dissidents turned to underground (*samizdat*) publications. Many dissidents were sent to psychiatric hospitals rather than imprisoned. In the mid-1970s the Helsinki Agreements (q.v.) were followed by the establishment of a Soviet group to oppose the misuse of psychiatry. The same agreements led the dissident scientist Yuri Orlov to establish a human rights 'monitoring group'. President Carter made human rights a major issue in US–Soviet relations in 1976. The revival of Cold War tensions in 1980 brought a new KGB crackdown on dissidents. Solzhenitsyn had already been exiled to the West and in 1986 he was followed by Orlov and Anatoly Scharansky. But others, like scientist Andrei Sakharov, remained in the USSR. It was Sakharov's release from internal exile in December 1986 which heralded a general release of Soviet political prisoners under Gorbachev.

Domino Theory   An idea first put forward publicly in April 1954 by President Eisenhower, who talked of the danger of 'falling dominoes' in South-East Asia. The danger, supposedly, was that the fall of Vietnam to Communism would be followed by the fall of neighbouring Laos and Cambodia; pressure would then be exerted on Thailand and, if that fell, on Malaya (where an emergency was in progress against Communist insurgents), Indonesia (where a strong Communist movement was liquidated in 1965) and the Philippines (a former US colony). The domino theory remained an argument for US involvement in Vietnam in the 1960s but was no more than a crude example of 'geopolitical' logic. It presumed a 'monolithic' Communist bloc and, when Vietnam did fall in 1975, it proved mistaken; despite the Communist triumph in Laos and Cambodia, Thailand remained pro-American.

'Dual-track': NATO's Cruise–Pershing decision   A number of developments affected America's NATO allies in the 1970s on the question of nuclear weapons: European leaders were concerned that their views were not being heard in the SALT II talks; the Soviets began to deploy new, mobile and MIRVed SS-20 nuclear missiles; there was considerable debate over 'limited nuclear war' in Europe; and the indecisiveness of President Carter created doubts about whether he would protect Europe in a confrontation with Moscow. In October 1977 West German Chancellor Schmidt said, in London, that a nuclear balance must be maintained in *Europe* as well as on a global scale.

In 1979 Carter met Schmidt, Giscard of France and Britain's Callaghan at Guadeloupe and agreed to match the Soviet SS-20s with ground-launched 'Cruise' missiles (GLCMs) and larger, medium-range Pershing

IIs. In December 1979 NATO confirmed this decision: 464 GLCMs would be deployed in various European countries and 108 Pershing IIs in Germany. However this decision was taken only in the belief that 'theatre' nuclear weapons would be controlled under a SALT III Treaty between the superpowers; actual deployment of the new missiles would be unnecessary and, it was hoped, the Soviets would agree to dismantle their SS-20s. But NATO's faith in a 'dual-track' policy – threatening to *deploy* new weapons while hoping for arms *control* – was soon undermined by the renewal of the Cold War following the Soviet invasion of Afghanistan. Deployment of the Cruise and Pershing missiles eventually took place in 1983 amidst considerable opposition from European peace movements and led the USSR to call off all nuclear arms talks.

Eisenhower Doctrine (5 January 1957)   A foreign policy doctrine put to Congress in the wake of the 1956 Suez Crisis and designed to cope with the danger of Communist exploitation of instability in the Middle East. President Eisenhower asked Congress for economic aid and for authority to use American armed forces to maintain the independence of Middle East states which faced 'overt armed aggression from any nation controlled by international communism'. The doctrine was criticised because it dealt only with one possible form of Communist action – armed aggression – which seemed least likely to arise. The doctrine failed to deal with such complex problems as Arab–Israeli tension and upset most Arab states because it seemed designed to make them take sides in the East-West conflict.

Eurocommunism   Exclusion from power, Khruschev's talk of 'national roads' to Communism, and the shock of the Soviet invasions of Hungary (1956) and Czechoslovakia (1968) all helped to undermine the loyalty of West European Communists to Moscow. In the era of detente after 1970, the French and Italian Communists felt able to develop their independence and appeal to liberal-democratic voters. In 1975, along with the Spanish Communists, they issued a declaration accepting free elections, a free press and other liberal principles. They could not, however, develop a joint approach to economic problems; the Spanish Communists failed to emerge as a strong force after the end of the Franco dictatorship; and the Soviet invasion of Afghanistan (1979) divided the Italian party from the more hard-line French, whose own electoral fortunes declined markedly in the 1980s. In retrospect Eurocommunism could be said to have thrived only in 1974–77.

Flexible response   Also known as 'selective' response, a military doctrine particularly associated with the Kennedy presidency, concerning nuclear targeting and the use of US forces abroad but also used to refer to NATO strategy in Europe after the late 1960s. When Kennedy became president the US 'Single Integrated Operational Plan' for war aimed at firing all nuclear weapons in a 'pre-emptive strike' against Russia. Joint Strategic Target Planning Staff had been created in August 1960, and the need for the US to launch a nuclear attack first ('on warning') was increased by the vulnerability of its command and early-warning systems. Difficulties with nuclear targeting made it easier to target Soviet urban–industrial centres rather than military installations.

Kennedy and Defense Secretary McNamara disliked such rigid plans which could well leave the USSR with enough nuclear weapons, even after a US 'first strike', to launch its own attack on America. As an alternative, 'flexible response' would pinpoint a range of targets in the hope that war could end without a full nuclear exchange. This included building a 'second strike' capability – giving the US the ability to hit back at Russia even after suffering an attack. McNamara created a 'Triad' of nuclear weapons systems – bombers, ICBMs and submarines – and in 1962 advocated targeting of Soviet nuclear forces ('counterforce strategy'). Flexible response proved enormously costly and raised complex issues of whether nuclear war really could be 'managed'. Furthermore the US was unable to target Soviet military installations with accuracy. So, in 1963, McNamara began to stress nuclear deterrence rather than flexible response (see Mutual Assured Destruction). Further studies by McNamara led to the adoption of flexible response by NATO in the 1960s, the idea being to avoid an outright nuclear exchange by gradual 'escalation' of any conflict in Europe. In a wider sense flexible response was also applied to the build-up of *conventional* forces under Kennedy designed to deal with a range of military threats, especially 'wars of national liberation' in the Third World.

Glasnost   Closely associated with Gorbachev's aim of *perestroika* in 1985, *glasnost* – or openness – was intended to bring greater self-criticism to bear in Soviet society so as to root out inefficiency and corruption in government and industry. The press became freer, industries were made self-managing and government bodies opened up to plural voting. Gorbachev hoped this would strengthen socialism, but it simply led opposition groups to criticise the Communist system itself and allowed a resurgence of nationalist feeling within the USSR from, for example, the Baltic provinces and the Caucasus.

Grand Design of Kennedy   The Kennedy administration came to power with a host of ideas for dealing with international problems and in North Atlantic affairs hoped to develop the idea of 'partnership'; Europe, in the post-colonial age, should be further encouraged to develop common institutions and so become an equal partner with America in defending Western values. To this end the administration supported British membership of the European Community, proposed a multi-lateral nuclear force for NATO and tried to overcome trade barriers between America and Europe through the 'Kennedy Round' of tariff reductions. But the 'Grand Design' was a vague concept. Europe actually remained very divided and France's General de Gaulle in particular was suspicious of US plans as a new way to dominate NATO.

Guam Doctrine or Nixon Doctrine   A doctrine first enunciated by President Nixon at a press conference on Guam Island on 23 July 1969. Nixon set out a number of principles to guide US policy, to ensure that there would be 'no new Vietnams'. The president said the US would fulfil its existing treaty commitments and would use nuclear weapons to defend its allies and vital interests, but that countries subjected to Communist aggression would have to be ready, first and foremost, to defend themselves. In Vietnam after 1969 the Saigon government was expected to rely on its own ground troops, and US forces were withdrawn, a policy known as 'Vietnamisation'. The Guam remarks were followed by other speeches which, in contrast to the 1947 Truman Doctrine (q.v.), showed a move towards retrenchment in US foreign policy.

Hallstein Doctrine   In September 1955 West Germany's Chancellor Adenauer visited Moscow and succeeded in establishing diplomatic relations. But he was deeply offended when, following his visit, the Soviets recognised East Germany as a sovereign state. As a result Adenauer's government defined the Hallstein Doctrine, named after Deputy Foreign Minister Walter Hallstein. Under the doctrine, West Germany broke off relations with any state which entered into diplomatic relations with East Germany. This discouraged international recognition of East Germany and underlined West Germany's claim to be the only real German state. Relations were maintained with Moscow but Adenauer broke off relations with Yugoslavia and Cuba when they recognised East Germany. In the 1960s the doctrine became increasingly untenable and West German policy changed to one of links with Eastern Europe under *Ostpolitik* (q.v.).

Historiography   The Cold War has been the centre of considerable historical debate, especially in the US. In the 1950s the *traditionalist* view was that the US had responded to a global Communist challenge, directed from Moscow, which represented a real threat to the capitalist West on the political, economic and ideological levels. Where criticisms were voiced they tended to be directed, as in the McCarthyite era (*c.* 1950–54), against US weakness. Thus Roosevelt was criticised for 'selling out' Eastern Europe at Yalta and Truman for 'losing' China to Communism in 1949. The 'China Lobby' was strong in Congress and in 1955 Congress forced the publication of the State Department's Yalta documents.

About 1960 a more critical *revisionist* or 'New Left' school began to emerge, which questioned US values. This gained force during the Vietnam War, when it seemed evident that US policy had been misdirected since 1945, and held sway in the 1970s. The New Left historians may be divided into 'hard revisionists', who were Marxist (and criticised the underlying economic motives behind US policy), and 'soft revisionists'. All revisionists argued that the US had had an active role in beginning the Cold War, using economic and military strength to intimidate the USSR and support a capitalist world order. The corollary of this was that the USSR was seen as defensive, with limited aims, and certainly not bent on world conquest.

With the end of the Vietnam War and the opening of the archives, the so-called 'post-revisionists' developed a more historically respectable approach to the early years of the Cold War. This group was never a single 'school of thought' and became ever more diverse as time went on. But their methodology was very different to that of the traditionalists, who were often little better than propagandists, or of the revisionists, whose world was dominated by Vietnam. Post-revisionists sought to stand back from Cold War arguments, to be more objective and sophisticated in their analysis and to concentrate not on apportioning blame for the Cold War, but rather on analysing the accidents, misconceptions and underlying forces which shaped it. Historians gained a better grasp of the Cold War with the opening of archives in the former Soviet bloc.

Hydrogen (or thermonuclear) bomb   The 'H' bomb (called the 'Super' by those working on it) was developed by the US after the Soviets exploded an atom bomb in September 1951, an event which led to fears that a Soviet H-bomb would follow. The first US bomb, 'Mike', was exploded in November 1952 in the Marshall Islands. One thousand times more powerful than the Hiroshima bomb, it destroyed an island and made a crater a mile across. A Soviet 'H' bomb was announced in August 1953. The US and USSR exploded 'deliverable' weapons in March 1954 and November 1955 respectively. At the same time both sides began to deploy effective, long-range strategic bombers, the Soviet M-4 'Bison' (later joined by the Tupolov 'Bear') and the superior American B-52 (deployed in June 1955 to succeed the huge, ungainly B-36). Britain exploded an 'H' bomb in 1957 and developed 'V' bombers (Valiant, Vulcan and Victor) as long-range weapons, but after around 1960 the principal delivery system became ballistic missiles.

Irangate (Contragate) scandal   On 3 November 1986 a Lebanese newspaper reported that President Reagan's former National Security Adviser

Robert McFarlane had secretly visited Iran earlier in the year, and that the US was supplying arms to the country. It was soon suspected that the US had been supplying arms in order to secure the release of US hostages held by Islamic fundamentalists in the Lebanon. Reagan, however, denied any 'arms for hostages' deal. The scandal worsened when it was discovered that arms had been secretly sent to Iran via Israel; not all the money raised could be accounted for, but some had been sent to the 'Contra' guerrillas who were fighting the left-wing Sandinista regime in Nicaragua. Reagan was opposed to the Nicaraguan government and finding it difficult to get funds for the Contras but denied knowledge of the scheme. Investigations directed attention at Admiral John Poindexter (who had succeeded McFarlane as National Security Adviser) together with Colonel Oliver North, one of his staff. The long-running scandal reduced faith in Reagan's ability to control the government, marred his last years as president and renewed distrust of the CIA and other government agencies.

Iron Curtain   A term made popular by Winston Churchill's Fulton speech of March 1946 to describe the barrier between Soviet-occupied areas and 'open' Western societies. The term had actually first been used in a book by Russian *émigré* Vassily Rozanov, in 1918, who wrote that 'an iron curtain is descending on Russian history', and was also used by Nazi propagandists in the last stages of the Second World War. Churchill first used the term in a telegram to President Truman on 12 May 1945, a few days after Germany's defeat.

Johnson Doctrine   Speech by President Lyndon Johnson on 2 May in 1965 in which he declared that 'The American nations cannot, and will not, permit the establishment of another Communist government in the Western hemisphere.' The doctrine was used to justify armed US intervention in the Dominican Republic (q.v.) to prevent a Castro-like regime coming to power there. At the time America had largely succeeded in isolating Castro's Cuba diplomatically within the Western hemisphere and had no wish to see Marxists exploit the economic problems of the region. The doctrine was called into question by the Allende regime in Chile (1970) and the Sandinistas in Nicaragua (1979), both of which were subjected to US pressure.

KGB (State Security Committee) and Soviet Intelligence   The Soviet secret police had originally been set up by Lenin in 1920 as the 'Cheka'. In 1934–41 such work was in the hands of the NKVD which, under the 'Kirov decrees', could arrest, try and execute people. The NKVD terrorised the population during Stalin's purges, whose victims included leading Communists and even some heads of the secret police itself (Yagoda and Yazhov). In 1941 the NKVD, then under Lavrenti Beria, lost control of several functions – including counter-espionage, the 'gulags' (labour camps) and the guerrilla war against Germany – to a new organisation, the NKGB, under Beria's close ally Vsevolod Merkulov. But the NKVD continued to control overseas intelligence and the internal police service. (Military intelligence was under a separate body, the GRU.)

In 1946 the NKVD became the MVD (Ministry of Internal Affairs) and the NKGB became the MGB (Ministry for State Security). They were used to destroy subversion in areas that had been newly occupied in the Western USSR, and carried out mass deportations of minorities. Beria remained in overall ministerial control of both and carried out the 1949 'Leningrad Purge'. But Stalin tried to weaken Beria by giving greater powers to the MGB's Viktor Abakumov (1946–51) and Semen Ignatiev (1951–53). In 1953 Stalin's death allowed Beria to take full control of the MVD and MGB again but other ministers were so fearful of him that he was overthrown, being replaced by Sergei Kruglov. It was then that Stalin's successors decided to form a new secret police-force under the direction of the Communist Party.

The KGB was formed in 1954 with the status of a ministry, but in practice it reported to leading party members. Secret trials under the Kirov decrees were ended so that the secret police could now arrest but not try people. The ordinary police and the Internal Troops (used to quell unrest) were under the Interior ministry. At the same time many of Stalin's victims were released from prison (about 15,000 in 1953–55) and 'rehabilitated', that is, treated as loyal citizens. These reforms were not designed to bring real political freedom but to prevent a return to Stalin's arbitrary rule. The KGB, reduced in size, was at the mercy of the party, not vice versa, but it continued to run a network of informers and to direct intelligence work abroad. The KGB helped to save Khruschev from the 1957 'anti-party plot' but supported his overthrow in 1964 and became particularly important under Yuri Andropov (q.v.). It successfully controlled all signs of dissidence until the mid-1980s.

At the peak of its power in the mid-1970s the KGB had about half a million staff including: border troops, seen by visitors at customs posts; signals forces, to control vital telecommunications in the USSR; uniformed guards at nuclear-weapons stores and government ministries; plain-clothes forces used against internal subversion and dissidents; the 'First Main Directorate', which gathered intelligence (including intelligence on Western technology), carried out covert operations and disseminated propaganda; and the 'Second Main Directorate' for counter-intelligence. The Soviets recruited spies in the West, including the Cambridge spy ring of Philby, Maclean, Burgess and Blunt, but numerous KGB officers were expelled from Western states. Under Gorbachev the organisation had to adjust considerably, becoming more open to outside observers and less active against internal opposition. Steps were taken to replace it in late 1991.

'**Linkage**' In general, any attempt to tie one foreign policy issue to another. The term became identified with Henry Kissinger and was an important accompaniment to America's policy of detente in the 1970s. Kissinger argued that if the Soviets wanted agreement with America on some issues, they must not try to take advantage of America in other areas. While accepting Soviet equality, 'linkage' would allow the US to manage Soviet power in a framework of co-operation; in return for strategic arms talks and agreement on trade and technology, the Soviets would have to help America settle Third World conflicts like Vietnam. 'Linkage' became – along with 'concreteness' (the need for firm agreements and not just a 'friendly climate' between Moscow and Washington) and 'restraint' (by the Superpowers in areas of conflict) – one of the key words in America's detente policy under Nixon. But the Soviet side, committed to support wars of national liberation, never accepted 'linkage', and their activities in the Middle East war (1973), Angola (1975) and Afghanistan (1979) did much to undermine detente.

Massive retaliation A nuclear doctrine enunciated by John Foster Dulles in January 1954 when he spoke of retaliation 'by any means' against the Soviets if they threatened US vital interests. The exact circumstances in which nuclear weapons would be used was left deliberately vague. The doctrine worried world opinion and was criticised by defence experts as unrealistic, the US president being unlikely to launch nuclear war except in a dire emergency. 'Massive retaliation' reflected US confidence about its nuclear superiority in the 1950s. Reliance on nuclear weapons in military planning also allowed the new Eisenhower administration to pursue a strong global containment policy while reducing the high spending on conventional arms by Truman during the Korean War. A policy of reliance on nuclear weapons and reduced conventional arms spending known in America as the 'New Look' was accepted by the National Security Council in October 1953. A similar policy was adopted by the USSR in 1955 and Britain in 1957. Under Kennedy a new doctrine, 'flexible response' (q.v.), superseded 'massive retaliation'.

McCarthyism A period in US history identified with Republican Senator Joseph McCarthy (1908–57), whose political career was undistinguished until February 1950 when, in a speech at Wheeling, West Virginia, he claimed to have a list of numerous 'known Communists' in the State Department. Despite criticisms from fellow senators and his inability to prove his claims, McCarthy won considerable support from the public, who were concerned with the advance of Communism since 1944. McCarthy became a household name and in 1951 he even launched an attack on former Secretary of State George Marshall. Re-elected in 1952, McCarthy became chairman of the Congressional 'Subcommittee on Investigations' and presided over a witch-hunt of public officials. Meanwhile a much wider witch-hunt had begun in US society, where people in all walks of life were liable to lose their jobs for any past association with left-wing causes. Even President Eisenhower was reluctant to criticise McCarthy who, however, eventually destroyed himself. His investigations of the Defense Department in 1954 were televised, allowing the US public to witness his ruthless tactics. In December of that year his actions were formally condemned by a Senate Committee and the US public, tired by his excesses, turned against him.

Missile experimental (MX)   A large ('heavy') successor to America's 'Minuteman' ICBM, with MIRV capability, conceived during the 1970s. President Carter decided in June 1979 to develop 200 MX missiles, partly in order to answer criticisms that he had been too moderate in the SALT II talks. Secretary of State Vance believed the missiles would be a valuable 'bargaining chip' in any SALT III talks. MX was seen as a match for the 'heavy' Soviet SS-17s, 18s and 19s, developed since 1973, which were believed to be targeted at Minuteman silos and could create a 'window of vulnerability' in US defences. National Security Adviser Brzezinski hoped MX would help America carry out its own 'silo-busting' tactics. The system, otherwise known as 'Peacekeeper', was also favoured by President Reagan after 1981.

Apart from the threat it posed to the nuclear balance, the system was enormously costly. It was developed alongside the new 'Trident II' for submarines, even though some experts believed one new missile system would be sufficient. More controversial were schemes to reduce MX's vulnerability to attack. Carter's plan for 'deceptive basing' was to put each missile on its own loop of railway in Nevada and Utah with twenty-three possible shelters for it to emerge from; this meant 4,600 shelters and would have represented the largest ever American public building effort. In 1982 Reagan proposed a 'dense pack' of only a hundred missiles within twenty miles of Warren Air Force base, but this would be costly *and* vulnerable to attack. The 1983 Scowcroft Commission on nuclear weapons questioned the 'window of vulnerability' but recommended 100 missiles in existing silos and also favoured a new, mobile, small 'Midgetman' missile, which the Soviets would find hard to target. Reagan's attempts to proceed with MX and Midgetman met Congressional opposition and in 1989 President Bush decided, in the short term, to build only fifty MX missiles.

Mutual assured destruction (MAD)   The decline of US nuclear superiority and the failure to develop an effective 'flexible response' (q.v.) to nuclear war led Defense Secretary McNamara after 1963 to talk of the 'assured destruction' of the USSR in any conflict. Meanwhile the Soviets deployed strategic nuclear bombers (after 1956), established their Strategic Rocket Forces (1959) and began, under Admiral Sergei S. Gorshkov, to build up a global navy which eventually included submarine-launched ballistic missiles (SLBMs). A Soviet submarine circumnavigated the globe in 1966. By about 1968, when the US decided to 'freeze' the size of its strategic nuclear arsenal and concentrate on technological improvements, a system of 'Mutual Assured Destruction' was therefore reached, also known as 'mutual deterrence', in which each side had rough 'parity' with the other. This was so even though the Soviet nuclear arsenal was primarily made up of ICBMs in 1968 while the US had a mixture of ICBMs, strategic bombers and SLBMs. The Nixon administration accepted what it termed 'sufficiency' in nuclear weapons and along with the USSR concluded the SALT I Treaty, implicitly on the basis of MAD – that is, on the understanding that neither superpower could hope to defeat the other in nuclear war without itself being destroyed.

After 1972 MAD was often called into question. US critics pointed out that the Soviets never used the term 'deterrence' and that Moscow might aim at a 'war-fighting' capability: Soviet propaganda claimed that Communism would triumph in *any* conflict, the Soviets retained a commanding advantage in conventional weapons in Europe (so that NATO would be the first to use nuclear weapons), and Soviet 'heavy' missiles – developed in the 1980s – seemed to aim at destroying America's 'Minuteman' ICBMs. But it seems the Soviets effectively believed in nuclear deterrence even if they did not use the term. As early as 1955 Khruschev wished to reduce conventional arms spending and rely on nuclear weapons for defence; unlike the West, the Soviets did not endorse ideas (seen in NATO's 'flexible response' tactics) for an 'escalated' conflict but instead foresaw only a massive nuclear exchange; and in January 1977 Brezhnev insisted that the USSR wanted 'sufficiency' not 'superiority' in nuclear weapons. In the 1970s 'limited nuclear war' was talked about in the European theatre but no expert ever showed how to 'manage' a protracted war in such a way that it did not lead to confusion, escalation and a full-scale nuclear exchange. Carter's 1980 Presidential Directive 59 (q.v.) and Reagan's desire to explore 'war fighting' revealed a continuing wish to escape the restraints of MAD, but without success. After 1987 both sides moved towards radical arms-reduction measures.

National Security Council and US foreign policy-making   Before 1939 the US had limited armed forces, no military alliances and traditionally pursued an 'isolationist' foreign policy. After 1945, however, Americans developed alliances with numerous countries (forty-eight in 1970), maintained substantial armed forces and pursued 'globalistic' economic and foreign policies. This placed enormous burdens on the international policy-making machine in Washington. The State Department (the US foreign ministry, founded in 1789) mushroomed in size to 113 sub-divisions by 1948. The powers of the president, which were defined only vaguely in the Constitution, grew enormously as US involvement abroad escalated, creating the image of an 'Imperial Presidency' in the 1960s. The armed forces were reorganised in 1947 under the National Security Act and placed under a single Secretary of Defense, with headquarters established in the Pentagon building. The same act also created the CIA (q.v.).

The National Security Council (NSC) was the body established under the 1947 Act to co-ordinate the work of the various parts of the US government on internal and external security. It appraises issues and advises the president. It is the highest policy-making body in the security field, and can be summoned immediately. The NSC's permanent members include the president, vice-president, the Secretary of State and Secretary of Defense, with two statutory advisers, the CIA director and the chairman of the Joint Chiefs of Staff (who represents the heads of the army, navy, air force and marine corps). Other appointments can be made by the president. The NSC eventually developed a large staff of its own in the White House.

Different presidents have used the foreign policy-making machine in different ways. Eisenhower favoured military-style efficiency, had a strong Secretary of State in John Foster Dulles, and appointed a 'special assistant' to run the NSC as a co-ordinating (not a policy-making) body. Kennedy extended the powers of the special assistant, who became known as the 'National Security Adviser', and created a special Executive Committee of the NSC to advise him on the Cuban Missile Crisis. Johnson felt the NSC to be too large and unwieldy, and preferred to hold intermittent 'Tuesday luncheons' with his close advisers. Under Nixon the National Security Adviser, Kissinger, and his White House staff had a far greater role than the Secretary of State, Rogers. Under Carter there was destructive rivalry between Security Adviser Brzezinski and Secretary Vance, with the president himself often indecisive. The Reagan years saw rivalry between Secretary of State Schultz and the Defense Secretary Weinberger, with a series of short-lived National Security Advisers. Under Bush however there was a close-knit group around the president (Baker at State, Cheney at Defense, Scowcroft in the White House), and Clinton too avoided putting too much power into the hands of one adviser.

Neutron bomb   Also called the Enhanced Radiation Weapon (EPW) the bomb, developed in the mid-1970s, used neutron radiation which does not give out the heat, blast and fall-out of atomic and hydrogen bombs. The ERW was particularly favoured by NATO's Supreme Commander Haig as a way to destroy Soviet tank formations, and President Carter decided to produce it in July 1977. The weapon was condemned by the Soviets as a 'capitalist bomb', designed to kill people without damaging property, and it was also criticised in Western Europe on moral grounds. In January 1978 the US told NATO that the neutron bomb would be deployed in Europe in 1980 unless the Soviets ceased deployment of their new intermediate-range SS-20s, but the decision led the Dutch defence minister to resign in March. Amid intense controversy West German Chancellor Schmidt announced, on 5 April, that he accepted production of the ERW, but only two days later Carter decided to postpone production of the weapon. Later, in August 1981, Ronald Reagan reversed Carter's policy and began to stockpile neutron bombs in the US.

Gorbachev's 'new thinking'   Gorbachev's talk of *glasnost* and *perestroika* in Soviet domestic politics was also accompanied by a radical 'new thinking' of foreign policy. In order to concentrate on domestic reforms the Soviet leader wanted to ease tensions with the West, where capitalism seemed as strong as ever. Also, to help reduce defence spending, and accepting that nuclear war was unthinkable, he wished to end involvement in overseas conflicts. 'New thinking' accepted that any idea of world-wide Communist revolution was impossible, and that the world had become a 'multipolar' one which could not be seen in simple terms of Communism versus Capitalism. Gorbachev also recognised that 'peaceful coexistence' and 'interdependence' had become a permanent state of affairs and that co-operation with the West was desirable. To achieve this he was ready to pursue dramatic reductions in nuclear and conventional weapons, to withdraw from Third World involvements like the Afghanistan war, to build co-operation across Europe and to re-establish links with a strong, independent China. Gorbachev's ideas did much to bring the Cold War to an end but did not strengthen the USSR's security in the way he had hoped.

New world order   A term which became increasingly popular after 1989 to describe the 'post-Cold War' situation in international affairs, or rather the 'new world' which leading statesmen hoped to create. The term was particularly identified with George Bush who, in April–May 1989, made a series of speeches on US foreign policy. These followed a full-scale review of policy, directed by the new president's National Security Adviser, Brent Scowcroft. The key speech was to the Texas A&M University on 12 May in which Bush accepted the Cold War was over, was ready to accept the USSR as a 'normal' part of international society and conceded that America's containment policy (q.v.) could be ended. But

Bush never defined the term 'new world order' himself. It simply seemed to sum up the US hope of shaping a more democratic world, with respect for the UN and the triumph of liberal values. It was challenged by Saddan Hussein's invasion of Kuwait. His defeat reinforced the concept, but subsequent conflicts in Bosnia and Somalia tarnished it and, with the Soviet threat removed, Americans were less willing to be active abroad.

Non-alignment   The Cold War led the US and USSR to see the world as rigidly divided into two armed camps. Not all states, however, wished to choose between East and West. Nehru's India, for example, was a member of the British Commonwealth but established links with China and Russia in the mid-1950s. In 1954 a visit to India by Chinese Premier Zhou Enlai led to the acceptance by both sides of 'five principles' (*pancha sheela*) for good relations. These were sovereignty, independence, equality, non-aggression and non-interference in each other's internal affairs. The principles were also accepted by the Soviets in 1955 when India's Pandit Nehru visited Moscow. Meanwhile, on 22 December 1954, India also made common cause with the Yugoslav leader, Tito, a Communist who had broken free of Soviet domination. A joint declaration was issued by Nehru and Tito in favour of a 'policy of non-alignment' which 'is not neutrality . . . and therefore passivity . . . but is a positive, active and constructive policy seeking to lead to collective peace'. The 1955 Bandung Conference, supported by Nehru, boosted the cause of non-alignment and identified it particularly with newly independent states, who had no wish to replace the imperialism of the past with US or Soviet domination. It became the first of many non-aligned Summits.

NSC-68   An important US policy document drawn up after the explosion of the first Soviet atomic bomb in 1949 and finalised on 7 April 1950. The document, largely the work of Paul H. Nitze, then head of the State Department's Policy Planning Staff, tried to define what US security policy should be in the face of a wide-ranging Soviet menace. For many years it remained secret, but its basic recommendations were well known. It became the blueprint for America's rearmament effort during the Korean War and also influenced the decision to build the hydrogen bomb, by advocating large military spending to demonstrate Western strength in the face of the 'Kremlin design'. Although a *defensive* document – it ruled out any idea of 'preventive war' against Moscow – it marked a major step away from George Kennan's original idea of containment (q.v.), putting more emphasis on military policy than on economic aid. It was followed by other annual 'Basic National Security Policy' documents which tried to give cohesion to US security planning.

Peace movement   Western peace movements, such as Britain's Campaign for Nuclear Disarmament (CND) or West Germany's Campaign

Against Nuclear Death, first had an impact around 1957 with the deployment of theatre nuclear weapons in Europe and growing evidence of the effects of nuclear fall-out after hydrogen bomb tests in the Pacific. The movements also represented the re-emergence of mainly middle-class dissidents in the West as the initial impact of the Cold War passed and the 'New Left' (as opposed to the old, Marxist Left) began to question post-war Western values. The movement, made up of diverse factors – intellectuals, pacifists, religious groups – declined in impact in the 1960s, when protest movements turned to other issues. However, opposition to nuclear weapons was always an important theme for left-wing socialists, and the peace movement gained a major boost in America and Western Europe after 1979 with NATO's 'dual-track' decision (q.v.) to deploy new missile systems. Groups like CND revived and reached their peak in 1983 when the NATO deployments took place, but they did little to sway the policies of leaders like Margaret Thatcher or Helmut Kohl and went into decline with the advent of Gorbachev.

Peaceful coexistence and Soviet foreign policy   When the Bolsheviks took power in Russia in 1917 they were committed to a Marxist ideology which saw all human activity as dominated by economic relationships; they were committed to a class struggle and hoped for a world revolution that would replace capitalism with Communism. Lenin interpreted late nineteenth-century imperialism as the 'highest form of capitalism', which exploited the world economy but would destroy itself because the rivalries of capitalist states inevitably led to war. (A Communist world would supposedly live in peace.) By 1920 however the Bolsheviks were isolated in the world and threatened by invasion from the West, so that Lenin talked of 'cohabitation' with capitalism to win a breathing space for the regime. By the 1930s Joseph Stalin had developed the idea of 'socialism in one country', which implied that the USSR could build Communism without world revolution. In the long term Moscow remained committed to the overthrow of capitalism, but the Communist International (q.v.) was used as an instrument of Soviet foreign policy rather than revolution.

In 1947 Cold War tensions led the Soviet Politburo member Zhdanov to reinterpret foreign affairs as a struggle between 'two camps', the socialist and capitalist, led by Moscow and Washington, with the socialists – in 1947 at least – on the defensive. But, despite Zhdanov's 'two camps' and the formation of Cominform (q.v.), Stalin effectively treated international affairs as a struggle between states, not ideologies. His successor, Khruschev, was after 1955 even more flexible. In addition to his de-Stalinisation (q.v.) policies, he talked of 'different roads to socialism' and established links with the emerging Third World. It was Khruschev who put new emphasis on the need for 'peaceful coexistence', ending the siege mentality of the 'two camps', arguing that war was not inevitable between East and West, and being ready to talk to Western leaders. However, while avoiding war Khruschev still hoped that the 'correlation of forces' in the world would shift in favour of Communism. In effect 'peaceful coexistence' remained a form of global class struggle, although it was seen to be longer-lasting than Lenin's 'cohabitation'. In particular Khruschev hoped after 1960 to exploit 'wars of national liberation' in the Third World against the West. Capitalism, Marxists argued, continued to exploit the developing world through an unfair world economic system (neo-colonialism) even after formal colonial empires had ended.

The Vietnam War could be seen as a success for Communism, and in the 1970s the USSR tried to exploit conflicts in Angola, Ethiopia and Afghanistan. But events in Afghanistan after 1979, the popularity of non-alignment for Third World states, and the continued domination of developing economics by the West undermined Soviet hopes. Furthermore, while the main capitalist states – the US, Japan, Western Europe – had remained reasonably united since 1945, it was Communist states who often fell out (Soviet–Yugoslav split; Sino-Soviet split; Somali–Ethiopian war). By 1985 it was evident that the Communist bloc was not at peace with itself, that capitalism was strong and that the 'correlation of forces' had not moved in the Soviet favour on any level – military, economic, cultural or technological. As part of Gorbachev's 'new thinking' (q.v.) on foreign affairs, 'peaceful coexistence' was viewed as a permanent state of affairs in which different economic systems lived together in an interdependent world. Ideology no longer prevented co-operation with the West, class struggle gave way to more traditional inter-governmental relations and the 'transition to Communism' was effectively abandoned.

Perestroika   By the time Gorbachev became Soviet leader in 1985 the Soviet economy had lost the momentum achieved in the early post-war years. Central planning was inefficient and, compared with the West, growth was low, management was inefficient and goods were of poor quality. Gorbachev therefore called for *perestroika*, or the 'restructuring' of Soviet society, to encourage better management, worker discipline and the use of technology. He saw this not as changing the fundamental nature of the USSR but as restoring socialism to the original ideas of Lenin. However, the Soviet people lacked the individual initiative, ideological commitment and technological ability to match Gorbachev's demands. Many Soviet people saw *perestroika* as just another government propaganda campaign, and, despite reforms in the late 1980s by Premier Ryzkhov, the economic situation grew worse. The reforms alienated Communist Party officials, who felt threatened by them, and divided the party, thus helping to destroy the USSR.

'Point Four' programme   In Truman's inaugural speech of January 1949, the re-elected president put forward a foreign policy programme, point four of which was to make 'the benefits of our scientific advances and industrial progress available for the improvement and growth of under-developed areas'. This followed the success of Marshall Plan aid to Western Europe and led to a number of programmes under the direction of the Technical Co-operation Administration. 'Point Four' did not have much success, however. The point was put into the speech to show the humanitarian side of US policy, but in practice the government wanted to restrain spending and to direct assistance at 'friendly' governments. The problems of the developing world were huge – decolonisation; population growth; illiteracy; lack of an economic infrastructure and capital – and required a far more significant programme to tackle them.

Presidential Directive (PD) 59   This was a step taken by President Carter in July 1980, in the wake of the Afghanistan crisis, to introduce greater 'selective targeting' into US nuclear war plans. Under the 1974 'Schlesinger Doctrine' the then Defense Secretary had extended nuclear plans to include more strikes on Soviet nuclear forces. This 'selective counter-force' strategy was possible because of greater accuracy of missiles, and ended the system where weapons were targeted at urban–industrial centres. PD-59, which was championed by National Security Adviser Brzezinksi and Defense Secretary Brown, widened the range of targets and was designed to cope with various war situations. The Directive was also designed to prove Carter's toughness in an election year. 'War fighting' plans were further developed under Ronald Reagan, but US nuclear strategy did not fundamentally change until the mid-1990s when the Russian threat seemed less significant than that of certain 'rogue states' (q.v.).

Rapacki Plan   This was a plan put forward by the Polish foreign minister, Adam Rapacki, on 2 October 1957 to the UN, proposing a nuclear-free zone in West and East Germany, Poland and Czechoslovakia. The area of the zone might later be expanded. The plan had Soviet support and came at the same time as ideas from the American George Kennan for the withdrawal of US and Soviet forces from Europe. But the plan also coincided with Russia's launch of the *Sputnik*, which terrified the West. Western countries rejected the Rapacki Plan because it would harm NATO defences.

Rogue states   A concept developed by the Clinton administration after 1993 to designate those countries which were a threat to the new, US-led liberal world order. With the collapse of Soviet Communism it became difficult to mobilise American opinion (which in any case had never fully adjusted to the Vietnam defeat) behind an active foreign policy. The failure to pacify Somalia in 1993 and the apparent intractability of the Bosnian civil war added to the sense of aimlessness in US foreign policy. Unfamiliar and complex challenges also surrounded such problems as 'global warming', the international narcotics trade and the interdependence of the world economy. But it was relatively easy to focus criticism on certain countries who were accused of sponsoring terrorism, aggression against their neighbours or maintaining Communist suppression. Apart from the Sudan and Colonel Gadaffi's Libya (both accused of sponsoring terrorism) the principal states which the Clinton administration criticised were:

(a) *Cuba*, still ruled by Fidel Castro, a thorn in America's side since before the Bay of Pigs in 1961 (q.v.), but more vulnerable after the collapse of the USSR, which had subsidised Castro's regime. After the defeat of the Nicaraguan Sandinistas in the 1990 election, Castro was diplomatically isolated in the Americas and subjected to increased economic pressures, notably with the 1996 Helms–Burton Act.

(b) *North Korea*, which still laid claim to South Korea and tried to destabilise it with the infiltration of agents and the assassination of political leaders (the worst case being the murder of seventeen members of a South Korean delegation to Burma in 1983). The strengthening South Korean economy and Soviet recognition of South Korea (1990) made the North more nervous and after 1991 it seemed to be developing nuclear weapons. In 1994 intense US pressure forced the North to terminate its nuclear programme and relations then eased. Facing mass starvation internally, the North agreed in 1997 to enter talks with the South, China and America to end the danger of war in the peninsula.

(c) *Iran and Iraq: the problem of 'dual containment'*. The Islamic Fundamentalist regime in Iran had treated America as 'the Great Satan' since the hostages crisis of 1979–80. But the US position in the oil-rich Persian Gulf was greatly complicated in 1990–91 when Saddam Hussein of Iraq (backed by the West against Iran in the 1980s) also became an opponent, thanks to his invasion in Kuwait. In the 1990s Washington pursued a policy of 'dual containment', keeping Saddam under UN sanctions whilst trying to persuade other states to limit trade with Iran and itself maintaining a freeze on Iranian assets. The policy proved something of a strain on American resources: Saddam periodically revived his threat to Kuwait or (in 1997–98) threatened to expel UN inspectors; and Iran was successful in establishing better relations with Russia, France and other states.

Second front   The major Soviet complaint against the Western Allies during the Second World War was their failure to open a 'second front' against Germany in the West at an early date. In 1941–42, with the bulk of the German army advancing into Russia, the Soviets desperately needed some respite. But an Anglo-American invasion of Europe required a build-up of men, *materiel* and landing craft in Britain and (as shown in the 1942 Dieppe raid) could be a costly failure if launched too early. The British and Americans agreed on the 'Germany First' principle by which Germany, as the strongest enemy state, should be defeated before Japan. But the British wanted to concentrate any attacks on Germany in the Mediterranean, an area of British influence which Churchill believed could be exploited as Hitler's 'soft underbelly'. In order to bring US troops into the fighting against Germany at an early date, President Roosevelt agreed to the invasion of North-West Africa in November 1942, and the success of this operation led in 1943 to the invasions of Sicily and Italy. Not until June 1944 was France invaded. Meanwhile it was the Soviets, fighting up to 200 German divisions, who turned the Nazi tide with enormous cost in 1942–43 at the battles of Stalingrad and Kursk. Soviet losses in the war were estimated at about 20 million, whereas the US and Britain combined lost less than a million dead. Soviet historians subsequently argued that the Western powers had deliberately tried to 'bleed' Russia.

Strategic Defence Initiative (SDI)   Usually referred to as 'Star Wars', the initiative was launched by President Reagan in a televised speech in March 1983, when he proposed to develop 'particle-beam' and laser weapons to shoot down incoming nuclear missiles before they hit the US. This followed the successful test of an American X-ray laser weapon and reports that the USSR had carried out an anti-satellite (ASAT) weapon test in space. SDI was favoured by a few individuals close to Reagan such as the scientist Edward Teller, and appealed to the president's belief that defensive weapons can always be justified on moral grounds. But the initiative had not been properly considered by the State or Defense Departments and it surprised Congress. The USSR argued that SDI broke the 1972 ABM treaty, that it extended the arms race into space and that it would upset the military balance.

The initiative proved a major complication in East–West arms talks (especially upsetting the 1986 Reykjavik Summit), yet the US found it impossible to develop an effective SDI system at any great speed. Research was costly and complex and any SDI system could expect to be faced by counter-measures such as 'decoy' missiles or a much-expanded

Soviet arsenal. Thus it would expand the nuclear arms race, not end it. From the first many scientists doubted the wisdom of 'Star Wars' and by the time Reagan's presidency ended it was clear that the only realistic space-based weapons systems were conventional (not beam) weapons.

Superpower   A term first used by the American political scientist W.T.R. Fox in his book *The Superpowers* (1944). Fox applied it to Great Britain as well as America and the USSR and saw it as designating a great power with global responsibilities. Actually it is debatable whether the USSR ever achieved true 'global' significance and the term 'superpower' was never popular in the USSR itself. 'Superpower' became popular in the West in the 1950s as a term referring to the US and USSR as, by far, the greatest economic and military powers on the globe and it remained in use thereafter, almost replacing the more traditional term 'Great Power'.

Third World   The spread of democratic ideas; the aspirations of all peoples to be represented in the UN; the defeat of colonial powers in the Second World War; the success of the anti-colonial powers, America and Russia; and the rise of native middle-class groups – all these factors helped to bring about a rapid decolonisation process around 1947–65. Western powers, particularly Britain and France, were the ones who had to cope with this process, which could prove difficult and costly, especially for France in Indochina and Algeria. The US, though nominally anti-colonialist, often found itself having to defend the colonial powers. The USSR was able to exploit the situation in order to establish allies among the former colonies, many of whom saw the Communist model of development as appropriate for them.

The mid-1950s saw countries like India, Egypt and Yugoslavia adopt a policy of 'non-alignment' (q.v.). This led to the idea of a 'third world', usually identified with the developing countries of southern Asia, Africa and Latin America, who had little direct interest in the Cold War and who, despite wide differences between themselves, had some common interests such as anti-colonialism, the need for economic development and opposition to racialism. In Asia and Africa many states won their independence in the years 1956–65, swelling the Third World movement and opposing 'neo-colonialism' (the continued, indirect domination of the developing world by advanced nations, using their economic power and such institutions as multinational companies). After 1965 these countries were able to use their combined strength at the UN to oppose both the US and USSR on some issues, but the diversity of the Third World made it impossible to maintain such unity consistently.

The growth of Third World interests had an important impact on the policies of East and West. The US launched the 'Point Four' programme (q.v.) for technical aid in 1949, and later US initiatives included the

Alliance for Progress (q.v.) and Peace Corps under the Kennedy administration, which had grandiose ideas of 'nation-building' in the developing world to create political systems and economic infrastructures. The
mid-1950s saw the USSR adopt a policy of visits to developing countries,
aid agreements and encouragement of socialist-style planning. In the
1960s, with less success, China too tried to launch a development aid
programme in certain Asian and African states. By the mid-1980s, however, costly government-sponsored aid programmes were less popular
and, with the end of the Cold War, the US pressed developing countries
to adopt more market-oriented policies. By then, with the power of the
oil-producing countries and the rise of the 'Asian Tigers' (Malaysia, Singapore, Indonesia, South Korea, Taiwan), the Third World had become
even more diverse in terms of wealth, political influence and interests.

Truman Doctrine   This was the doctrine put forward by President Harry
Truman in an address to a joint session of Congress on 12 March 1947.
Following information from the British that they could no longer supply
financial assistance to the Greek government in its struggle with Communist guerrillas, nor to the Turkish government which had been under
Soviet diplomatic pressure, Truman asked that America should supply
such assistance. The president accompanied his request with a descrip-
tion of a world divided between totalitarian and democratic ways of life,
declaring: 'I believe that it must be the policy of the US to support free
peoples who are resisting attempted subjection by armed minorities or
by outside pressure.' The doctrine has been seen as the US declaration
of Cold War, the end of isolationism and beginning of a policy of support for regimes solely on grounds of their anti-Communism.

War Powers Act (7 November 1973)   The principal measure enacted by
Congress after the Vietnam War to restrict the 'Imperial Presidency' in
foreign affairs. The Act states that a president can commit US troops to
combat only (a) if war is declared (the prerogative of the Senate under
the US constitution); (b) if Congress allows it; or (c) when the US or its
armed forces are attacked. In the last case the president should seek
Congressional support within sixty days; after ninety days Congress can
override any presidential veto and terminate a military commitment.
The Act was criticised as hamstringing executive action, but in the 1980s
its provisions proved ambiguous, allowing President Reagan to carry out
military action in the Lebanon, Grenada and against Libya.

Watergate scandal   A major scandal which destroyed the Nixon presidency, called the integrity of the United States government into question
and helped to cripple US foreign policy in 1973–74. During the 1972
re-election campaign a group of seven men, some former members of

the CIA, broke into the Watergate building, which was the Democratic Party's Washington headquarters. They were caught and, in January 1973, tried and sentenced. Until then the incident had created little trouble for Nixon, but the *Washington Post* newspaper accused the White House of involvement in political 'dirty tricks'. In February the Senate set up a committee under Sam Ervin to investigate the case and various revelations followed about links between the president's staff and the Watergate burglars. In April the crisis began to dominate political life, evidence of a presidential 'cover-up' emerged and the White House Chief of Staff, H.R. Haldemann, was forced to resign. In May the Senate hearings began and soon produced evidence that was directly damaging to Nixon, especially from a former White House legal adviser, John Dean.

Despite promises to co-operate with enquiries, Nixon aroused suspicion when he at first refused to release tape-recordings which, it was revealed, he had made of White House conversations. There was further uproar in October when the president sacked one of the investigators, Special Prosecutor Archibald Cox. In 1974 the press and Congress began to look at other aspects of secrecy in government, including the activities of the CIA. In late July Nixon was forced, by the Supreme Court, to hand over tape-recordings which revealed his early involvement in a 'cover-up' of links between the White House and the Watergate burglars. Congress then seemed likely to impeach him, and Nixon resigned.

SECTION EIGHT

Strategic nuclear weapons: the US and Soviet balance, 1956–79

The nuclear arms race began in 1949 when the Soviets exploded their first atom bomb. At that time the US had a stockpile of about a hundred weapons, and had developed the ungainly B-36 bomber to deliver them. But it was only *c*. 1956 that the superpowers developed reliable long-range bombers to carry hydrogen bombs. Figures in the following tables cover the years 1956 to 1979. For ceilings and arsenals after that date, see entries for SALT II, START I and START II in Section Four.

1. Strategic bombers

1956	1960	1965	1970	1975	1979
US 560	550	630	405	330	316
USSR 60	175	200	190	140	140

2. Inter-continental ballistic missiles (ICBMs)

1960	1962	1964	1966	1968	1970	1972	1974	1979
US 20	295	835	900	1,054	1,054	1,054	1,054	1,054
USSR 30	75	200	300	800	1,300	1,527	1,587	1,398

Note: In the 1970s both superpowers were able to put multiple warheads (MIRVs) in each missile. In 1972 the total number of US warheads on ICBMs was 1,474 and after 1974 was 2,154. The Soviets began to use MIRVs after 1973. In 1979 they had 4,306 warheads on ICBMs.

3. Submarine-launched ballistic missiles (SLBMs)

1962	1965	1968	1972	1975	1979
US 145	500	656	656	656	656
USSR 45	125	130	497	740	989

Note: US deployment (of Polaris) began in 1960. Soviet submarine deployment in 1961. In 1972 the MIRVs allowed the US to put 3,384 warheads on SLBMs, rising to 5,120 in 1979. In 1979 the Soviets had 1,309 warheads on SLBMs due to MIRVs – well behind the US.
Sources: *The Military Balance* (annual); J.M. Collins, *US–Soviet Military Balance*, 1960–80 (Washington, 1980).

SECTION NINE

Bibliography

This bibliography is intended to provide a selection of about a hundred of the best books written in English on the Cold War. Since the post-war period is an expanding area of historical interest, the potential list of books is large and ever-growing. It would be impossible to list them all, but I have tried both to cover the full range of the Cold War and to point out several types of sources, including general introductory texts, detailed studies of major issues and memoirs by those who took part in events.

Those wishing to look at published original documents can consult the official collections, *Foreign Relations of the United States* (Government Printing Office, Washington) and *Documents on British Policy Overseas* (HMSO, London), which are growing in number every year. A useful selection of documents on American policy in the early period is Etzold, Thomas H. and Gaddis, John L. (eds), *Containment: Documents on American Policy and Strategy, 1945–50* (Columbia University Press, New York, 1978). Those wishing to study Vietnam should refer to Porter, Gareth (ed.), *Vietnam: the Definitive Documentation of Human Decisions, 1941–75* (2 vols, Heyden, London, 1979).

1. General

Of the general works on post-war international history, one of the most comprehensive and easily available introductions is Calvocoressi, Peter, *World Politics since 1945* (6th edn, Longman, London, 1991), but see also the two-volume study by Dunbabin, John, *The Cold War: the Great Powers and their Allies* and *The Post-Imperial Age: the Great Powers and the Wider World* (both Longman, London, 1994). Specifically on the Cold War issues, general accounts covering the whole post-war period include Crockatt, Richard, *The Fifty Years War: the US and the Soviet Union in World Politics, 1941–91* (Routledge, London, 1995), Ball, S.J., *The Cold War: an International History, 1947–91* (Edward Arnold, London, 1998) and Ashton, Stephen R., *In Search of Détente: the Politics of East–West Relations since 1945* (Macmillan, London, 1989). Dockrill, Michael, *The Cold War, 1945–63* (Macmillan, London, 1988) provides a short introduction to the Cold War down to the Cuban Missile Crisis. One of the most stimulating thinkers on the Cold War is the American historian, John L. Gaddis whose general essays include *Russia, the Soviet Union and the United States* (2nd edn, McGraw-Hill, New York, 1990), *The Long Peace, Inquiries into the History of the Cold War* (Oxford University Press, London and New York, 1987), and *We Now Know: Rethinking Cold War History* (Clarendon Press, Oxford, 1997), although another essential work is his *Strategies of Containment* (Oxford University Press, London and New York, 1982), specifically on American foreign policy. On US foreign policy throughout the Cold War see also Ambrose, Stephen E., *Rise to Globalism: American*

Foreign Policy since 1938 (7th edn, Penguin, Harmondsworth, 1993) – which is very readable, if rather critical in its interpretation – or Spanier, John, *American Foreign Policy since World War II* (14th edn, Holt, New York, 1997). Important aspects of US policy are discussed in Lafeber, Walter, *Inevitable Revolutions: the US in Central America* (Norton, New York, 1993), Smith, Peter H., *Talons of the Eagle: Dynamics of US–Latin American Relations* (Oxford University Press, New York, 1990), Brands, H.W., *Into the Labyrinth: the US and the Middle East, 1945–93* (McGraw-Hill, New York, 1994) and Foot, Rosemary, *The Practice of Power: US Relations with China since 1949* (Clarendon Press, Oxford, 1995).

On the Soviet Union, Ulam, Adam B., *Expansion and Coexistence: Soviet Foreign Policy, 1947–73* (Praeger, New York, 1974) remains comprehensive but dated, down to the Brezhnev era. General texts on Soviet foreign policy have yet to absorb new archive material, but see Nogee, Joseph L. and Donaldson, Robert H., *Soviet Foreign Policy since World War II* (2nd edn, Pergamon, New York, 1986), or Bialer, Seweryn, *The Soviet Paradox: External Expansion, Internal Decline* (I.B. Tauris and Co., London, 1985) is also a helpful interpretation.

On European issues see De Porte, A.W., *Europe between the Superpowers* (Yale University Press, New York and London, 1986) or Duignan, Paul and Gann, L.H., *The Rebirth of the West: the Americanization of the Democratic World 1945–58* (Blackwell, Cambridge, MA, 1992) on the early period, or Young, John W., *Cold War Europe, 1945–91: a Political History* (2nd edn, Edward Arnold, London, 1996), and on the Atlantic Alliance, Powaski, Ronald, *The Entangling Alliance: the US and European Security, 1950–93* (Greenwood, Westport, CT, 1994) or Kaplan, Lawrence S., *NATO and the US: the Enduring Alliance* (Twayne, Boston, 1988). A particularly important aspect of Atlantic relations is discussed in Bartlett, C.J., *The Special Relationship* (Longman, London, 1992) and Dobson, Alan P., *Anglo-American Relations in the Twentieth Century* (Routledge, London, 1995). On the Far East, see Yahuda, Michael, *The International Politics of the Asia-Pacific, 1945–95* (Routledge, London, 1996).

One vital feature of the Cold War was the role of the intelligence services. On the Americans, see especially Andrew, Christopher, *For the President's Eyes Only* (HarperCollins, London, 1995), Ranelagh, John, *The Agency: the Rise and Decline of the CIA* (Simon and Schuster, New York, 1986) or, as an investigation of the role of intelligence in a democracy, Johnson, Loch K., *America's Secret Power: the CIA in a Democratic Society* (Oxford University Press, Oxford, 1989). On the Soviet side, Andrew, Christopher and Gordievsky, Oleg, *KGB: the Inside Story* (HarperCollins, London, 1991) is essential. Another important issue is the advent of nuclear weapons. Their impact on world affairs is analysed in Freedman, Lawrence, *The Evolution of Nuclear Strategy* (2nd edn, Macmillan, London, 1989), although for the uninitiated, Newhouse, John, *The Nuclear*

Age: From Hiroshima to Star Wars (Michael Joseph, London, 1989) is an alternative.

2. The early Cold War – 1940s and 1950s

Most works on the Cold War deal, of course, with shorter periods. The years 1941–50 have attracted special attention since they saw the emergence of East–West tension as the vital element in world affairs. A brief introduction to this period is McCauley, Martin, *The Origins of the Cold War, 1941–1949* (2nd edn, Longman, London, 1995), although a wider focus is provided in Loth, Wilfried, *The Division of the World, 1941–55* (Routledge, London, 1988). Those interested in historiography ought to refer to earlier works such as Feis, Herbert, *From Trust to Terror* (Norton, New York, 1970), a 'traditional', pro-American account of Cold War origins; or Kolko, Joyce and Gabriel, *The Limits of Power: the World and US Foreign Policy, 1945–54* (Harper and Row, New York, 1972), a classic left-wing interpretation affected by Vietnam. Questioning of US policy, however, predated the Vietnam War, as can be seen in Williams, William A., *The Tragedy of American Diplomacy* (Delta, New York, 1962), a seminal 'revisionist' essay. Another seminal work was Gaddis, John L., *The US and the Origins of the Cold War* (Columbia University Press, New York, 1973) while Yergin, Daniel, *Shattered Peace: the Origins of the Cold War and the National Security State* (Penguin, Harmondsworth, 1980) tried to fuse revisionist and traditional elements. The 1980s and 1990s have seen a greater attempt to 'stand back' from Cold War issues and find a truer historical perspective on events. Interesting works include, on US policy, Messer, Robert L., *The End of an Alliance: James F. Byrnes, Roosevelt, Truman and the Origins of the Cold War* (University of North Carolina Press, Chapel Hill, 1982), Larson Deborah W., *Origins of Containment: a Psychological Explanation* (Princeton University Press, Princeton, NJ, 1985), Patterson, Thomas G., *On Every Front: the Making and Unmaking of the Cold War* (rev. edn, Norton, New York, 1992) – which, despite its title, mainly concerns the Truman years – and Eisenberg, Carolyn, *Drawing the Line: the American Decision to Divide Germany* (Cambridge University Press, Cambridge, 1996).

On key US policy-makers, see Pemberton, William E., *Harry S. Truman* (Twayne, Boston, 1989), Brinkley, Douglas, *Dean Acheson and the Making of US Foreign Policy* (Macmillan, London, 1993) and Mayers, David, *George Kennan and the Dilemmas of US Foreign Policy* (Oxford University Press, New York, 1988). On European issues an excellent collection of essays is Becker, Josef and Knipping, Franz, *Power in Europe: Great Britain, France, Italy and Germany in a Post-war World, 1945–50* (De Gruyter, Berlin, 1986), although on French policy see also Young, John W., *France, the Cold War and the Western Alliance, 1944–49* (Leicester University Press, London, 1990), on the division of Germany, Deighton, Anne, *The Impossible Peace:*

Britain, the Division of Germany and the Origins of the Cold War (Oxford
University Press, London, 1990) and on Yugoslavia, Heuser, Beatrice,
Western Containment, Policies in the Cold War: the Yugoslav Case (Routledge,
London, 1990). A key issue in forcing America into an active foreign
policy was the economic state of Western Europe, on which see Hogan,
Michael J., *The Marshall Plan: America, Britain and the Reconstruction of
Western Europe, 1947–52* (Cambridge University Press, Cambridge, 1987),
or Milward, Alan S., *The Reconstruction of Western Europe, 1945–51*
(Methuen, London, 1984), both thoughtful and substantial works.

Memoirs on the 1940s abound. The presidential memoirs by Truman,
Harry S., *Year of Decisions, 1945* and *Years of Trial and Hope, 1946–52*
(Hodder and Stoughton, London, 1955 and 1956) are rather uninform-
ative. Far better is Secretary of State Dean Acheson's *Present at the Creation*
(Hamish Hamilton, London, 1970). Great Britain still had a major role
to play in world events at this time and a very important memoir is
Churchill, Winston S., *The Second World War* (6 vols, Cassell, London,
1948–54), especially *Triumph and Tragedy* (which, however, exaggerates
Churchill's war-time fear of the Soviets). From the British side, see also
Foreign Secretary Anthony Eden's *The Reckoning* (Cassell, London, 1965),
which covers 1938–45, and *Memoirs: Full Circle* (Cassell, London, 1960),
which covers 1951–56. Soviet memoirs on this period are predictably
thin but Djilas, Milovan, *Conversations with Stalin* (Hart-Davies, London,
1962) provides recollections of Stalin by a Yugoslav dissident.

The most recent overall discussions of the abundant evidence on US
policy in the 1940s include Woods, Randall B. and Jones, Howard, *Dawn-
ing of the Cold War: the US Quest for Order* (University of Georgia Press,
Athens, 1991) and Leffler, Melvyn, *A Preponderance of Power: National
Security, the Truman Administration and the Cold War* (Stanford University
Press, Stanford, CA, 1992). Work on the Soviet side has been revolution-
ised by the opening of archives to researchers. Some of the more interesting views on Stalin's foreign policy before 1991 were to be found
in Mastny, Vojtech, *Russia's Road to the Cold War: Diplomacy, Warfare and
the Politics of Communism* (Columbia University Press, New York, 1979),
McCagg, William O., *Stalin, Embattled, 1943–48* (Wayne State University
Press, Detroit, 1978) and Taubman, William, *Stalin's American Policy: From
Entente to Détente to Cold War* (Norton, New York, 1982). But there are
now at least three important works which have exploited the Soviet
archives on the early Cold War: Mastny, Vojtech, *The Cold War and
Soviet Insecurity, the Stalin Years* (Oxford University Press, Oxford, 1996),
Kennedy-Pipe, Caroline, *Stalin's Cold War* (Manchester University Press,
Manchester, 1995) and Zubok, Vladislav and Pleshakov, Constantine, *Inside
the Kremlin's Cold War: From Stalin to Khruschev* (Harvard University Press,
Cambridge, MA, 1996). A large number of works have been published
on British policy, but see especially Kitchen, Martin, *British Policy Towards*

the Soviet Union during the Second World War (Macmillan, London, 1986) on the war years, and Bullock, Alan, *Ernest Bevin: Foreign Secretary, 1945– 51* (Heinemann, London, 1983) on post-war issues. Kent, John, *British Imperial Strategy and the Cold War* (Leicester University Press, Leicester, 1993) underlines the importance of imperial issues for British policy-makers; and Young, John W., *Winston Churchill's Last Campaign: Britain and the Cold War, 1951–55* (Oxford University Press, Oxford, 1996) investigates Churchill's attempts to end the Cold War in the 1950s. Much attention has focused on the forging of the Anglo-American 'special relationship'. Harbutt, Fraser J., *The Iron Curtain: Churchill, America and the Origins of the Cold War* (Oxford University Press, Oxford, 1986) is a more stimulating interpretation than Edmonds, Robin, *Setting the Mould: the US and Britain, 1945–50* (Oxford University Press, Oxford, 1986) but the latter is more comprehensive. On nuclear issues in this period, Alperowitz, Gary, *Atomic Diplomacy: Hiroshima and Potsdam* (rev. edn, Penguin, New York, 1994) is critical of US policy, and Herken, Gregg, *The Winning Weapon: the Atomic Bomb in the Cold War, 1945–50* (Knopf, New York, 1982), an antidote, whilst on the USSR, see Holloway, David, *Stalin and the Bomb* (Yale University Press, New Haven, CT, 1994).

In 1950 world attention focused on the Far East where, as discussed in Stueck, William W., *The Korean War: an International History* (Princeton University Press, Princeton, NJ, 1995), the West had found a new Communist opponent in China. On the background to the Korean War, the best introduction is Lowe, Peter, *The Origins of the Korean War* (2nd edn, Longman, London, 1994) but, on the origins of US links to Japan, see also Schaller, Michael, *The American Occupation of Japan: the Origins of the Cold War in Asia* (Oxford University Press, New York, 1985). On the war itself there are numerous studies but see especially Whelan, Richard, *Drawing the Line: the Korean War, 1950–53* (Faber, London, 1990) and Goncharaov, Sergei, et al., *Uncertain Partners: Stalin, Mao and the Korean War* (Stanford University Press, Stanford, CA, 1993). Korea deepened Cold War animosities and led to the militarisation of Western policies, including German rearmament, on which see Fursdon, Edward, *The European Defence Community: a History* (Macmillan, London, 1980).

The late 1950s proved years of continuing crisis, although after the death of Stalin there were meetings between Soviet and Western leaders. Work on archival sources in the US has led to a more positive appreciation of President Eisenhower's policies, as seen in Divine, Robert A., *Eisenhower and the Cold War* (rev. edn, Oxford University Press, Oxford, 1998), Ambrose, Stephen E., *Eisenhower: the President, 1952–69* (George Allen and Unwin, London, 1984) and Pach, Chester J. and Richardson, Elmo, *The Presidency of Dwight D. Eisenhower* (University of Kansas Press, Lawrence, 1991). But a lot of attention is still given to his Secretary of State, on whom see Immerman, Richard H., *John Foster Dulles and the*

Diplomacy of the Cold War (Princeton University Press, Princeton, NJ, 1990).
On their overall approach to the Cold War, see Dockrill, Saki, *Eisenhower's New Look National Security Policy* (Macmillan, London, 1996). On
the Soviet side in this period we are fortunate enough to have the revealing if rambling memoirs of the Communist General Secretary himself.
Talbott, Strobe (ed.), *Khruschev Remembers* (André Deutsch, London, 1971)
can now be supplemented by Schechter, Jerrold (ed.), *Khruschev Remembers: the Glasnost Tapes* (Little Brown, Boston, 1998).

3. The 1960s and the Vietnam War

In contrast to Eisenhower, recent work on President Kennedy has tended
to be adversely critical, as seen in Paterson, Thomas G., *Kennedy's Quest
for Victory: American Foreign Policy, 1961–63* (Oxford University Press, Oxford, 1989), but those seeking a more positive approach can still refer to
such works as Schlesinger, Arthur M., *A Thousand Days: John F. Kennedy
in the White House* (André Deutsch, London, 1975). On the Cold War in
the early 1960s, see Beschloss, Michael, *Kennedy Versus Khruschev* (Faber
and Faber, London, 1991) or Ausland, John C., *Kennedy, Khruschev and
the Berlin–Cuba Crisis* (Scandinavian University Press, Oslo, 1996). The
key event of these years has now been fully documented but remains
the subject of changing views: compare Garthoff, Raymond, *Reflections on
the Cuban Missile Crisis* (rev. edn, Brookings Institution, Washington, 1989),
and Kennedy, Robert F., *Thirteen Days: a Memoir of the Cuban Crisis* (Norton,
New York, 1969). One of the best memoirs on this period is by a US
official: Ball, George, *The Past has Another Pattern: Memoirs* (Norton, New
York, 1982). But from the Soviet side, for this and later periods, see
Dobrynin, Anatoli, *In Confidence* (Times Books, New York, 1995) by the
Soviet Ambassador to Washington, 1962–86.

After Kennedy, of course, much attention has inevitably been paid to
the Vietnam War, on which an enormous amount of material is available. On the long-term background to the war, see especially Blum,
Robert, *Drawing the Line: the Origins of the American Containment Policy in
East Asia* (Norton, New York, 1982) and Short, Anthony, *The Origins of
the Vietnam War* (Longman, London, 1989). However, there are also
several full, rewarding studies on the war as a whole: see especially Young,
Marilyn, *The Vietnam Wars* (HarperCollins, New York, 1991), Schulzinger,
R.D., *A Time for War: the US and Vietnam, 1941–75* (Oxford University
Press, New York, 1997), Smith, Ralph B., *An International History of the
Vietnam War* (4 vols, Macmillan, London, 1983–90), Herring, George
C., *America's Longest War: the US and Vietnam, 1954–75* (New York, 1986),
and on the Johnson years, Gardner, Lloyd C., *Pay Any Price* (Ivan R. Dee,
Chicago, 1995).

4. Detente and the New Cold War – 1970s and 1980s

The strains of Vietnam on the US helped to make the 1970s the decade of detente. An excellent introduction to detente, thoughtful and comprehensive, is Bowker, M. and Williams, P., *Superpower Détente: a Reappraisal* (Sage, London, 1988), but also good is Stevenson, Richard W., *The Rise and Fall of Détente: Relaxations of Tension in US–Soviet Relations, 1953–84* (Macmillan, London, 1985). On the vital years under Nixon, Szulc, Tad, *The Illusion of Peace: Foreign Policy in the Nixon Years* (Viking, New York, 1978) is very full, Litwak, Robert S., *Détente and the Nixon Doctrine: American Foreign Policy and the Pursuit of Stability, 1969–76* (Cambridge University Press, Cambridge, 1984) a more interesting overall interpretation and Thornton, Richard, *The Nixon–Kissinger Years* (Paragon, New York, 1989) perhaps the easiest introduction. For a right-wing criticism of detente, see Pipes, Richard, *US–Soviet Relations in the Era of Détente* (Westview Press, Boulder, CO, 1981). On Soviet policy in this period a number of studies exist, including Edmonds, Robin, *Soviet Foreign Policy: the Brezhnev Years* (Oxford University Press, Oxford, 1983), Ulam, Adam, B., *Dangerous Relations: the Soviet Union in World Policies, 1970–82* (Oxford University Press, Oxford, 1983) and Gelman, Harry, *The Brezhnev Politburo and the Decline of Détente* (Cornell University Press, Ithaca, NY, 1984). Away from the focus on Superpowers, see also Dyson, Kenneth (ed.), *European Détente: Case Studies of the Politics of East–West Relations* (Pinter, London, 1986) or Mastny, Vojtech, *Helsinki, Human Rights and European Security, 1975–85* (Duke University Press, Durham, NC, 1986). And on the key nuclear arms agreements, see Newhouse, John, *Cold Dawn: the Story of SALT* (Pergamon-Brassey, London, 1979), and Talbott, Strobe, *Endgame: the Inside Story of SALT II* (Harper and Row, New York, 1979).

Some of the best work on this period comes from the leading actors in these events. Inevitably much attention has centred on the supposed architect of 1970s detente, Henry Kissinger, whose memoirs, *The White House Years* (Weidenfeld and Nicolson, London, 1979), covering 1969–73, and *Years of Upheaval* (Weidenfeld and Nicolson, London, 1982), covering 1973–74, are a mine of information – but carefully written to defend the author's case. To put them into context, see Isaacson, Walter, *Kissinger* (Faber and Faber, London, 1992), Schulzinger, Robert D., *Henry Kissinger: Doctor of Diplomacy* (Columbia University Press, New York, 1989); and see also Nixon, Richard, *RN: Memoirs of Richard Nixon* (Sidgwick and Jackson, London, 1978), one of the best presidential autobiographies. The key text on the 1970s, tracing the rise and decline of detente, is Raymond Garthoff's monumental *Détente and Confrontation: American–Soviet Relations from Nixon to Reagan* (rev. edn, Brookings, Washington, 1994).

As detente gave way to a New Cold War in the late 1970s, US policymakers found themselves divided, and there are again three intriguing (and contrasting) memoirs available from the President, Secretary of State and National Security Adviser: Carter, Jimmy, *Keeping Faith: Memoirs of a President* (Collins, London, 1982), Vance, Cyrus, *Hard Choices: Critical Years in American Foreign Policy* (Simon and Shuster, New York, 1983), and Brzezinski, Zbigniew, *Power and Principles: Memoirs of the National Security Adviser, 1977–81* (Farrar-Strauss-Giroux, New York, 1983). Another memoir that is very detailed on arms control talks in the 1970s and 1980s is Nitze, Paul H., *From Hiroshima to Glasnost: a Memoir* (Weidenfeld and Nicolson, London, 1989), and on the Soviet side the essential account is Gromyko, Andrei, *Memories* (Hutchinson, London, 1989), which is predictably dry and propagandistic. The best study of US foreign policy in the late 1970s is Thornton, Richard, *The Carter Years: Towards a New Global Order* (Pentagon, New York, 1991). For the period of Ronald Reagan's presidency, the president's own memoirs, *An American Life* (Hutchinson, London, 1991), despite enormous length, are disappointingly sparse on new material. A little better on the early years is Haig, Alexander M., *Caveat: Realism, Reagan and Foreign Policy* (Weidenfeld and Nicolson, London, 1984), by Reagan's first Secretary of State. Superior to both is Schultz, George P., *Turmoil and Triumph* (Scribner's, New York, 1993). Among academic studies Hyland, William, G., *Mortal Rivals: Superpower Relations from Nixon to Reagan* (Random House, New York, 1987) charts the return to Cold War, and the extent of US–Soviet alienation is highlighted by Talbott, Strobe, *Deadly Gambits: the Reagan Administration and the Stalemate in Nuclear Arms Control* (Pan, London, 1985). Two left-wing criticisms of Western policy in the early 1980s were Chomsky, Noam, Steele, Jonathan and Gittings, John, *Superpowers in Collision: the New Cold War of the 1980s* (Penguin, Harmondsworth, 1984), and Halliday, Fred, *The Making of the Second Cold War* (2nd edn, Verso, London, 1986). On key problems affecting East–West relations in this period, Ascherson, Neal, *The Polish August: the Self-limiting Revolution* (Penguin, Harmondsworth, 1981), Arney, George, *Afghanistan* (Mandarin Paperback, London, 1990) – a general history of the Afghan War, 1979–88 – and Bulloch, John and Morris, Harvey, *The Gulf War: Its Origins, History and Consequences* (Methuen, London, 1989), on the Iran–Iraq conflict, were written for the popular market but are none the worse for that. On Afghanistan, see also Hyman, Anthony, *Afghanistan under Soviet Domination* (Macmillan, London, 1992). Patman, Robert G., *The Soviet Union in the Horn of Africa: the Diplomacy of Intervention and Disengagement* (Cambridge University Press, Cambridge, 1990) shows what quality of academic research can be done on recent history.

5. The end of the Cold War

On the Gorbachev period and the end of the Cold War, the memoirs by Schultz and Reagan remain useful on the US side, but see also Baker,

James A., *The Politics of Diplomacy* (Putnam, New York, 1995). Mikhail Gorbachev has published his own *Memoirs* (Doubleday, New York, 1996) and see also Shevardnadze, Eduard, *The Future Belongs to Freedom* (Sinclair-Stevenson, London, 1991). Very useful is Beschloss, Michael and Talbott, Strobe, *At the Highest Levels: the Inside Story of the End of the Cold War* (Little Brown, Boston, 1993), based on interviews with the key players. But see also Garthoff, Raymond, *The Great Transition: American–Soviet Relations and the End of the Cold War* (Brookings, Washington, 1994), Oberdorfer, Don, *The Turn: How the Cold War Came to an End* (Jonathan Cape, London, 1992) and on one of the most dramatic developments, Zelikow, Philip and Rice, Condoleeza, *Germany Unified and Europe Transformed* (Harvard University Press, Cambridge, MA, 1995), by two policy-makers from the Bush White House. On developments since the collapse of the Cold War there is as yet a limited amount of high-quality reading but on certain key questions see Cox, Michael, *US Foreign Policy after the Cold War* (Pinter, London, 1995), Park, W. and Rees, G. Wyn, *Rethinking Security in Post-Cold War Europe* (Longman, London, 1998) and Blackwill, Robert and Karaganov, Sergei (eds), *Damage, Limitation or Crisis? Russia and the Outside World* (Brasseys, London, 1994). There is also a memoir for 1991–93 by Yeltsin, Boris, *The View from the Kremlin* (HarperCollins, London, 1994).

SECTION TEN

Maps

Map 1 Cold War Europe, 1945–89

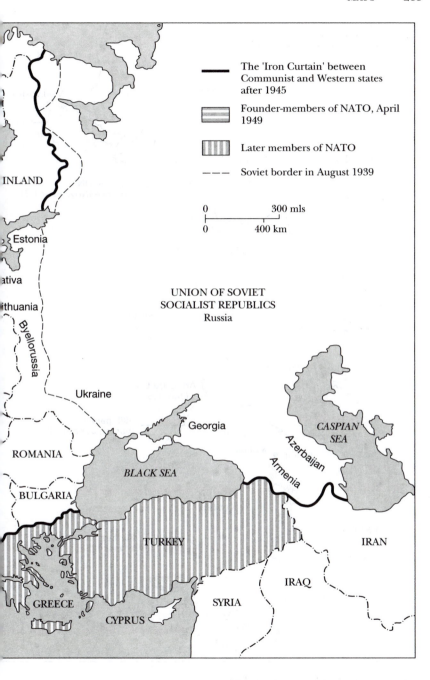

The 'Iron Curtain' between Communist and Western states after 1945

Founder-members of NATO, April 1949

Later members of NATO

Soviet border in August 1939

| 0 | 300 mls |
| 0 | 400 km |

INLAND

Estonia

ativa

ithuania

Byellorussia

Ukraine

UNION OF SOVIET
SOCIALIST REPUBLICS
Russia

Georgia

CASPIAN
SEA

Azerbaijan

Armenia

ROMANIA

BLACK SEA

BULGARIA

TURKEY

IRAN

GREECE

IRAQ

CYPRUS

SYRIA

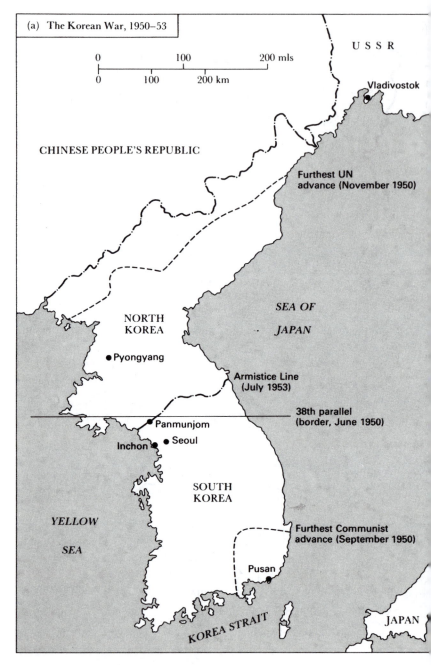

(a) The Korean War, 1950–53

USSR

Vladivostok

CHINESE PEOPLE'S REPUBLIC

Furthest UN
advance (November 1950)

NORTH
KOREA

SEA OF

JAPAN

● Pyongyang

Armistice Line
(July 1953)

38th parallel
(border, June 1950)

● Panmunjom

Inchon ● Seoul

SOUTH
KOREA

YELLOW

Furthest Communist
advance (September 1950)

SEA

Pusan

KOREA STRAIT

JAPAN

Map 2   The Cold War in the Far East

(b) Indo-China

CHINESE PEOPLE'S
REPUBLIC

NORTH VIETNAM

Dienbienphu

BURMA

Hanoi

Haiphong

LAOS

GULF OF

TONKIN

Vientiane

Partition line 1954–75
(demilitarised zone)

Hue

Da Nang

THAILAND

Pleiku

Bangkok

CAMBODIA

SOUTH
VIETNAM

Phnom Penh

GULF OF

THAILAND

Saigon
(Ho Chi
Minh City)

SOUTH

CHINA

SEA

| 0 | 100 | 200 mls |
| 0 | 100 | 200 km |

Map 3 The Middle East

KAZAKHSTAN

KAZAKHSTAN

KIRGHIZSTAN

UZBEKISTAN

TURKMENISTAN

TAJIKISTAN

CHINA

1948 Cease-fire
Line

Kabul

Kashmir

Islamabad

IRAN

AFGHANISTAN

Karachi

PAKISTAN

INDIA

Strait of Hormuz

Muscat

Rann of
Kutch

ARABIAN
SEA

OMAN

Underlined – members of Baghdad Pact in 1955–58

Areas occupied by Israel in the 1967 war

International borders

Borders of republics of the USSR
(independent after 1991)

0   300 mls

0   300 km

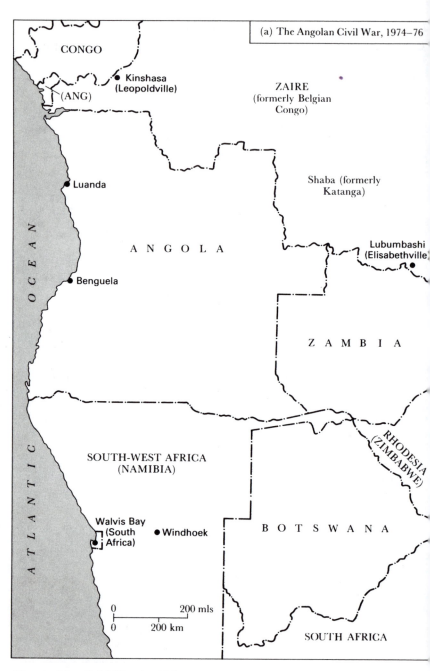

(a) The Angolan Civil War, 1974–76

CONGO

Kinshasa
(Leopoldville)

(ANG)

ZAIRE
(formerly Belgian
Congo)

Luanda

Shaba (formerly
Katanga)

A N G O L A

Lubumbashi
(Elisabethville)

Benguela

O C E A N

Z A M B I A

A T L A N T I C

SOUTH-WEST AFRICA
(NAMIBIA)

RHODESIA
(ZIMBABWE)

Walvis Bay
(South
Africa)

Windhoek

B O T S W A N A

0   200 mls
0   200 km

SOUTH AFRICA

Map 4   The Cold War in Africa

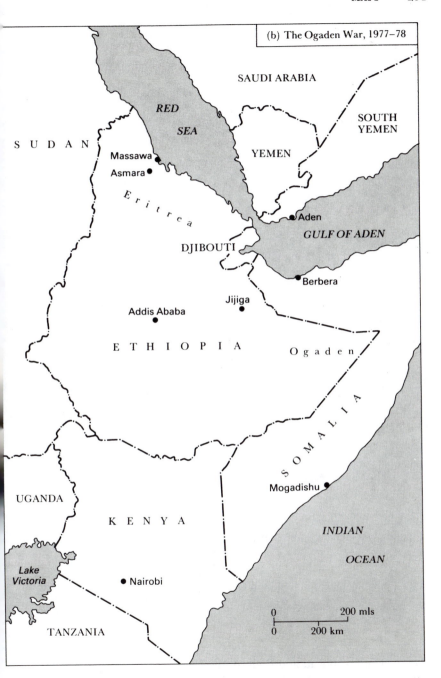

(b) The Ogaden War, 1977–78

SAUDI ARABIA

RED
SEA

SOUTH
YEMEN

SUDAN

YEMEN

Massawa

Asmara

E r i t r e a

Aden

GULF OF ADEN

DJIBOUTI

Berbera

Jijiga

Addis Ababa

ETHIOPIA

O g a d e n

S O M A L I A

UGANDA

KENYA

INDIAN

OCEAN

Mogadishu

*Lake
Victoria*

Nairobi

0   200 mls

0   200 km

TANZANIA

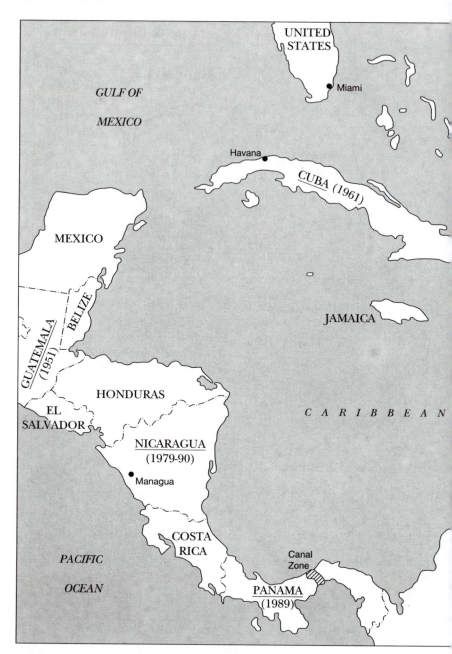

Map 5 The Caribbean and Central America. *Note*: The underlined countries subject to US military intervention (Dominican Republic, Grenada, Panama, Haiti), CIA-backed invasions (Guatemala, Cuba) and diplomatic and economic pressure (Nicaragua)

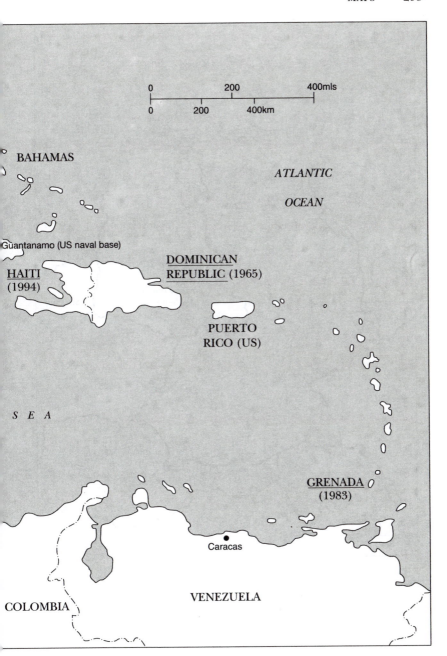

BAHAMAS

ATLANTIC

OCEAN

Guantanamo (US naval base)

HAITI
(1994)

DOMINICAN
REPUBLIC (1965)

PUERTO
RICO (US)

S E A

GRENADA
(1983)

Caracas

COLOMBIA

VENEZUELA

0   200   400mls
0   200   400km

Map 6 Cold War Germany, 1945–90

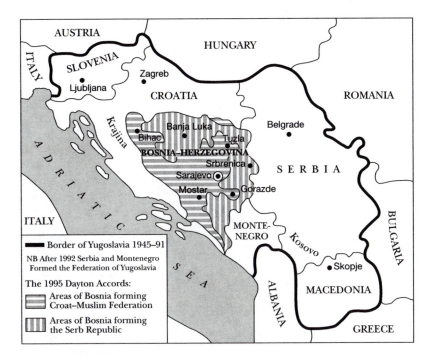

Map 7 The break-up of Yugoslavia

Map 8   Post-Cold War Europe, after 1993

Members of the European
Union as of January 1995

Borders of the former Soviet Union

ARM.   ARMENIA
LUX.   LUXEMBOURG
SWITZ. SWITZERLAND

0   300 mls

0   400 km

FINLAND

ESTONIA

RUSSIA

LATVIA
LITH-
UANIA

KAZAKHSTAN

BELARUS

UKRAINE

TURKMENISTAN

MOLDOVA

ROMANIA

GEORGIA   AZER-
                         BAIJAN
ARM.

BULGARIA

TURKEY   IRAN

GREECE   SYRIA   IRAQ

CYPRUS

Index